ADVANCED LEARNER'S DICTIONARY *Of* PSYCHOLOGY

ADVANCED LEARNER'S DICTIONARY *Of* PSYCHOLOGY

Compiled & Edited by
A Team of Experts

ANMOL PUBLICATIONS PVT. LTD.
NEW DELHI - 110 002 (INDIA)

ANMOL PUBLICATIONS PVT. LTD.
4374/4B, Ansari Road, Daryaganj
New Delhi - 110 002

Advanced Learner's Dictionary of Psychology

First Edition, 2000
Reprint, 2002
ISBN 81-261-0485-6

[Responsibility for the facts stated, opinions expressed, conclusions reached and plagiarism, if any, in these volumes is entirely that of the Editor. The Publishers bear no responsibility for them whatsoever.]

PRINTED IN INDIA

Published by J.L. Kumar for Anmol Publications Pvt. Ltd., New Delhi and Printed at Mehra Offset Press, Delhi.

Preface

This *Advanced Learner's Dictionary of Psychology* is basically designed for students and teachers as well. It is the result of a careful analysis of the needs of advanced level students and should be an invaluable aid in their day-to-day learning.

As it is extremely difficult to limit the contents of such a dictionary at 'Advanced' level standard, many headwords are included that are above this level and that may be of interest to Advanced Learners. A few headwords that are not strictly scientific are also included because of their common usage in everyday scientific terminology. It has been our aim to provide explanations that are easily understood, whilst maintaining academic standards.

We have tried to include the more important terms used at advanced level, but would welcome any comments regarding serious omissions or indeed about the content of any of the entries.

We would like to thank all the people who have cooperated in producing this dictionary. We are also grateful to many people who have given additional help and advice.

—Editors

A

Abasement: The need to comply, to surrender, to confess, to atone, to accept punishment.

Abdominal reflex: A contraction of muscles in the abdominal wall in response to a sudden stroking of the skin in that region.

Abducens or abducent nerve: The sixth cranial nerve. The abducens carries a motor component to the lateral rectus muscle of the eye and a sensory component media-ting proprioception from the same muscle.

Aberration: A departure from normal, a temporary lapse from normalcy; idiosyncratic or peculiar behaviour.

Ability grouping: The practice of sectioning pupils into relatively homogeneous groups according to their scholastic ability.

Ability: The power to perform an act. An ability may be innate or it may be the result of practice. *Ability*, as distinguished from *aptitude*, implies that an act can be performed now, whereas *aptitude* implies that training or education will be necessary before an act can be performed at some future time. *Capacity*, often used as a synonym for *ability*, usually implies an ability that can be fully developed in the future only under optimal conditions of training.

Ability test: Refers to a standardised examination for the purpose of measuring either general ability or some specialized ability.

Ablation experiments: Animal experiments wherein portions of the brain are excised after a habit like maze-learning has been established. The relationships between the amounts of destroyed tissues and their location on the one hand, and retention of the skill, on the other hand are then noted by the observer.

Abnormal pasychology: The branch of psychology that investigates abnormal behaviour.

Abnormal: 1. Diverging widely

from the normal; descriptive of behaviour deviating markedly from what is considered normative, healthy or psychologically desirable from an adjustmental point of view. The term often carries a strong connotation of undesirability or pathology, but it is also occasionally employed to characterize extreme superiority or supernormality.

2. in statistical distributions, descriptive of scores that are atypical or outside the normal or expected range of scores. The terms *abnormal* and *normal,* though used extensively in both technical and popular writing, are difficult to define precisely. Some authorities have suggested that abnormality be defined in statistical terms—that individuals who fall outside certain limits along the normal probability curve be considered abnormal. The difficulty with this definition lies in deciding where to establish limits or cutoff points. Others have suggested that normalcy and abnormality be defined in terms of cultural standards, thus allowing considerable latitude for cultural relativity.

Some writers have suggested that normalcy be defined partly in subjective terms, or in terms of the individual's feelings of adequacy, happiness, and relatedness to others. In applying such a definition, considerable latitude must be allowed for clinical judgment.

Abortive jump: It is the manner in which rats avoided bumping their noses and falling into the net, by learning to strike the barrier with their paws and to turn their heads aside.

Aboulia: Refers to chronic indecision, with eventual loss of initiative. It is a pathology of conation.

Abreaction: The discharge of tension by reliving in words, feelings and actions a traumatic experience in the presence of an analyst.

Abrosia: It is a condition of fasting. In some types of hysteria *(anorexia)* and in catatonia, negative impulses may induce refusals to eat.

Abscissa: 1. The horizontal or x axis on a two-dimensional graph. In learning curves, for example, the independent variable of time or trials is usually plotted along the abscissa, and the dependent variable of or successes along the ordinate, or vertical axis. 2. the distance (x distance) from a particular point to its origin, measured along a line parallel to the horizontal axis.

Absent-mindedness: Not paying attention to those phases of a situation which, other persons consider to be of major importance.

Absolute accommodation: The accommodation of either eye separately.

Absolute brilliance limen: It is the minimum intensity of brilliance needed to elicit a sensation of just noticeable difference from the other parts of the visual field.

Absolute error: The observed value or score plus or minus the true value or score. The true value is usually taken to be the mean of the measurements. Thus, the absolute error is a positive or negative deviation on either side of the mean.

Absolute impression: A judgment of intensity, brightness, weight, etc., when the stimuli are presented without any standard for comparison. The statement "This baby is heavy" illustrates and absolute impression.

Absolute judgment: In a series of judgments, an evaluation of the first of a pair of stimuli before the second is presented. Such judgments are made after the subject has become familiar with the series, and they are therefore not truly "absolute," but the result of his having built up a subjective scale against which the judges a given member of the series.

Absolute luminosity: It is the luminosity expressed in absolute terms.

Absolute measurement: Any measurement taken without regard to algebraic sign.

Absolute pitch: Refers to the pitch of a tone as a function of its rate of vibration.

Absolute zero: Refers to the point on a psychological scale where the variable being measured ceases to exist.

Absorption: A state of preoccupation or high degree of attention to one object or activity.

Abstract ability: Refers to the ability to use abstract ideas in problem solving end in dealing with novel situations.

Abstract average: An average substituted for individual items in subsequent mathematical operations.

Abstract idea: A generalized idea representing some aspect of a class or group of objects apart from particular or concrete objects themselves. *Mammal* is an abstract idea embracing a wide range of different vertebrates whose young are born alive and who are suckled after birth by the mother.

Abstract intelligence: It is the ability to use symbols and concepts while dealing with unfamiliar problems and difficulties. This type of intelligence can be measured by verbal and mathematical symbols and abstract concepts.

Abstract intelligence: The ability

to deal with abstract concepts and relationships effectively.

Abstract: That which has been taken out of the whole or is being considered apart from its constituent elements.

Acceptance: 1. Characterized by a positive or adient attitude. 2. in clinical practice, recognition of the individual's worth without implying either approval of his conduct or emotional attachment on the part of the therapist.

Accessory nerve: The eleventh cranial nerve. This nerve is a helper, or accessory, to the vagus, or tenth nerve, and is distributed with it to the muscles of the pharynx and larynx.

Accessory parts: All parts of sense organs except the receptor cells themselves. Accessory parts contribute to the more effective functioning of sense organs.

Accident proneness: Refers to the tendency for certain persons to have a disproportionately large number of the accidents occur within a given group of employees.

Accidental error: Error in measurement that results from variable and unknown causes and can neither be predicted nor controlled. If it is assumed that all measurements are, to some degree, inexact, then the means of a series of measurements is the best estimate of the true value. An accidental error is a deviation from this value.

Accommodation time: It is the time that lapse between a change in viewing distance and the achievement of accommodation.

Accretionary growth: Refers to multiplication of tissues without qualitative change in the functions of an organ or an organism.

Acculturation: It is the process of absorbing the folkways and mores of a culture that originally was alien to the immigrant.

Accuracy test: Any test that emphasizes accuracy of performance independent of the time it takes to complete it.

Accuracy, compulsion: Refers to pathological zeal in accurate work, even with minute details and trivia. It is considered to be a maladjustive habit whereby the individual seeks to escape from anxiety conflicts.

ACE test: The American Council on Education test of intelligence, designed primarily for college freshmen.

Acetylcholine (ACH): A complex organic compound liberated at the endings of parasympathetic fibbers and at muscle end plates. Acetylcholine is a neurotrasmitter.

Acetylcholinesterose (ACHE): The enzyme that breaks down acetyl- choline at the transmitter site, thus stopping its effects.

Achievement age: It is the calendar or chronological age equivalent to a given level of proficiency on an achievement test.

Achievement motive: Refers to the tendency to strive for success or the attainment of a desired end.

Achievement quotient: The ratio of achievement age as measured by actual performance in school or on a standardized test and the level of performance expected. *Abbr.* A.Q. The expected level of performance may be indicated by the child's chronological age or it may be estimated by finding his mental age.

Achievement test: A measure of the individual's present ability to perform a task. Achievement tests measure how well the subject has profited by learning and experience as compared to others. Achievement tests are not designed to measure the individual's future potential, which is measured by aptitude tests.

However, it is recognized that it is impossible to measure aptitude without measuring achievement. Moreover, because it is impossible to measure all aspects of a complex skill or group of skills by means of a single test, batteries or groups of achievement tests are commonly employed in educational and industrial practice.

Achilles tendon reflex: Refers to contraction of the muscles of the calf when the tendon back of the heel is sharply tapped.

Achondroplasia: Refers to defects in the cartilage at the epiphytes of long bones; children with this disorder have difficulty in locomotion.

Achromatic response: It includes several subcategories for responses determined by texture, shading, or any factor not involving colour.

Acouasm: Refers to a subjective noise in the ears which may be due to impacted cerumen, charges of air pressure in the middle ear, blocked eustachian tubes, quinine, or inflammation of tympanum or middle ear.

Acoustic spectrum: Refers to the range of sounds audible to the human ear—from 20 to 20,000 Hz in young adults.

Acoustics: It is the science of sound also refers to the properties of a room that influence the distinctness with which sounds can be heard.

Acquired: Characteristic of behaviour learned through practice or experience, in contrast to behaviour that is innate or inherited. Since psychologists believe that all behavior is a joint function of both heredity and environment, the terms *acquired* and *innate* are ordinarily not used as absolute qualifiers. When responses, such as reflexes, are primarily the result of the individual's biological endowment, they are characterized as innate; when responses, such as riding a bicycle or talking, are primarily dependent upon learning, they are characterized as acquired.

Act psychology: A viewpoint taken by Franz Brentano to the effect that the subject matter of psychology should be acts, as opposed to contents. Brentano held that mental acts referred to contents, but were not identical to them. If, for example, we see a color, the act of seeking is a process that leads to a content of what is seen.

However, the content itself was held to be not psychological, but physical. Act psychology arose in opposition to structuralism, founded by Wilhelm Wundt which held that the subject matter of psychology was conscious contents to be studied by means of the method of introspection.

The act psychologists rejected introspection in favor of phenomenological observation. Act psychology made no important positive contributions to psychology, but was important as a challenge to the dominant structuralism of the times and as a forerunner of functionalism.

Act psychology: Refers to the view point that emphasises activities, rather than contents of consciousness.

Act regression: The reappearance of a previously extinguished conditioned response when a barrier is interposed to a conditioned response related to the extinguished response.

Acticipation method: It is a technique used in verbal learning where the subject is prompted upon hesitation and corrected up on making an error.

Action current: The change in electrical potential in nerves and muscles that is correlated with activity.

Action potential: The change in electrical potential associated with the activity of nerves and muscles.

Action research: A program of research whose ends are practical as opposed to theoretical.

Action system: The complex of nerves, muscles, and glands that participate in a response.

Activation pattern: On the electroencephalogram refers to a fast irregular wave pattern accompanying arousal.

Activation: Arousal or preparation for action. The term is generally used to characterize the influence of one organ on another. For example, the reticular formation alerts or activates the cerebral cortex, and for this *r* son is sometimes called the reticular activating system.

Activation: Means arousal or preparation for action. For example, the reticular formation alerts or activates the cerebral cortex.

Activation-deactivation adjective checklist: A personality inventory designed to assess the testee's customary level of activation.

Active avoidance: Refers to a learning situation wherein the subject must perform a specific act so as to avoid punishment.

Active therapy: 1. An analysis in which the therapist assumes a more directive or active role than is customary, for the purpose of breaking down resistance. 2. more generally, *active therapy* implies any psychotherapeutic situation in which the therapist taken an active, as opposed to a passive, or nondirective, role.

Activity drive: Refers to the hypothetical drive to account for an animal activity even though all physiological drives are satiated.

Activity quotient: It is a proposed index of emotionality using the ratio of activity words to qualifiers in a sample of the individual's speech or writing.

Activity sampling: The determination of what an individual does during a specified period of time.

Activity system: A group of closely interrelated behaviours that serve the same general function. For example, crawling, running, walking, and hopping are mall forms of locomotor behavior and constitute an activity system.

Activity system: Refers to a group of closely interrelated behaviours which serve the same general function. For example, crawling, running, walking, and jumping.

Acuity grating: Refers to a printed square of closely spaced, alternating black and white lines used to, determine the minimum separability of objects necessary for their perception as two.

Acupuncture: Refers to a technique that is used for producing regional anaesthesia. Anaesthesia is produced by inserting a long thin needle at the critical point and either twirling it or passing a mild electric current through it.

Acute Preparation: An animal that must be destroyed for humane reasons it- the termination of an experiment involving radical surgical procedures.

Ad hoc: Refers to a hypothesis or hypothetical explanation developed to explain a particular set of data that does not fit into an existing theoretical framework.

Ad lib: Refer to ad lib body weight, that is the weight approached by a fully nature organism given unlimited access to a balanced diet, i.e., one on ad lib feeding.

Adaptive act: It is the basic unit of behaviour involving a motivating stimulus and a sensory situation leading the animal to make responses which reinforce behaviour leading to a goal, there by satisfying the motivating condition.

Adaptive behaviour: Refers to the behaviour that helps the individual interact more effectively with his environment.

Addiction: It is the state of being physically dependent upon a drug. In general, addiction means increased tolerance to a drug, physical and psychological dependence, and withdrawal symptoms when administration of the drug is stopped.

Additive scale: A scale whose units can be summated since they are equal at all points along the scale. A yardstick is, an additive scale.

Adipocytes: Means fat cells. It his been found that obese people have more and larger adipocytes than those of normal weight.

Adjuvant therapy: Supplementary or corollary techniques used in therapy.

Adler, Alfred: Austrian psychiatrist, founder of Individual Psychology. Adler, an opthalmologist, became interested in the then controversial theories of Sigmund Freud, and in 1902 he joined the Vienna Pscyhoanalytic Society, which Freud had founded.

Adler's formulations concerning inferiority feelings and compensatory striving for power as basic factors in personality development precipitated an open break with Freud in 1911. With a substantial group of followers,

Adler established a new theoretical system which became known as Individual Psychology (*q.v.*). In his lectures and books he addressed himself not only to specialists in his field, but also to intelligent laymen, educators, and all those concerned with the welfare of children. He also founded a number of child-guidance clinics, several of which are still active. His influence, long overshadowed by that of freud, has in recent years achieved increased recognition, and his teachings can be seen to underlie many contemporary developments in personality theory and psychotherapy.

Adolescence: It is the period of development marked at the beginning by the onset of puberty and at the end by the attainment of physiological or psychological maturity.

Adrenergic: Means having an adrenaline-like action or characterizing the action of autonemic fibbers of the sympathetic nervous system which secrete sympathin, an andrenaline-like product.

Adrenocorticotrophic Hormone (ACTH): A hormone secreted by the anterior pituitary that functions in the growth and development of that adrenal cortex. It also plays a critical role in the continued functioning of the adrenal cortices by stimulating the production of glucocorticoids and has been implicated in subpressing the production of testosterone.

Adult intelligence: The measured intellectual level at which the curve of mental growth has ceased to rise. It is estimated at between 16 and 19 by most authorities, but some would advance the point to the early twenties.

Aerobic: Pertaining to or characteristic of organisms that need or are not destroyed by free oxygen.

Affective congruency: Consistency between an individual's feelings about a segment of his self concept and related behavior and the feelings of others toward these same components.

Affective congruency: Refers to the consistency 'between an individual's feelings about a segment of his self concept and related behaviour and the feelings of others toward these same components.

Affective logic: It is made up of sequences of judgments or reasoning that superficially resemble logical chains of reasoning but upon closer examination are found to be linked by emotional factors.

Affective psychosis: Psychotic reaction especially characterized by severe emotional disturbances, like those occurring in manic, depressive reaction.

Affective ratio *(Rorschach)*: It is the ratio of the total number of responses to the coloured cards to the total responses to the uncoloured cards.

Affective syndrome organic: Refers to persons displaying serious disturbances of mood that are traceable to some particular organic factor, generally a toxic reaction to a drug or a metabolic disturbance.

Affective-arousal theory: A

theory proposed by D.C. McClelland that assumes motives arise from changes in the affective states. Specifically, it is held that motives arise when learned cues reinstate emotional or affective states originally associated with discrepancies in the individual's level of adaptation. Mild discrepancies result in pleasant states; extreme discrepancies in strongly unpleasant states.

Afferent code: Refers to the pattern of neural input to the brain corresponding to the pattern of environmental stimulation.

Afferent stimulus interaction: (*Hull*) the postulate that all afferent impulses interact in such a way as to modify one another.

Afferent: Refers to the conduction of nerve impulses from the periphery to or toward the central nervous system.

Affiliation *(Murray)*: Refers to the need for friendly association with others; formation of friendships; joining of groups.

Affordance: Refers to the "invitational" quality of a percept or an event. In a sense, affordance refers to the intrinsic properties of items and events.

Afterimage: It is the continuation of a sensory experience after removal of the stimulus. In visual experience, after images may be positive or negative. If positive, they are of approximately the same hue and brightness as the original stimulus. If negative, they are less saturated, duller, and approximately the complementary colour of the original stimulus.

Age norm: The average score on a standardized test observed in a large, representative sample of children at a particular age.

Age-grade scaling: The standardising of educational materials by determining the norms for a Population of children who are at the appropriate grade level for their age.

Agenesis: Lack of reproductive capacity or Complete or partial failure of an organ or organ part to develop properly.

Agent: Refers to anything that produces an effect. The "thing" may be a chemical substance, a force, a person, a group of persons, etc.

Aggregation theory: A theory of intelligence according to which abilities are a function of dispersed localized areas in the cerebral cortex.

Agnosia: Refers to partial or total inability to attach meaning to sensory impressions. Agnosia may take place in any sensory modality and is generally the result of brain injury.

A-ha experience: Refers to the feeling that accompanies the moment of insight, that instant when the various disparate aspects of a problem-solving situation suddenly fit together to yield the solution.

Albedo: The reflectance of any surface particularly, the percentage of light that is reflected by a surface measured against the total light-falling on that surface.

Albinism: A category of pigment disorders characterized by a less than normal production of melanin in the skin.

Alcohol hallucinosis: Refers to a syndrome of vivid auditory hallucinations following the sudden cessation of alcohol intake after an extended history of alcohol abuse.

Alcohol withdrawal: Refers to an organic mental disorder that is characterized by coarse trem or of the hands, eyelids and tongue, nausea, weakness, sweating, depressed, mood anxiety and irritability.

Aldosterone: The most active of the mineralocorticoids produced by the adrenal cortICts, aldosterone is important in the regulation of the metabolism of sodium, potassium and choline.

Alexia: Means without words. A languagerelated disability characterized by the partial or complete loss of the ability to identify the printed word. The disorder is often quite specific in that alexics do not have impairment of vision and can identify spoken words normally. Sometimes called *word blindness* and *visual aphsia.*

Alexithymia: It is a disruption in both affective and cognitive processes. It is not treated as a "true" Psychiatric syndrome. Typically the alexithymic person has relatively undifferentiated emotions and thinking tends to dwell excessively on the mundane.

Algesimeter: It is a device for measuring sensitivity to pain. A variety of such devices exists. In all cases, the basic data are the subjects' reports of subjective experience.

Alimentary canal (or tract): The system of organs made up of a tubular passage from mouth to anus that serves digestive functions. It includes the mouth, pharynx, esophagus, stomach, small and large intestines, and the rectum.

Allele: One of a pair of genes located at corresponding positions on a pair of chromosomes. Each pair of alleles controls or influences a specific trait, like eye colour. One allele is generally dominant and the other recessive.

Allelotropia: Refers to the apparent shifting in lateral position of an element in the visual field when a similar element is presented to a disparate position in the other eye.

Allergy: It is a condition of heightened sensitivity to foreign substances that would be harmless to most people but, in the susceptible individual, causes reactions ranging from mild irritation to shock and, in rare cases, death.

Allochiria, Allocheiria: Refers to a condition wherein touch is referred to a corresponding point on the opposite side of the body being stimulated.

Allophone: Refers to one of two or more elementary sounds in a particular language that differ in acoustic or articulatory properties but without conveying any difference in meaning.

Alpha block: Refers to the inhibition of the resting alpha wave of 8-10 Hz by asynchronous and rapid beta waves when a novel stimulus is presented.

Alpha blocking: A change in the alpha rhythm of an EEG because of any shift away from normal, waking, relaxation. Alpha rhythms may be "blocked" by the person orienting toward a stimulus such as a sound or light, by a state of apprehension or anxiety, or by a mental activity such as performing multiplication covertly.

Alpha examination: Refers to a group verbal test made up of eight subtests; the Army Alpha Test was administered extensively to military personnel during World War I.

Alpha motor neuron: Refers to one of the large motor neurons that controls the voluntary or skeletal muscles.

Alpha response: It is a rapid, low-amplitude response that is assumed to be an unconditioned response that develops as a result of sensitisation during training.

Alpha rhythm: The alpha rhythm has a normal frequency of 8-12 cycles per second and an amplitude of 5-15 microvolts. It is, affected by age, drugs, mental activity, sleep, and sensory stimuli.

Alpha, beta, gamma hypotheses: These are three hypotheses that state the relationship of frequency of repetition to rate of learning. Alpha: frequency promotes learning; Beta: frequency has no influence; Gamma: frequency hinders learning.

Altercasting: Means influencing the role of another by choosing a specific role oneself, thereby, reducing alternative behaviour for the other.

Alternate form: It is a scaie of items quite similar to another scale such that the two arc considered as different versions of the same test.

Alternate-response test: Refers to any test that presents two responses for each question, the subject is required to choose the correct alternative.

Alternating personality: A dual personality, one component of which tends to alternate in its appearances with the other component.

Alternating perspective: A drawing that creates a sense of the third dimension in that part of the figure alternately closer and farther away as the figure is fixated.

Alternating perspective: Refers to the shift in perspective that takes place when one fixates on a particular stimulus for a period of time.

Alternating vision: Refers to the use of first one and then the; other eye in seeing. For most purposes one of the eyes is dominant over the other, whose sensory information is suppressed.

Alzheimer's disease: It is a progressive form of presenile dementia that is superficially similar to senility except that it strikes relatively early in life.

The first sign is impaired memory, generally followed by disturbed speech and thought and ultimately complete helplessness.

Amaurotic idiocy: Refers to a group of related, genetically transmitted diseases which are marked by retardation and vision deficits and produced by faulty metabolism.

Amazon: Refers to a myth of a race of, female Greek warriors, a tall, muscular woman. Such women are falsely considered as lesbians, there is no relationship-between a woman's physical stature and her sexual preferences.

Ambiequal: Refers to one who is well balanced in extratensive and introtensive tendencies; neither egocentric not excessively dependent upon others.

Ambiguity tolerance: It is the ability to withstand conflicting or complex situations without undue psychological distress.

Ambulatory psychotherapy: Refers to outpatient treatment of persons suffering from psychological disorders.

Ames room: It is a specially constructed room designed by the artist/psychologist Adelbert Ames. It provides a striking demonstration of the cues for depth perception,

The room is of distorted construction, three of the walls are actually trapesoidal and the ceiling slants markedly. However, due to the use of the cues of shading, size constancy and interposition, the room appears normal to an outside observer.

Looking into the room produces many illusions, objects and persons appear distorted particularly in their apparent size, round objects seem to roll uphill, etc.

Amnesia: Refers to any partial or complete loss of memory. Amnesic syndrome which is "physiological" is caused by some form of damage to brain tissue or "psychological" which is caused by any of a variety of factors including alterations in the memorial code or neurotic reactions.

Amytal: Sodium Amytal. It is the proprietary name for one of the barbiturates used extensively as a sedative and hypnotic. It is also called "truth serum," because under its influence inhibitions may be lowered with the result that the individual will discuss his problems more freely. Contrary to popular opinion, criminals do not confess against their will when given hypnotic drugs.

Anabolic: Means, promoting a buildup or restoration of a structure or body. Anabolic agents like testosterone or similar steroids stimulate anabolism.

Anabolism: Refers to conservation phase of bodily metabolism where in tissues are restored and built up, in contrast to catabolism or the expenditure and breaking down of tissue.

Anaglyph: Refers to a picture printed in two complementary colours slightly offset from each other so that when viewed through lenses of corresponding colours (one colour to each eye) the effect is one of stereoscopic depth. This process is that used in the production of 3-D movies.

Anaglyptoscope: It is a device which shifts the angle of lighting on a test object, resulting in a reversal of areas of shadow and light. It is used to demonstrate the role of shadows in the perception of depth.

Anal expulsive (Stage): Some psychoanalytic theorists hypothesise two distinct aspects to the anal stage, one characterized by anal expulsiveness, where in pleasure is derived from the passing of phases, and the other characterized by anal retentiveness, wherein pleasure is associated with the withholding of phases.

Anal sadism: It is a form of sadism originating in an individual's resentment due to punishment he received during toilet training.

Anal sadistic: Refers to any sadistic pleasure hypothesized to originate in the *anal stage.* Such behaviour derives from harsh punishment during toilet training.

Analog: A thing or event is said to be an analog of another if' there 'is a coherent correspondence between their parts, function, roles, etc.

Analogical reasoning: Reasoning by which decisions about objects, events or concepts depend upon perceived similarities in the relationships between pairs.

Analogies test: A test wherein a relationship between two terms is given and the person is asked to complete an analogous relationship.

Analogy: It is the a functional correspondence in organs that are anatomically different or found in different species.

Anal-sadistic stages: Refers to an infantile period of development characterized by anal eroticism and sadistic impulses directed toward the parent.

Analytical psychology: 1. Any system of psychology that attempts to reduce phenomena to their constituent elements. 2. Jung's system of psychoanalysis. Analytical Psychology, founded by Carl Jung of Zurich, Switzerland, was originally modeled after Freud's psycho-analysis. However, almost from the beginning, Jung began to deviate from Freud, and the final break came in 1912 with the publication of *The Psychology of the Unconscious*, in which Jung presented his new interpretation of the libido. The libido, according to Jung, is the general life energy of "life urge," and this primal energy is not, as Freud had argued, necessarily manifested as the sexual drive; it may show itself at one time as sexual energy, at another as a creative or artistic form of behavior, or in still another setting as a striving for superiority. The psychological process by which libidinal energy is transformed into cultural activities is the symbol. Symbols emerge in the unconscious part of the psyche.

Some of these belong to the primitive, collective unconscious modern man has inherited from his jungle ancestors. Others belong to the personal or individual unconscious, which develops out of repression from the individual's past. The primal symbols Jung called *archetypes* and these are universal.

Some of the more common archetypal symbols are those for the Mother, the Hero, the Flood, the Cross, which are found again and again in the world's myths and literature. As these are made available to the conscious mind they become a powerful guiding force in a man's behaviour, particularly in its religious and ethical aspects.

Archetypes of special significance in the individual personality are the persona, the shadow, the anima and animus, and the self. The persona is the mask that the individual presents to the world. The shadow is the dark, destructive side of personality. The anima is the female component of the male personality representing a kind of ideal woman which the man seeks.

The animus is the corresponding male arche-type in the woman. The self is the core of personality around which the other archetypes are integrated. Jung also emphasized the bipolar nature of mind. The best-know of these dimensions is the introversion- extroversion polarity, or the inward-and outward-directed poles of personality. Extroverts are those whose personalities are directed outward, along social lines—men of action, rather than men of thought, finding value in objects and persons rather than in their own psyches.

Introverts, on the other hand, are directed inward, finding value in their own ideas and feelings, and tending to avoid the world of action and social affairs. Jung also believed that there were four main kinds of mental activity constituting two pairs of polar opposites: thinking, and feeling, and sense perception and intuition. Combining the four main types of mental activity with extroversion and introversion, Jung developed his theory around eight basic types of individuals. The masculinity-femininity dimension of the psyche is another important bipolar opposite. In treating his patients. Jung attempted to bring to consciousness the repressed side of the psyche. Thus, in treating men, the feminine unconscious could be made available and its intuitive, artistic aspects utilized in enriching the individual's life. Jung's system of therapy, like Freud's consisted of the use of free association and dream interpretation.

However, Jung used dream analysis in order to understand the individual's current problems and future aspirations rather than solely as a basis for understanding the role of past experience as a cause of psychic difficulties. Jung also emphasized a more active form of therapy than Freud's, not hesitating to intervene with interpretations and suggestions.

Anaphylaxis, psychological: Refers to psychological hypersensitivity resulting from a previous traumatic experience so that later presentation of the original circumstances causes deep psychological distress.

Anchedonia: Absence of hedonic tone or pleasantness unpleasantness in situation that normally elicit such emotional reactions.

Androgyneity: In anthropology refers to the concept that the individual has bipolar potentiality in sex until he is turned into a definite sex by tribal ritual.

Anesthesia; Anaesthesia: Refers to a complete or partial loss of sensitivity to external and/or internal stimuli due to drugs, lesions, or functional causes.

Angell, James Rowland: American psychologist and leader in the functionalistic movement Angell studied at Michigan under John Dewey and at Harvard, where he came under James's influence. After graduate study at Halle, Germany, he taught for one year at the University of Minnesota, and then spent the next twenty-five years as a teacher and administrator at the University of Chicago. It was there that he assumed leadership of the functionalist school. Upon leaving Chicago, Angell became president of Yale—the first president of that institution who was not an alumnus. Following his retirement from academic life in 1937, he served as educational counselor with the National Broadcasting Company.

Angell is notable among the functionalists for developing the movement into a full-fledged school of psychology. He is also recognized his administrative ability in making the department at Chicago the most influential of its day. Among his many students and associates were John B. Watson and Harvey Carr, both of whom became leaders of schools in their own right.

Anger: A state of an acute emotional reaction elicited by any of a number of stimulating situations, including threat, overt aggression, restraint, verbal attack, disappointment, or frustration. It is characterized by strong responses in the autonomic nervous system, specially by emergency reactions of the sympathetic division and by implicit or overt attack responses that may be either somatic or verbal.

Angina: Refers to a feeling of suffocation, of being choked. It is a disease of the pharynx characterized by attacks of choking.

Angular gyrus: A convolution of the cerebral cortex located in the posterior portion of the lower parietal region near the posterior end of the upper temporal fissure. Broadmann's number 39. Believed to be associated with speech functions.

Aniconia: Absence of mental imagery.

Anima: 1. In Jung's early formulations, the part of personality in close contact with the unconscious, in contrast with the persona, which represents the social self. 2. in later formulations, an archetype representing the feminine characteristics, in contrast to *animus*, which represents masculine characte-ristics.

Animal magnetism: Refers to hypnotism in which the hypnotic state was induced by the flow of magnetism from the operator to the subject.

Animal psychology: It is a branch of psychology that deals with the systematic study of animal behaviour, particularly from a comparative point of view.

Animal: Refers to a member of one of the two divisions of living Organisms distinguished from plants (the second of the two) primarily by lack of photosy-nthesising ability. In psychology, references to animals typically mean organisms lower than man.

Ankle clonus: It is the process of repetitive contraction-relaxation of the ankle muscles and is a common Symptom of neurological disease's of the central nervous system.

Anterior horns: Refers to the ventral portion of the gray matter in the spinal cord. These are the site of origin on the large motor neurons controlling muscular movement.

Anthropology: It is the study of mankind. It includes archeology, linguistics, psychology, sociology and smatterings of *biology*, anatomy, genetics and compa-rative literature.

Anthropology: The science of man, including his physical characte-ristics, his cultures, and his races. Broadly, anthropology is divided into *physical anthropology*, which includes the study of anatomy and the anthropometric characte-ristics of various groups, and *cultural anthropology*, which is the study of nonliterate cultures.

Anthropometry: The science of measurements of bodily form, particularly the proportions and relative frequency of occurrence of physical characteristics among the different races, cultures, sexes, etc.

Anthropomorphism: 1. Attributing human characteristics to gods, animals, or inanimate objects. 2. interpreting the behaviour of lower forms in terms of human abilities or characteristics.

Anthropopathy: Attributing human feelings or emotions to gods or animals.

Antidiuretic hormone (ADH): It is a hormone released by the posterior pituitary which increases the capacity of the kidney tubules to reabsorbe water, thus reducing urinary output.

Antihistamine: Refers to any substance or agent that inhibits or blocks the effect of *histamine.* They are useful in controlling rashes and allergic reactions due to release of histamine and are helpful to sufferers of hayfever. They are also used as mild sedatives as they tend to produce drowsiness in most (but not all) persons.

Anti-intraception: Refers to a tendency to be opposed to that which is subjective, imaginative, humanistic. It is considered as a characteristic of the *authoritarian personality*.

Antimania drugs: Drugs which are used for the treatment of *hypomania* and *manic-depressive psychosis*. The drug of choice here is one of the lithium compounds. These drugs also help in preventing the depressive aspect of manic-depression.

Antimetropia: Refers to condition wherein the two eyes have differences in refractive power, *e.g.,* one eye is myopic-and the other hyperopic.

Antisocial personality: A behavioural disorder characterized by truancy, delinquency, promiscuity, theft, vandalism, fighting, violation of common social rules, poor work record, impulsiveness, irrationality, aggressiveness, reckless behaviour, and inability to plan ahead. The particular pattern of behaviour varies from individual to individual.

Antonym test: It is a verbal test where the subject is given a word and must supply its antonym as quickly as possible.

Anxiety neurosis: A neurosis wherein the most prominent symptom is anxiety that cannot be identified with any particular cause and that in many cases is pervasive and affects major areas of the individual's life.

Anxiety reaction: Complex response pattern characterized by strong feelings of anxiety and accom-panied by somatic symptoms, such as palpitations of the heart, choking, tightness of the chest, trembling, faintness, etc.

Anxiety tolerance: The level of anxiety the individual can stand without serious psychological harm or maladjustment.

Anxiety: 1. Feeling of mingled dread and apprehension about the future without specific cause for the fear. 2. a chronic fear of mild degree. 3. strong, over-whelming fear. 4. a secondary drive involving an acquired avoidance response. In the presence of the conditioned stimulus (usually shock) the animal subject displays behavior interpreted as evidence of anxiety, including urination, defecation, attempting to flee the apparatus, etc. 5. The inability to predict the future or to resolve problems because the individual's construct system does not seem to apply to ongoing events.

Anxiety-relief responses: In behavior therapy, a technique in which the word "calm" is associated with the termination of an electric shock with the objective that the patient will eventually be able to reduce anxiety by thinking of the word in anxiety-arousing situations.

Aphrasia: Refers to the functional inability or refusal 6 utter correct words or phrases even though separate words may be spoken.

Apomorphine: It is a drug which mimics the action of dopamine. (q.v.) at the synapse. It may be used to induce vomiting.

Applied psychology: That branch of psychology that utilizes the principles and discoveries of psychology for practical ends. The applies psychologist may "borrow" principles or discoveries from the theoretical psychologist, or he may conduct his own research program. Discoveries in practical fields are then added to the general fund of psychological knowledge. Thus, applied psychology an theoretical psychology are complementary, each contributing to the other.

Apport: Refers to the hypothesised moving of an object to a particular place by paranormal means.

Apprehension: It is the act of seizing or of grasping. Apprehension is generally considered as a rather primitive, immediate act and distinguished from *comprehension,* that involves more in the way of reflection and interpretation.

Apprehensiveness: Refers to a relatively mild sense of anxiety about upcoming events, an uneasiness about future happenings.

Approach-approach conflict: It is a situation wherein the individual is drawn toward equally attractive but incompatible goals. For example, a college senior might receive equally attractive offers from two professional courses to which he has applied.

Arachnoid layer: It is the delicate membrane intermediate between the pia mater and dura mater in the brain and spinal cord.

Arborisation: Interlacing, branching. Used of nerve processes that display treelike conformations.

Area sampling: Refers to the use of all respondents in a given geographical area. For example, all respondents in a square mile in a given city.

Argot Means slang. A specialized slang that reflects the common and unique experiences of a particular group. Originally, argot was reserved for the language of criminal groups, now it is more widely used.

Armed forces qualification test:

A preliminary screening test consisting of several subtests designed to provide scores of performance on verbal, arithmetic, spatial and mechanical skills as well as a single general score.

Army alpha (and beta) tests: Two general tests of intelligence used in screening recruits for the U.S. Army in World War I. The Beta was a performance test designed for illiterates and recent emigres to America whose English was poor; the Alpha was a standard examination that drew heavily on verbal skills.

Artificial intelligence: The solution by computers or information processing systems of tasks that normally require human intelligence.

Artificialism: Refers to child's tendency to explain-natural phenomena in terms of intentions. For example, when asked why the clouds move the child answers, "The clouds move because they want to."

Asceticism: It is a way of living based upon voluntary, abstention from sensual, physical pleasures and emphasizing simplicity and self-disciplinc.

Asexual: Means reproduction that does not involving the union of sex cells from two different individuals.

Assay: Means to examine by test or trial. Hence, the analysis of any complex subject (*e.g.,* a' chemical substance, a drug) to determine its components.

Assets-liabilities technique: A therapeutic procedure wherein the client compiles two lists of his or her behavioural and personality characteristics, one containing traits regarded as being of value (assets) and the other listing traits seen as personal liabilities. The technique is generally used in behaviour therapy for specifying the goals for the client.

Association neuron: Refers to one of the neurons in the central nervous system which connect sensory and motor neurons or, connect any two centres in the brain

Association test: It is a psychometric or experimental procedure that is designed to assess the subject's reactions to stimuli of various sorts. In *free association* tests, the subject is allowed to respond with word that comes into his mind.

In *controlled association* tests he must respond according to a predetermined category, such as synonyms, antonyms, etc.

Association-reaction time: It is the elapsed time between a Stimulus word and the response in a word association test.

Associative learning: Learning as the formation of bonds between ideas, or stimulus-response units.

Associative memory: The remembering of a past experience or an idea by recalling something associated with it. Thus, revisiting a town after many years' absence may recall a series of long-forgotten incidents each associated with one or more of the others.

Associative shifting: (*Thorn-dike*) The principle that responses learned to one set of stimuli may be learned to a new set provided that the overall situation is kept similar. Thorndike considered conditioning a form of associative shifting.

Associative strength: The strength of a stimulus-response connection in verbal learning as measured by the frequency with which a given stimulus evokes the response, or as measured by its persistence in memory.

Associative thinking: Refers to the thinking that depends on past associations. A train of thought where one idea leads to another illustrates this form of thinking.

Associative thinking: Thinking that depends on past associations. A train of thought where one idea leads to another illustrates this form of thinking.

Assumption: It is a premise or supposition that something is true for the purpose of theoretical development. The term includes *hypothesis,* a principle to be tested experimentally, and *postulate,* a principle assumed to be true for the purpose of developing a theory.

Astigmatism: Refers to the failure of the light entering the eye to come to a focal point due to irregularities in the curvature of the refracting mechanism mostly the cornea.

Asynergia: Refers to inability to carry out complex motor activities involving coordination between different muscle groups.

Atomism: The theory that psychological phenomena are best studied and understood when reduced to their constituent parts or elements. The term is chiefly used with derogatory implications by the opponents of this point of view.

Atropine: It is a drug which acts to block the action of acetylcholine at certain synaptic sites. Once widely used in eye examinations to relax the iris and in research, on thirst to block salivation.

Attitude: A relatively stable and enduring predisposition to behave or react in a certain way toward persons, objects, institutions, or issues. Looked at from a slightly different point of view, attitudes are tendencies to respond to people, institutions or events either positively or negatively. Attitudes typically imply a tendency to classify or categorize.

Thus, one with a favorable attitude toward the Democratic party is likely to react factorably to all Democrats, disregarding their unique characteristics as individuals. Similarly, if the individual holds the attitude that "All Jews are aggressive" he will respond to Jewish people as if they were aggressive, whether or not they are in fact aggressive.

The source of attitudes are cultural, familial, and personal. That is, we tend to assume the attitudes that prevail in the culture in which we grow up. A large segment of these are passed on from generation to generation within the family structure. But some of our attitudes are also developed as adults on the basis of our own experience.

Social psychologists believe that important sources of adult on the basis of our own experience. Social psychologists believe that important sources of adult attitudes are propaganda and suggestion from authority, business, educational institutions, and other agencies that seek to influence conduct.

Because attitudes differ in degree as well as in kind, psychologists have devised techniques for the measurement of attitudes. Several types of attitude scales have been developed for use with individuals and groups, and mass techniques of public-opinion polling have been developed for the assessment of national attitudes.

Attribution theory: The position that without necessarily being aware of doing so, individuals employ a number of tests to determine whether another person's words and deeds reflect his underlying characteristics or are merely forced responses to a given situation.

A-type personality: A personality pattern characterized by competitiveness, aggressiveness, high achievement, impatience and restlessness. Presumed to be associated with proneness to coronary disease.

Authoritarian personality: A personality pattern characterized by strongly held beliefs, prejudices, and ethnocentrism. Such individuals tend to be highly conventional, submissive to authority, puritanical in sexual attitudes, disciplinarians, and inflexible in attitudes and behaviour.

Aversive behaviour: Refers to the study of behaviour under conditions of noxious stimulation. It includes the three major phenomena of *escape learning, avoidance learning* and the effects of *punishment*.

B

Balance theory: the position that people prefer to hold consistent and compatible beliefs while avoiding those that are inconsistent and incompatible.

Ballistic movement: a smooth, projectilelike movement in which the limb "follows through." Time-and-motion experts consider ballistic movements more efficient than other types of movements.

Bandura, Albert: American psychologist. Bandura was born December 4, 1925, in Mundara, Alberta, Canada. He grew up in the Province of Alberta, where he received his early schooling. He received his B.A. degree from the University of British Columbia in 1949, earning his M.A. and Ph.D., from the University of lowa. He served a year's clinical internship at the Wichita Guidance Center after receiving his doctorate and then accepted an appointment to the department of psychology at Stanford University, where he has remained ever since. In 1974 he was awarded the endowed chair, The David Starr Jorgan Professor of Social Science. Throughout his career at Standford, Bandura has been a leader in developing social learning theory, an attempt to apply a modified form of behaviourism, stressing a cognitive approach, to the understanding of human behavior with clinical applications.

Bandura has published numerous technical articles in professional journals and several influential books, *Social Learning and Personality Principles of Behaviour Modification, Aggression and Social Learning Theory*. In 1972 he received the Distinguished Scientist Award from the American Psychological Association, and in 1974 was elected president of that organization.

Basic personality: the constellation of personality traits common to individuals in a given culture which results from common childhood experience and training.

Basic skills: a term used in

educational literature to refer to the fundamentals of reading, writing, and arithmetic, whose mastery is needed to progress normally at higher levels. Behavior therapy is based on experimental studies of conditioning, both of the classical and operant varieties. Joseph Wolpe's publication, *Psychotherapy by Reciprocal Inhibition,* is considered one of the landmarks in the development of behavior therapy.

Utilizing the concept of reciprocal inhibition, which refers to the discovery that a response incompatible with another will inhibit the former, Wolpe demonstrated that individuals suffering from anxiety reactions could be trained to over come their problem by pairing imagined anxiety-producing situations with physical relaxation. Because anxiety and relaxation are incompatible responses, as relaxation increases, anxiety decreases. Care is taken to ensure that the imagined anxiety-producing situations are introduced in a hierarchy of low to high anxiety-induction in order to ensure gradual learning to cope with even the most severe situations.

Desensitization may also involve the gradual introduction of feared stimuli or situations. Fear of snakes has been overcome by introducing the subject to snakes in a cage at a distance, then having the subject gradually approach and touch the cage. The therapist may then remove the snake and handle it as the client watches.

The client eventually is encouraged to touch and handle the snake himself. Aversive techniques may also be employed by behaviour therapists to overcome undesirable behaviours such as excessive smoking, drinking, or homo-sexuality. For example, the alcoholic may be given a drug (antabuse) that induces nausea if the ingestion of alcohol occurs while the drug is in the bloodstream. After a number of such pairings of the drug with alcohol ingestion, drinking becomes aversive. Similarly, electric shock paired with nude photographs of the same sex may be used in the treatment of homosexuality.

Among operant techniques derived from the experimental analysis of behavior by B.F. Skinner and his associates, the most widely used is the token economy, which involves a program of contingency reinforcement for behavioral responses that the therapist considers desirable. For example, a mentally retarded child may be trained to brush his teeth by reinforcing him with a token which can be "spent" for candy, television watching time, etc.

similarly, the adult mental patient may be reinforced with tokens for behaving in ways that the staff deems desirable or more adaptive. The utilization of the token economy is based on the theory of generalized reinforcers that acquire their reinforcing effect thought association with primary reinforcers.

Behaviour determinant: (*Tolman*) any variable that is a necessary antecedent condition for behaviour to occur.

Behaviour therapy: The systematic application of learning principles and techniques to the treatment of behavior disorders. Behavior therapists assume that disorders are learned ways of behaving that are maladaptive and consequently can best be modified in more adaptive directions through relearning. In contrast to traditional forms of psychotherapy, behavior therapy minimizes the client's verbal explorations toward the eventual restructuring of personality by removing repressions and achieving insight. Instead, a direct attack is made on the client's symptoms.

Thus, if the client complains of anxiety, the behavior the-rapist does not attempt to trace the history of the problem back to childhood but instead initiates a program of reconditi-oning reconditioning designed to alleviate the symptoms of anxiety in those situations in which the client finds them most troublesome.

Behaviour: 1. any response(s) made by an organism. 2. specifically, parts of a total response pattern. 3. an act or activity. 4. a movement or complex of movements. Although American psychologists are generally in agreement that the subject matter of psychology is behavior, there is considerable divergence of opinion as to precisely what ought to be included under the category of behavior. Taken in its broadest sense, behavior includes anything the individual does or experiences.

Ideas, dreams, glandular responses, running, maneuvering a space ship—all are behavior. In a narrower sense, *behavior* can be defined to include only objectively or publicly observable responses. This definition would exclude such conscious phenomena as thinking, perceiving, judgment, and the like, except as these may be studied through their consequences in behavior. Few psychologists today define their subject matter so rigidly as to exclude any major segment of human activity.

Most behaviorists, however objectively oriented they may be, believe that there is room in psychology for inferred or intervening variables. Thus, the term *behavior* no longer implies the strict behaviorism championed by Watson and the opponents of structuralism. In general, American psychology has become behavioristic in method, but in spirit it is sufficiently broad to include the study of all important segments of human activity.

Behavioural contagion: the lessening of restraint as a result of observing others behave in a certain way.

Behavioural dynamics: the pattern of motives that underlies behavior.

Behavioural genetics: a branch of psychology concerned with the investigation of genetic or hereditary influences on behavior.

Behavioural homology: the generalization that behavioural patterns form a continuity from species to species. Thus, fear responses in lower forms correspond in function and pattern to fear in man.

Behavioural oscillation: (*Hull*) variations in reaction potential from moment to moment. Behavioral oscillations follows the normal frequency curve.

Behavioural pattern: any complex act made up of recognizably individual components that are organized into a whole. Riding a bicycle is an example of a complex behavioural pattern made up of mounting, pedaling, steering, braking, etc.

Behavioural rehearsal: In behavior therapy, the utilization of role playing by therapist and patient with the goal of helping the patient overcome deficits in interpersonal behaviour.

Behavioural sciences: the sciences that study the activities of man and the lower animals by means of naturalistic observation and experimentation. These include psychology, sociology, and social anthropology.

Behavioural: a term used to distinguish sciences whose aims and methods, are objective as opposed to subjective or mentalistic.

Borderline intelligence: An intellectual level between retardation and normalcy. An IQ in the 70's may be characterized as borderline, but the determination of normalcy or retardation must always be an individual matter, taking into account not only the measured intellectual level but social and legal factors as well.

Brain: The mass of nervous tissue within the skull. Its principal parts are diagrammed in the accompanying figure. Working up from the top of the spinal cord, we first come to the *medulla*, which is essentially an enlargement of the upper cord where it connects with the brain. Running through the medulla on the way to and from the brain are the various spinal pathways. The medulla also contains a number of *nuclei* or centers, that are important in the regulation of vital functions, such as respiration and circulation. To the rear of the medulla lies the *cerebellum*, or "little brain."

The cerebellum is the chief organ for the control of coordination and posture. It receives fibers from the kinesthetic and vestibular pathways and has abundant interconnections with the cerebrum. The *pons* (Latin for "bridge") lies above the medulla and is a bridge between the two halves of the cerebellum in that fibers connecting the right and left hemispheres of that organ pass through the pons.

The pons also has a number of nuclei or centers for the origin and termination of cranial nerves serving the head. The *midbrain* connects the pons and medulla to the brain proper and also contains reflex centers important in vision and hearing. The rest of the brain is known as the *forebrain* and is the most highly developed part of the brain both in man and the higher animals. Referring again to the figure, we see that the thalamic region of the forebrain lies above the midbrain. The *thalamus* is a great relay station where incoming sensory impulses are shunted to appropriate higher centers. The *hypothalamus* lies downward and forward from the thalamus. It is not a lower extension of the thalamus with similar functions. It is important in a number of *motivational* and *emotional* aspects of behaviour. An important part of the forebrain is the *limbic system*, which consists of the *cingulate cortex* an old part of the cortex that lies deep within the longitudinal fissure, the *septal region*, the *fornix*, the *hippocampus*, the *amygdala*, and according to some authorities, the hypothalamus.

The limbic system is important in emotional reactions. For example, the destruction of the amygdala nuclei will turn ferocious animals into docile creatures. The septal region has been identified as one of the socalled pleasure centers of the brain. The hippocampus has been implicated in conditioned fear reactions and possibly in short-term memory storage. The functions of the cingulate gyrus and fornix are not yet completely understood.

The *reticular formation* is a loosely organized network of cells extending from the region of the medulla upward to the level of the thalamus and hypothalamus. This system is a nonspecific cluster of centers that receives afferent impulses as they branch off from afferent neurons arriving from the various sense organs. From the reticular formation impulses are relayed to subcortical centers and to the cerebral cortex, which contains the higher brain centers.

Conversely, neurons originating in the higher centers and in the subcortical nuclei give off branches as they travel through the reticular formation before entering the spinal cord. Thus, the reticular system acts as a two-way communication center intermediate between the great steam of incoming sensory impulses and the rest of the brain. One function of the reticular formation is to serve as a cortical activation center. When bursts of sensory impulses are streaming in from the peripheral sense organs, the system goes into activity, thus "alerting" the rest of the brain. It is possible that the system may also serve as a switching center that determines to what parts of the cortex impulses will be shunted. Because the reticular system also mediates between outgoing impulses from the cortex to the muscles, it may well be that if also determines to what extent motor processes will be aroused by environmental stimulation.

It is even possible that we may have to modify some of our traditional thinking about the cerebral cortex as the sole center of consciousness in factor of assigning this role to the effects of the reticular activating system as they impinge upon the cortex. We have now reached the *cerebrum*, which is the largest, most conspicuous part of the central nervous system in higher animals. It is divided into the *right* and *left cerebral hemispheres*, which are connected to each other by the *corpus callosum*. The outer half-inch layer of the cerebrum known as the *cerebral cortex* consists of *gray* matter and takes its appearance from the fact that the cell bodies of neurons have a grayish tint. Below the surface most of the brain consists of *white matter*, or the whitish axons and dendrites of the fibers traveling to and from the cortex.

The cerebral cortex is covered with invaginations, or fissures, which provide natural anatomical land-marks by means of which various lobes and functional areas can be distinguished. Neurologists believe that the cerebral cortex became invaginated in the course of evolution when it developed so rapidly that it could not fit inside the skull without folding. It has also been suggested that by wrinkling, more tissue surface is exposed to the cerebral blood supply—an advantage for an organ that demands a large volume of blood. The most important of these invaginations is the *central fissure*, which begins in the center of the cortex at the longitudinal fissure and runs downward and somewhat forward until it meets the *lateral fissure* which runs along the side of the brain. The tissue ahead of the central fissure makes up the *frontal lobe*. The *parietal lobe* lies to the rear of the central fissure, roughly under the corresponding parietal bone of the skull. The *occipital lobe* is not precisely delineated by fissures, but is located in the back of the brain.

Functional areas of the cortex. Traditionally, the functional areas of the cortex have been divided into two broad categories (1) *primary sensory and motor areas* (2) *associative areas*. The primary areas are those that either receive (sensory) impulses from lower centers or, in the case of the motor areas, initiate voluntary movements. the association centers may be thought of as the integrating and interpreting areas of the brain. These are the centers responsible for the so-called "higher" mental processes of thinking, learning, perceiving, etc. We shall examine each of these two kinds of cortical areas in some detail. The motor system can be broadly divided into two main divisions, *pyramidal* and *extrapyramidal*. the pyramidal system originates in the per central gyrus in the frontal lobes of the cerebral cortex. It takes its name from the fact that the cell bodies of the cortical neurons are shaped roughly like a double pyramid. From the cortex the fibers stream downward through the medulla, where approximately 80 percent cross over before continuing to the lower parts of the spinal cord.

The remaining 20 percent cross just before terminating in the spinal cord. Consequently, the pyramidal system is completely *contralateral*, in that the right precentral gyrus controls the left side of the body and the left gyrus controls the right side. Moreover, the upper part of the motor areas of the cortex controls the lower limbs, while the lower portion of the gyrus controls the muscles in the head. There is a disproportionate amount of tissue devoted to more mobile parts of the body such as the thumb, eyes, and mouth. The larger, less mobile portions of the body are represented by the relatively small amounts of cortex. If the precentral gyrus is stimulated by a weak electric current, movements are elicited in the corresponding part of the body. Indeed, our detailed knowledge of this area's functions was largely determined in this manner. If the area is destroyed, as frequently happens in older persons as a result of a stroke (cerebral hemorrhage), then the limbs and face on the opposite side become partly or totally paralyzed, depending on the extent of the damage. The extrapyramidal system is made up of all the other areas of the brain that contribute to muscular movements. Of these, the most important is the *premotor association area,* which lies immediately in front of the primary motor area. Its function is to lend skill and coordination to voluntary movements. When the area is removed in animals, the animal shows weakness and poor coordination on the affected side, and an inability to carry out skilled acts.

Clinical studies of human patients with brain injuries in the motor association area and nearby regions often reveal the presence of *apraxias*, or the inability to carry out purposeful acts, such as lighting a cigarette, playing a piano, or solving a simple motor problem. These difficulties are much more likely to occur if the injury is on the *dominant* side of the brain. The most important of the primary sensory areas are the *somaesthetic, visual,* and *auditory*. the somaesthetic (*soma* = body; *esthetic* = feeling) region lies just beyond the central fissure in the postcentral gyrus.

A *gyrus* (pl. *gyri*) is a strip of cortical tissue lying between two folds. It receives impulses from all over the body, mediating touch, pressure, temperature, sensitivity, and kinesthesis. Again, as is true of the motor region, the relationship is a crossed-over and upside-down one. In individuals whose somaesthetic region has been exposed during surgical operations, electrical stimulation of the area results in verbal reports to the effect that the patient feels sensations of warmth, numbness, and muscle movements in various parts of the body.

Destruction of the somaesthetic region results in reduced tactile sensitivity and a greatly raised two-point threshold. Apparently the sense of pain is not represented cortically. The somaesthetic (and other areas of the brain) can be cut, stimulated, or destroyed without arousing pain. Indeed patients undergoing brain surgery are usually conscious, the only anesthesia employed being local, to the scalp. Plain, therefore, is apparently mediated by subcortical centers in the thalamus. The primary visual area is located in the occipital lobe.

The optic neurons from the retina terminate in the very tip of the occipital lobe, where the nervous impulses arising in the retina are interpreted as lights. Careful studies of the relationship between the retina and the primary visual areas indicate that there is a point-for-point correspondence between the retina and the occipital cortex.

However, the optic neurons partly cross on their way to the brain. Consequently, injury to one of the primary visual centers results in one-half blindness in each eye (hemianopsia). If, for example, the right visual cortex were destroyed, the individual would be blind in the right half of each retina. Since the lens refracts light entering the eye in such a way that it crosses over, the left half of each visual field would be affected.

Electrical stimulation of the primary visual area gives rise to reports of pinpoints of light, whirling colors, starlike patterns, and, sometimes, particular colors. The primary auditory area is located in the temporal lobe. Each auditory cortex receives fibers from both ears. Electrical stimulation of the auditory cortex causes sensations of humming or buzzing. Interestingly, there is evidence that the organization of high, medium and low-pitch appreciation found in the cochlea is preserved in the auditory cortex. If pitch is dependent on the place stimulated in the sense organ, as Helmholtz supposed, then some kind of localization in the cortex would be demanded in order to preserve the organization of high, medium, and low pitches found in the cochlea.

The centers for taste and smell are not so clearly localized, are highly complex, and are only poorly understood. We need not attempt to trace them here. it is interesting to note, in light of evolutionary theory, that the centers for smell are extensive in man and are located in the older portions of the brain, phylogenetically speaking, where they have been overshadowed by evolutionarily more recent parts of the cerebral cortex.

The associative areas of the cortex are less specifically localized than the primary sensory areas. However, it is possible to state a general principle to the effect that with each primary area there is a nearby region of the cortex whose functions are associative. Thus, there are *somaesthetic, auditory*, and *visual association* areas adjacent to their corresponding primary areas. The association areas are able to retain information from past stimulation and relate it to incoming impulses. If, for example, we are shown a common object, such as an orange, the impulses generated by the retina and transmitted to the primary visual area are relayed to the visual association area. This "information" about the color, texture, and shape of an orange has been retained from past experience and we therefore recognize the stimulus as an orange.

Persons with injuries in the association areas are said to suffer fom *agnosia*, a condition characterized by an inability to recognize objects on the basis of the affected sense modality. A person with *visual agnosia,* for example, might not recognize a key visually even though he could tell what it was if he were allowed to feel it. Similarly, if blindfolded, persons suffering from *somaesthetic agnosia* would be unable to distinguish among a number of blocks of different geometric shapes.

Closely related to the motor and premotor areas of the cortex is a complex center known as *Broca's area,* or the *speech center.* This center is usually located on the left side of the brain and in this respect is unlike other cortical centers, such as Wernicke's area in the upper temporal region, which are represented bilaterally. Injuries to the speech center and to other language centers have been studied exhaustively since World War I, when many soldiers suffered lesions of the brain in combat.

Speech disorders that are a consequence of such injuries are called *aphasia,* or the inability to pronounce words, or if words are pronounced fluently, to put them together in meaningful sentences; (2) *alexia* or the inability to read; (3) *agraphia,* or the inability to write; (4) *amnesic aphasia,* or the inability to remember words. Because of the actual destruction of cortical tissue in aphasias, patients suffering from these disorders are very difficult to retain, although some relearning if possible if the damage is not too extensive. Finally, there is a relatively large mass of tissue on the frontal poles of the brain known as the *frontal association area.* This region, unlike the other association areas, is not closely linked with a specific primary area. Instead, its functions are general and involve the planning, management, and control of behavior.

Persons suffering injuries to the frontal lobes are likely to be impulsive, inconsiderate, excessively emotional, and lacking in good judgment. In a sense, then, the prefrontal association areas are the general head-quarters of the brain, exerting an over all controlling and guiding function on behavior. Recent studies of persons whose brains have been "split," that is, whose corpus callosum has been cut, reveal that the two cerebral hemispheres have different functions. In general, the left side of the brain is the dominant or major side, the right, the minor side.

The left side functions primarily in language, analytical thinking, and mathematical skills. The right side functions in spatial perception, in musical and other forms of artistic appreciation. *The fibers of the brain.* A detailed description of the neurons of the brain would carry us far afield. However, brief mention will be made of several features. Microscopic sections of the cerebral cortex show that it is exceedingly complex. It has been estimated that the cortex alone contains some nine billion neurons. The cell bodies of the cortical neurons are connected with the lower centers by *projection fibers*, which stream up and down from the midbrain and fan out upon the cortex as if they were "projected" like a picture on a screen. The cortical neurons are also richly interconnected by *association fibers*, which travel from the anterior of the cortex to the occipital regions and to all points between. The right and left hemispheres are also interconnected across the corpus callosum.

C

C Factor: The factor of cleverness, quickness in 'thinking, revealed in some factor analyses of intelligence tests.

Cable properties: Properties which characterise the ability of axons to conduct impulses passively in a decremental fashion, achexia; cachexis. It is a condition of extreme malnutrition.

Cachexia: Means, bad condition, due to ill health, malnutrition, physical wasting away.

Cacogeusia: Pathological condition wherein 'ordinarily palatable foods produces a disgusting, putrid taste.

Cacosmia: Refers to an abnormal condition wherein pleasant or neutral smelles are experienced as foul and disgusting.

Caffeinism: Refers to caffeine intoxication. Its symptoms are nervousness, anxiety, insomnia. In sensitive persons as little as 250 mg can produce these effects.

Calcarine cortex: Refers to the cerebral cortex that surround the calcrine fissure in the occipital lobe. It contains the primary visual area.

Calcarine fissure: Refers to an invagination on the medial surface of the occipital lobe that separates the cuneus from the lingual gyrus.

California psychological inventory: Ages 13 plus. Similar to the MMPI for use with normal populations. Contains 480 items to be answered "true" or "false." Yields scores on dominance, Self-Acceptance, Responsibility, Socialization, Self-Control, Achievement, and Femininity.

California test of personality: A questionnaire type of personality inventory yielding scores on self-reliance, personal worth, sense of freedom, belongingness, various social skills, and total adjustment. Available for all grade levels and adults.

Caloric nystagmus: Nystagmus induced by irrigation of the ears with warm or cold water.

Caloric nystagmus: Refers to nystagmus induced by irrigation of the ears with warm or cold water.

Camera: Refers to a chamber, room, cavity, box, etc. Used in anatomy for internal chambers and in experimental research for specially constructed chambers.

Canalization: Means The narrowing or restricting of alternative ways of behaviour so as to select one in preference to others.

Cancellation test: It is a speed test wherein the subject is asked to cancel out a certain symbol whenever it appears scattered at random among a pattern of similar symbols.

Candela: The primary standard unit for measurement of the luminous intensity of light. It is the amount of light radiating from a bar of pure platinum held at the solidification temperature (2,042°K) through a 1.5 mm aperture.

Cannula: Refers to a small tube inserted into the body for the extraction or introduction of substances.

Canon: Refers to any working principle or formula and is generally reserved for important, fundamental principles that are likely to lead to meaningful truths.

Canonical: Characterising or relating to elements or events that are ordered or structured according to some principle or model.

Capacity: In computer sciences and cognitive science refers to the amount of information which a given system can handle; e.g., channel capacity, storage capacity.

Capgras syndrome: Refers to the delusion that "doubles" have replaced persons whom one knows.

Cardinal point: Refers to that point in a quantitative series of sensations at which the differential threshold begins to increase in accordance with Weber's law-that is, in proportion to the magnitude of the stimulus rather than in an absolute manner.

Cardinal trait: It is a pervasive and outstanding characteristic which influences nearly all of an individual's behaviour.

Carpal age: Refers to the degree of bony development as judged by ossification of the carpal, or wrist, bones.

Case study: Refers to the detailed account of a single individual. This is used in psychotherapy, "where as complete a compilation as possible is made on a single person. In clinical psychology and psychiatry, disciplines which were originally nonexperimental in their approach, case studies often became the basis for generalized theoretical principles.

Caseworker: Refers to any health-related professional (of para professional) who handles individual case over an extended period of time.

Castration complex: (Psychoan.) in the male refers to the infantile fear of losing the genital organs. In the female, the fantasy that the girl once possessed the penis but lost it by castration.

Catabolism: It is the processes that is involved in tearing down tissues and expending energy, with the resulting accumulation of waste products.

Cathexis: Cathection: Refers to the investment of the libido on an object, on another person, or on the self.

Ceiling effect: Refers to the maximum score on a test or a limit on the performance on some task.

Cell assembly: A hypothetical functional organization of neurons formed by repeated stimulation during practice. According to Hebb, cell assemblies are further organized into more complex assemblies, or phase sequences, which mediate learned experiences and skills. It is assumed that such assemblies need not be constantly active in order to mediate a memory but are activated by incoming impulses. Thus, to use Hebb's example, seeing part of a triangle will activate an entire phase sequence and give the perception of triangularity.

Cell body: It is the integral "life support" component of a neuron. It contains the nucleus and other supporting structures.

Cenogamy: A form of marriage where two or more men and two or more women unite into a single marital tie.

Censorship: It is the process responsible for selecting, accepting, or rejecting from consciousness ideas, memories, and impulses arising from the unconscious. It is a joint function of the ego and superego.

Central motive state: Hypothetical processes in the central nervous system employed in accounting for the physiological motives and certain other forms of behavior.

Central motives states are persistent and do not require additional outside stimulation once under way. They result in selectivity of reception and response and are sometimes responsible for the direct emission of behavior, such as that which occurs in response to releasers.

Central tendency: Refers to tendency for judgments, ratings, or estimates to gravitate toward the center of a scale.

Central: Refers to something in the middle, or in the main portion of a body or a structure.

Centralism: Centralist psychology the position that behavior as defined in its broadest sense is a function of the central nervous process—in short, of the brain. By contrast, the *peripheralist* stresses events that take place on the periphery—that is, in the receptors, the muscles, and the glands.

The centralist denies that behavior is nothing but effecter processes. He points to the brain as the control and integrating center mediating stimulus and response. Even those centralists who are willing to make effector behavior the fundamental unit of psychology seeks its explanation in the central nervous system. They emphasize cognition, attitudes, and problem solving, while the peripheralists stress drive, habit, and motor responses.

The middle-of-the-road psycholo-gist sees room for both points of view and stresses the interaction between central and peripheral processes. He emphasizes behaviour as dependent upon the interaction of environmental and organismic factors. The environment, he points out, can influence the organism only by way of the peripheral receptor mechanisms as these feed impulses to the brain. But the effecters, which in turn influence the environment, are under the direction of the central nervous system. Moreover, he points to the fact that behavior is not simply response to stimuli but response to stimuli as influenced by the organism. Thus, all three factors, environmental, peripheral, and central, are important. See also Peripheralism.

Centralism: Refers to the view that behaviour could only be understood and explained through appeals to brain processes and brain function.

Cephalocaudal: Any thing pertaining to the dimension of the body between the head and tail.

Cerebellum: The smaller of the two main divisions of the brain. The cerebellum is an important organ of motor coordination.

Cerebral hemispheres: Refers to the two symmetrical hemisph-erical halves of the *cerebrum.*

Cerebrum: It is the largest and most important division of the brain. It consist of two hemispheres, each containing a number of cortical (surface) and subcortical centers that mediate sensory, motor, and complex ideational activities.

Cerveau isole: Refers to an experimental animal whose brain has been transected at the upper level of the midbrain between the inferior and superior colliculi.

Chancroid: It is a veneral disease that is characterised by the eruption of a sensitive, inflamed ulcer in the genital area. Treatment is usually with antibiotics.

Character analysis: Psychoanalysis oriented toward dealing with the client's character defeness.

Character structure: The unity of integration of character traits.

Character trait: 1. A relatively consistent and persistent form of behavior as viewed from the moral or ethical point of view 2. (*Psychoan*) an inherited tendency.

Character: Refers to a consistent and enduring property or quality by means of which a person, object, or event can be identified.

Characterology: 1. The field of psychology concerned with the study of character and personality. 2. a pseudo-science that attempts to discover character traits by means of external signs, such as hair color, length of fingers, nasal configuration, etc.

Charpentier's law: According to it the product of the area of the image and the light intensity is a constant for threshold stimuli in the fovea.

Chemoreceytor: Refers to those sense organs which are responsive to chemical action.

Chlorolabe: It is a green-sensitive pigment found in the cones the retina.

Chorea: Refers to any neurological disorder that is marked by muscular twitching and jerky, involuntary movements, *e g.*, Funtington's chorea, Sydenham's chorea.

Chot: Refers to an uncoordinated response elicited by a sudden, stimulus for which the organism is not prepared.

Chromosome: A dark staining body in the nucleus of the cell. These bodies carry the genes or elementary units of heredity. In the human species there are 22 pairs of chromosomes plus the two sex determiners, or a total of 46. In the female, the sex determiners form an additional pair, the XX chromosomes; in the male they are unpaired, the XY chromosomes.

Chronaxie: A value used to express the sensitivity of a nerve to stimulation. It is measured by first determining the threshold of the nerve, the amount of direct current that when applied indefinitely would just excite it. This value is then doubled and the amount of time this current; must be applied before the nerve responds is the chronaxie.

Chronobiology. Refers to the study of biological rhythms, biological clocks, circadian rhythms, etc.

Chronograph: Refers to a device that records and presents graphic records of time intervals.

Cilia: Means Eyelashes or Hairlike processes projecting from the surface of various cells (e.g., in the bronchi), sing cilium.

Cingulotomy: A form of psychosurgery wherein fibers in the cingulate cortex are severed. It is used in severe cases of manic-depression or severe anxiety.

Circadian: Pertaining to rhythmic biological cycles occurring at approximately 24-hour intervals.

Clang association: Refers to an association in a verbal task wherein two words or other stimulus items become linked due, to acoustic similarity.

Classical psychoanalysis: Psychoanalysis based on Freudian doctrine and procedure.

Classification test: 1. A test that requires the subject to sort objects into categories. 2. a test used to classify people, such as an aptitude test when employed for the purpose of classifying students into instructional sections.

Classificatory scale: A simple nominal scale in which names or classifications are assigned to objects. *Syn.* Nominal Scale.

Client-centered therapy: A system of psychotherapy based on the assumption that the client or subject is in the best position to resolve his own problems provided that the therapist can establish a warm, permissive atmosphere in which the client feels free to discuss his problems and to obtain insight into them. In client-centered therapy, the therapist assumes a non-directive role he does not advise, interpret, or intervene except to offer encouragement and occasional restatements of the client's remarks for the purpose of emphasis and clarification.

Clinic: Refers to a place organized for the diagnosis and treatment of physical and mental disorders.

Clinical grouping: The classification of persons into relatively homogeneous groups according to their symptomatic behavior.

Clinical method: A variety of techniques including interviews, questionnaires, tests, projective techniques, and diagnostic observation. The purpose of the clinical method is the practical one of diagnosing the cause of a disorder and prescribing for its treatment. In addition, most clinics maintain training and research programs for the transmission and diffusion of knowledge.

Clinical psychology: It is the branch of psychology that deals with the application of clinical methods to persons suffering from behaviour disorders.

Clinical psychology: The branch of psychology that specializes in the application of clinical methods to per sons suffering from behavior disorders.

Clinical type: Refers to any individual case wherein the symptoms and behaviours conform to one of the many identifiable syndromes of clinical psychology and psychiatry.

Cluttering: Refers to rapid, often incoherent speech characterised by eliding words and syllables.

Coacting group: Refers to a group working side by side on a common project but without communication or interaction between the members.

Coccyx: Refers to the small bone at the base of the spine in man and tailless apes. It is formed from four fused rudimentary vertebrae.

Codeine: An opium alkaloid obtained from morphine. It is an, analgesic and has sedative properties and is commonly used in low does as an analgesic and a cough suppressant.

Cognitive psychology: 1. The branch of psychology that includes the study of psychology that includes the study of processes involved in sensing, perceiving, remembering, and thinking. 2. a point of view in psychology that stresses the importance of purpose, knowing, understanding, and reasoning in behaviour.

The cognitive point of view was first emphasized by the Gestalt psychologists in their investigations of perception, learning, and thinking, particularly as they opposed traditional associationistic theories and methods of research involving these processes. For decades beginning in the 1930s, Jean Piaget, the famous Swiss psychologist, emphasized the cognitive approach in his research on the development of understanding in the child. In the 1930s and 1940s, E.C.

Tolman attempted to make the cognitive point of view compatible with behaviouristic methods in the study of animal learning. Using the maze as a model, he argued that the animal learns by developing a cognitive map of the apparatus. More recently cognitive psychology has come to be identified with the point of view that the organism is an information-processing system analogous to electronic detection, storage, and retrieval systems. For specific examples of cognitive approaches.

Cognitive science: Refers to a cluster of disciplines that 'studies the human mind. It includes cognitive psychology, epistemology, linguistics, computer sciences, artificial intelligence, mathematics and neuropsychology.

Cognitive structure: The organization of the perceptual world into a unified and hierarchical pattern of beliefs, attitudes, and expectancies.

Cognitive theory of learning: Any theory of learning that postulates intervening variables of a cognitive nature in order to explain learning. In contrast, stimulus-response theories emphasize reinforced responses and avoid the use of central cognitive constructs as explanatory concepts.

Cohort: Refers to an ancient Roman military unit consisting of from 300 to 600 soldiers. In demography, a number of persons all possessing a common characteristic; for example, a group of children born in the same year. In ethology, a number of organisms of a given species that function together as a group.

Coition: Coitus Refers to sexual intercourses; the union of the male and female genitals with orgasm. Coition is the process in general whereas coitus is a specific—act of intercourse.

Cold: Refers to the sensation normally aroused by a stimulus whose temperature is below skin temperature.

Colour mixer: It is an electric apparatus which rotates interleaved coloured discs rapidly so as to achieve fusion of the colors.

Colour naming. It is a scoring category for naming the coloured cards with appropriate Colour names as a form of response.

Colour primary: Refers to one of those colors which, when mixed in proper proportions, yield all other colors including white within this definition, red, green, and blue are the primaries.

Colour shock. Refers to scoring category for an emotional response to a coloured card.

Colour temperature: It is the temperature of a black body at which it yields a Colour matching that of a given sample of radiant energy. The temperature is measured on the Kelvin or absolute scale.

Colour: Refers to the subjective sensation associated with light. Colour experience depends on three components of the physical energy: wavelength, *purity* and *intensity*. Wavelength corresponds to the psychological attribute of *hue* purity to *saturation* and intensity to *brightness.*

Coma: It is an abnormal state of deep stupor with total absence of consciousness, loss of all voluntary behaviour and most reflexes.

Communication: Means the transmission of energy changes from one place to another, as in nervous transmission.

Communications theory: The branch of psychology that deals with communication in all its phases—human, mechanical, institutional. The related disciplines of physiology, neurology, and electronics are included as they apply to communications. Particular emphasis is lent to developing models and parallels between human communication and machines.

Communications unit: In communications theory, an ensemble consisting of a *sender,* which encodes messages that are then transmitted in signal form through a *channel* to a *receiver* where they are then decoded. Analogies are drawn between electronic communications units and the human organism. The sense organs are receivers that transform stimuli (encoding) into signals (nervous impulses) that are sent through the channels of the nerves to the brain, where they are interpreted (decoded).

Comparative psychology: The branch of psychology that investigates behavioral differences among the various species from a comparative point of view.

Comparison stimulus: Refers to a stimulus, or part of a series of stimuli, that is compared with or judged against a standard stimulus.

Compensation idea: Means the substitution in fantasy or in dreaming of a superior image for an inferior one.

Complaint character: Refers to a person who displays neurotic self-effacement, deference and inappropriate yielding.

Completion test: A type of test designed such a way that the subject must supply the answer by filling in blank spaces,

Complication experiment: Refers to experimental procedure the data from which gave rise to Titchener's law *of prior entry.*

Complication: Refers to a combination of sensations derived from different receptors, like the sight and smell of a rose.

Composite: Refers to unitary experience or whole made up of elements belonging to several other experiences.

Compound eye: A type of eye

found extensively in insects, it is made up of a number of rudimentary optical systems which focus images at slightly different points in order to form a mosaic instead of a single image.

Compound reaction: Forms of the reaction-time experiment wherein the subject either must recognize the stimulus before reacting or must discriminate between two or more stimuli.

Computational metaphor: Refers to the use of computers as models of human functioning and to the extended notion that human cognition is a computational process.

Conation: Refers to that aspect of the mental 'processes that have to do with volition, striving willing.

Concept acquisition: Refers to the process by which one learn& ("acquires") a concept not known before,

Concept discovery: Refers to the process by which one discovers which of several previously learned concepts is the proper one for a given situation.

Concrete image: Refers to a memory image which is recalled in terms of the sensory qualities of an object, like the feel of a hammer or the odor of a skunk.

Concrete intelligence: Refers to the ability to deal effectively with practical or concrete situations and relationships.

Conduction aphasia: Refers to a speech disorder involving the inability to repeat words as a result of damage to the conduction pathways between Wernicke's area and Broca's area.

Conduction unit: It is a system of neural connections or bonds that function in a certain adaptive act.

Cones Refers to the photoreceptors in the retina which mediate colour vision. They are most densely packed in the fovea and thin out toward the periphery.

Confidence limits: Refers to the limits outside of which an event is not expected to table place *by* chance with more than some specified probability.

Conformity: Refers to tendency to allow one's behaviour to be 'governed by prevailing attitudes and opinions.

Confound: Means to fail to separate two variables so that their effects cannot be independently ascertained.

Congenital deafness: Deafness already present at birth due to the defects in the development of the middle or inner ear.

Connection: Refers to any linking between two phenomena, whether physical or mental.

Connector (Nouron): Refers to neuron that lies between and connects two other neurons or a receptor and an effector.

Conscience: Refers to the individual's system of moral values the sense of right and wrong in conduct formerly believed by the theologians to be an innate character but now generally, held by psychologists to be learned.

Conscious experience: It is that awareness of a mental process of perception, emotion, motivation, etc.

Consciousness: Coexisting mental states with no awareness or incomplete awareness between them. Morton Prince coined the term to describe cases of dissociation in which multiple personalities exist in the same individual with only incomplete awareness of each other.

Consequent: Refers to an event or phenomenon Which occurred following some other event such that it "invites" the inference that it was caused by that event.

Constancy hypothesis: The assumption that there is a one-to-one relationship between stimulus variables and responses regardless of surrounding conditions, provided that the sense-organ-stimulus relationships remain the same. The constancy hypothesis is attributed to the structuralistic and behavioristic schools of psychology by the Gestalt psychologists, who take a relativistic point of view and hold that responses are always relative to the total complex of stimulating conditions as they interact with organismic factors.

Constancy: It is the tendency for perceived objects to give rise to a the same perceptual experiences even though there in may be wide differences in the conditions of observation.

Continence: Means self-restraint with respect to: (1) retention of urine, feces and other bodily discharges; (2) sexual impulses.

Contingency table: Refers to a table showing the frequencies of occurrence of categories of events in vertical and horizontal rows.

Continuant: In phonetics, a distinctive feature for distinguishing the sounds of a language.

Continuity theory of learning: The postulate that in discrimination learning there is an increment of learning for every rewarded or reinforced response to the stimulus.

Contradictory: Refers to either of two propositions such that if one is true the other necessarily is false and vice versa.

Contrary: Refers to either of two propositions such that if one is true then the other cannot also be true although both of them may be false.

Contrast: A marked awareness of the differences between two stimulus conditions resulting from bringing them together.

Control series: Refers to a series or measurements or experiments-designed to test the validity of a previous experiment or set of observations.

Control: Means, the exercise of the scientific method by which the various treatments in an experiment are regulated such that the causal factors may be unambiguously identified.

Converse: Refers to a proposition derived by conversion (reversing the terms) of another proposition.

Convulsion: A general seizure involving rapid spasmodic contraction and relaxation of the musculature.

Convulsive therapy: Any form of somatic therapy in the treatment of mental disorders that utilizes induced convulsions.

Coolidge effect: It is the phenomenon by Which the males of many species will show high continuous sexual performance for extended periods of time With successive introductions of new, receptive females.

Coordination: Means smooth, harmonious functioning of bodily parts, particularly muscles.

Coping Behaviour: Refers to the characteristic way in which the individual deals with his social and physical environment specially as he mobilizes his resources to handle stress.

Coping behaviour: The characteristic manner in which the individual deals with his social and physical environment, particularly as he mobilizes his resources to handle stress.

Copulin: Refers to a vaginal pheromone isolated in rhesus monkeys that stimulates the male to copulate. The level of secretion is highest at the time of ovulation, thereby maximizing impregnation.

Cornea: It is the transparent outer layer of the eye that covers the iris and the pupil. It is completely free of blood vessels and functions as a refractor of light.

Corpuscle: Refers to a free-floating cell in the blood or a small, specialized organ in the skin like a touch corpuscle.

Correction: Refers to the manipulation of data in, such a way as to minimize errors of observation and chance.

Correlate: Refers to any of two variables or factors which are Systematically related to each other; that is, they "co-relate".

Correlation hierarchy: A correlation table in which the magnitude of the coefficients falls off progressively from one corner to the other three. In such cases, the correlations could be accounted for as originating from a general factor and specific factors.

Correlation table: It is a statistical technique used for showing the relationship between two variables to be correlated.

Correlation, tetrachoric (rt): Refers to correlation which is based on two variables each of which is expressed as a dichotomy (two-valued).

Corresponding points: Refers to retinal points in the two eyes which give rise to a single visual impression when stimulated simultaneously.

Cortical deafness: Refers to deafness due to injury to the areas for hearing in the cerebral cortex.

Corticalization: Refers to the gradual subsuming of control of behavioural and psychological processes by the cerebral cortex. It can be seen as an evolutionary process.

Cortin: It is a complex secretion of the adrenal cortex and contains several hormones. Cortin is important in the control of salt intake and in the regulation of the gonads.

Counselling: Refers to a wide variety of procedures for helping individuals achieve adjustment, like giving of advice, therapeutic discussions, the administration and interpretation of tests, and vocational assistance.

Counterinvestment: Means attaching an opposite feeling to a repressed idea or impulse. For example, showing hatred for a person whom one unconsicously loves.

Couvade: It refers to the custom among nonliterate peoples of the father taking to bed at the birth of a child as if he were suffering the pains of childbirth.

Crawling: Refers to infantile locomotion in a profit position by means of the arms pulling the body forward as the legs or knees push.

Creole: In studies of language, refers to a pidgin which has become the dominant verbal communication system for 'a people and has acquired its own native speakers.

Criterion: Refers to an independent, outside measure against which a test can be validated or a standard of judgment or belief

Critical: Pertaining to an important or crucial judgment or evaluation,' or a decisive point or the point of transition in a phenomenon or event.

Crossed reflex: Refers to a reflex on the contralateral (opposite)

side of the body from that stimulated.

Crossing over: In genetics refers to the mutual exchange of genes between two chromosomes. The exchange takes place between corresponding genes on homologous chromosomes during meiosis.

Crowding: Refers to the sensation of stress and unpleasant feelings that are associated with settings involving a high density of people.

Crucial experiment: Refers to a test or experiment which is critical for the acceptance of rejection of a hypothesis or theory.

Crystallized intelligence: Refers to intellectual ability as dependent on I factors 'and learning as these interact with fluid intelligence

Cue: Refers to a learned signal for guiding or controlling behaviour or a stimulus used by the organism in making a discrimination.

Cultural anthropology: That branch of anthropology concerned with the structure and functioning of nonliterate societies.

Cultural assimilation: The process of learning the customs and other group characteristics that make it possible for the individual to be fully incorporated into a group.

Cultural conflict: The opposing forces that impinge upon individuals or groups who hold allegiance to two different cultures.

Cultural determinism: The assumption that culture is responsible for the development and limitations in behaviour patterns characteristic of a society.

Cultural items, Refers to test items which are heavily loaded with information which can be acquired only in a specific culture or subculture and, are thus unfair to anyone not belonging to that culture.

Cultural lag: Refers to the carry over of customs, attitudes and cultural products after these become dated or obsolete relative to the standards set by another culture or subculture.

Culture complex: Refers to an organised set of social attitudes and behaviour patterns which form an integrated whole ; for example, all activities associated with the hunting, preparation, and eating of meat.

Culture contact: Refers to any form of interaction between persons of two distinct cultures which results in mutual modification of the culture through reciprocal assimilation

Culture Fair Intelligence Test: 1. The hypothesis that all societies tend to evolve in the same way. That is, all societies pass through the hunting, pastoral, agricultural, and industrial stages of evolution. 2. the theory that the individual child tends to pass through stages typical of his race and that his education should be planned accordingly.

Culture: It is the sum total of the customers, arts, science, and religious and political behaviour taken as an integrated whole that distinguishes one society from another.

Cumulative record: Refers to a continuous record to which data are added in summative form.

Cumulative scale: It is an attitude scale wherein the items have been arranged in such a way that a response to any given item may~ be taken as indicative of agreement with all items of lower rank.

Cuneate nucleus (or cuneus): Refers to grouping of neurons located in the lower medulla which relays neural impulses from the upper trunk and arms to the somatic sensory areas of the brain.

Cupula: Refers to a gelatinous body in the ampulla of the semicircular canals wherein the hair cells of the *crista* are embedded.

Curare: Refers to d-Tubocurarine. It is a chemical substance found in certain South American plants which causes paralysis in striated muscles. It acts by blocking cholinergic transmission at the myoneural junction by competing with acetylcholine at the receptor sites. Its major medical use is to induce muscle flaccidity for surgery, but it has also served psychology in a number of experiments that showed that a paralysed animal can still learn a stimulus-response connection even through the overt response itself cannot be made during the, actual training trials.

Curiosity: Refers to the tendency to explore, to investigate, to seek knowledge. Curiosity is considered by some psychologists as one of the primary drives, 'along with sex, hunger, thirst, etc.

Custodial care: Refers to the minimal institutional care-of mental Patients without any therapy.

Custodial case: Refers to an individual who needs institutional care due to mental illness or criminality.

Cutting score: Refers to a critical score which serves as a dividing point in a distribution of scores

Cybernetics: A discipline primarily concerned with control mechanisms and their associated communications systems, particularly those that involve feedback of information to the mechanism about its activities.

Cybernetics: The science of

control mechanisms and their associated communications systems. Cybernetics cut across engineering, psychology, physiology, economics, and medicine. Illustrative problems that have been studied by cyberneticists, such as control systems in guided missiles, the production of artificial limbs, and the development of machines enabling the blind to read.

Cyclic disorder: Refers to a mental disorder, like manic depressive psychosis, which tends to recur periodically.

Cycloid: Characterising a personality pattern which shows relatively marked alternations of depression and excitement.

Cyclothymia: It is a tendency toward alternating periods of elation and depression which is serious cases, is manifested as manic-depressive psychology.

Cytogeneties: It is a branch of the study of heredity specialising in the, structure and function of chromosomes and genes.

Cytogenic syndrome: Refers to a condition marked by a variety of physical and behavioural symptoms due to some abnormality in the size, number, or shape of the chromosomes.

Cytology: The branch of biology concerned with the study of cells.

Cytosine: It is one of the four nucleotide bases that make up deoxyribonucleic acid and ribonucleic acid.

D

Dactology: It is the art of communication by making use of signs made with the fingers.

Damping: The checking or attentuation of vibrations in a sounding body by internal and external friction.

Dance therapy: It is based on the use of the physical and esthetic aspects of dance as a therapeutic medium.

Dancing mania: Refers to an epidemic of obsessive dancing, that has appeared from time to time in Europe.

Dark light: Not light at all. It refer to the fact that the receptors in the eye have a level of spontaneous activity that, under the proper conditions can be phenomenologically real and detected as a sense, of "Light".

Day blindness: Refers to an abnormality of the eye in which the individual sees better in dim light.

Day residue: Refers to the fragments of recent experiences during waking hours that emerge as dream images.

Daydream: Refers to mental meandering, fantasies while one is awake. Interestingly, a good deal of research suggests that daydreaming is associated with mental health and stability.

Deafness, nerve: Refers to deafness caused by any neurological impairment of the auditory receptors in the cochlea or the auditory nerve.

Death feigning: Refers to a response to threatening situations which a number of species have developed. The organism goes into a state of tonic immobility and seems to be dead.

Death instinct: Refers to the instinct for destruction and death, and when fused with pleasure, inward and outward directed drives for pain.

Death wish: Refers to an underlying element of the death instinct. It typically stands for a hypothesized motivational syndrome which is arguably responsible for individuals who consistently put themselves into situations which are life-threatening.

Debility: Refers to weakness in function, loss of ability. Generally of organic and motor functions, sometimes of cognitive.

Debriefing: It is the process of telling the subject in an experiment what it was about and, when necessary, revealing any deception or withholding of information that may have been a necessary element in the study.

Debug: Means to detect, identify and correct an error in a program, a research project, a logical argument, a complex piece of equipment, etc.

Decibel: It is a unit of measurement of the perceived differences in sound. The decibel is a 10 x $\log_{10}$ of the ratio between thresh hold intensity of 1000 Hz 2nd a comparison sound. A bel is ten times the threshold intensity. A whisper is about 10 decibels, conversation about 60, and thunder about 120.

Deciduous teeth: Refers to the first, or baby teeth, that give way to the permanent teeth.

Decile: Refers to any one of 9 points which divides a distribution of ranked scores into equal intervals. Each interval, thus, contains 1/10th of the scores.

Declarative: It is a speech act wherein one tells someone something, i.e., one makes a declaration.

Decoding: An information theory, the process by means of which a receiver translates signals into messages. By analogy, stimuli may be treated as signals, which the receptors encode into nervous impulses, which are decoded by the brain.

Decoding: It is the process by means of which a receiver translates signals into messages.

Decompensation: Refers to a progressive loss of normal functioning in favour of Psychotic behaviour, or disorganization of the Personality under stress.

Decorticate conditioning: Refers to a conditioned response that has been established in the absence of the cerebral cortex.

Decorticate: Refers to the state of being without a cortex. Certain classes of behaviour requiring little or no functioning of the "higher mental processes" are sometimes referred to as decorticate activities. Sometimes the term is used of species of animals that never evolved a neocortex; e.g., avians.

Decrement: Refers to any decrease in anything. The term is used, of behavioural performances, of knowledge, of memory, etc.

Decryption: Within cryptography, it is the act or process of converting a coded message back into normal form; decoding

Deep: Means below the surface, as in anatomical descriptions of underlying organs and tissues. In acoustics, Pertaining to low-pitched tones. In vision, Pertaining to richly saturated colours. In. Psychoanalysis, characteristic of material which the client brings to the analysis which derives from early life experiences or from experiences which have been repressed.

Deep sensitivity (or sensibility): Refers to sense of pressure, the receptors for which are in deep subcutaneous layers of the skin or in muscles.

Defence reflex: A reflexive response, like as the sudden withdrawal of a limb to a painful stimulus.

Defense mechanism: Refers to any behaviour pattern which protects the psyche from anxiety, shame, or guilt. Some Common defense mechanisms are: repression; regression; projection identification; fantasy; compensation; sublimation; reaction-formation; aggression.

Defensiveness: Refers to the personality characteristic of being overly sensitive to criticism.

Deference: Refers to the need to admire and follow a leades, or to serve a superior happily.

Deficiency: Means a lack of something, a condition wherein some important element is missing.

Definition: A boundary between two classes or phenomena. For example, a figure may be said to have good definition if it stands out clearly from the background because of having a well-defined border.

Definitional validity: It is the assumed validity of a test whose items are taken as the definition of the variable to be measured.

Deflection: A defense mechanism which functions by diverting attention or awareness away from the object that arouses anxiety.

Defusion: Refers to a separation of the life and death instincts mostly fused in the unconscious.

Degenerate: Refers to one who deviates markedly from normal standards of acceptable conduct. Refers to individuals who have committed sexual offences and in such/cases implics a constitutional deficiency.

Dehoaxing: Means revealing any deceptions practised on a subject during an experiment.

Deiter' cells: These are elongated supporting cells present in the outer portion of the organ of Corti in the cochlea.

Delayed reaction: A response in a reactiontie experiment that does not occur immediately. In discrimination reaction time, for example, more complex conditions than are found in simple reaction time may lead to a short delay. The delay was formerly attributed to ideational processes.

Delayed reaction: Refers to a response in a reaction-time experiment which does not occur immediately.

Delayed reinforcement: 1. In classical conditioning, reinforcement that is not administered until a period of time has elapsed between the presentation of stimulus and the emission of a response. 2. In operant conditioning, a delay between the emission of a response and the administration of the reinforcement.

Delayed response: An experimental situation wherein an animal reacts to a stimulus a considerable time after the stimulus has been removed. For e.g, the stimulus might be food placed under one or two cups while the animal watches but is restrained from appro-aching until a specified delay period has passed. The ability to delay is a function of phylogenetic level.

Delayed reward: Refers to the presentation of the reward following an interval of time after the subject has made his response.

Delinquent: Refer to someone who commits a crime or who violates a legal code.

Delirium: Refers to disoriented condition having clouded consciousness, generally accompanied by hallucinations, illusions, misinterpretations of events and a mostly confused quality with reduced capacity to sustain attention to things in the environment.

Delphi methods: It is a procedure used for predicting future events based on the pooling of judgements made by a number of experts.

Delta Rhythm: An electroencephalographic wave of 1-3 Hz of high voltage (150 microvolts) that is characteristic of deep sleep.

Delusion of persecution: A delusion, characteristic of the paranoid individual, that he is the victim of efforts to injure him or to cause him to fail in some way. The belief often takes the form of an imagined conspiracy in which the patient's physical and family are thought to have joined in the effort to damage the patient.

Delusion or reference: A false belief that the behaviour of others has malign significance for the self.

Delusion: A false belief which cannot be modified by reasoning or a demonstration of the facts. Delusion should be distinguished from illusion, that is a distorted perception, and from hallucination, that is a false perception.

Demand character: Refers to the need-arousing attributes of objects. A shiny red apple "demands" to be eaten; a striking painting "demands" to be looked at.

Dementia, alcoholic: Refers to dementia observed in the last stages of severe, chronic alcoholism.

Dementia: Refers to a deterioration of intellectual, judgmental, and emotional Processes that are characteristic of certain forms of senility and psychoses.

Democratic atmosphere: A leadership situation in which the members of a group are allowed to participate in planning, are told in advance what the group's goals are, and are encouraged to discuss and criticize group activities.

Demography: The study of population variables including geographic distribution, vital statistics, physical situations, and the like.

Demonology: It is a legitimate area of study of folklore and cultural myths concerned with demons and spirits.

Demonomania: Refers to the delusion on the part of an individual that he is under the influence of a demon or evil spirit.

Dendrite: It is the receiving end of a neuron. It is the first part of the neuron to receive impulses conveyed toward the cell body from other neurons or receptors.

Denial: A defense mechanism which simply disavows or denies thoughts, feelings, wishes or needs which cause anxiety.

Density: It is the attribute of solidity or compactness that according to some psychologists, tones possess.

Dental age: It is a measure of the child's dental development comparing the number of permanent teeth that nave erupted to the average number for the child's age.

Dental: Refers to a speech sound that is produced by placing the tongue against the teeth.

Deoxyribonucleic Acid (DNA): A large complex molecule consisting of four nucleotide base& (adenine, guanine, cytosine and thymine) and a "backbone" of a sugar molecule (specifically, 2-deoxy-D-ribose). The nucleotide basis are arranged in pairs down the center of the double-helix-shaped molecule and it is the specific arrangement that carries the genetic code determining the functioning of every cell. The code is based on sequences of 3 nucleotide bases each specifying one of 20 amino acids, Since there are 64 possible arrangements there is considerable flexibility in the arrangement and more than enough to code any given protein's sequence of amino acids. Each of the chromosomes in the nuclei of all cells is made up of DNA; it is, therefore, the chemical basis for all heredity and the carrier of all genetic information.

Dependence, psychological: Refers to drug dependence characterized by a pervasive drive to obtain and take the substance It is used for dependencies on drugs whose action does not produce fundamental biochemical changes like that continued doses of the drug are required for normal functioning. Drugs like marijuana are cited as likely to Produce Psychological dependence with habitual use.

Dependence: It is a relationship of causality between two phenomena, in such a way that a change in one is accompanied by a change in the other.

Dependency: Refers to a condition wherein one individual must rely upon another, or upon society, for his maintenance.

Dependent personality: A personality pattern characterized by lack of independence, passivity, low self-confidence, and a tendency to submit to others.

Depression: Refers to, a state of despondency characterized by feelings of inadequacy, lowered activity, and pessimism about the future or in Pathological cases, an extreme state of Unresponsiveness to stimuli, along with self-depreciation, delusions of inadequacy, and hopelessness.

Depressor nerve: It is a branch of the vagus (Xth cranial) nerve that functions to lower blood pressure.

Deprogramming: It is a procedure used for reversing the effects of extreme indoctrination characteristic of brainwashing in cults. The victim is encouraged to think critically, flexibly, and independently after removal from the cult.

Depth analysis: psychoanalysis is often called-depth analysis as the assumption is that the analysis is probing deeply below the well-defended conscious level of mind to the, underlying dynamic factors which presumably Motivate the person.

Depth interview: Refers to an interview which attempts to get at underlying or dynamic factors which motivate the individual and are responsible for observed behaviour patterns.

Depth perception: It is the perception, of depth, viewing the world in three dimensions. It refer to the distance of objects from the viewer and also refer to the three-dimensionality of objects themselves.

Depth psychology: A system of psychology that assumes behavior is to be explained in terms of unconscious processes. The Freudian and Jungian systems of psychoanalysis exemplify depth psychology.

Deranged: Means disturbed or disoriented. Used with regard to cognitive, intellectual abilities.

Dereistic: Characterizing thinking that is autistic or governed by personal factors.

Derivation: Refers to that which is the result of a formal set of inferences the outcome of a deductive process.

Derived emotion: Refers to an emotional reaction associated with the outcome of any intense motive or instinct, like joy or despair.

Derived need: It is a need developed from or learned by close association with a primary need.

Derived property: In psychology refers to the postulate that parts derive their characteristics from the whole.

Derived scale: Refer to any scale which is a result of a transformation from another scale.

Derived score: Refers to any score which is a result of a transformation from another score, e.g., the z-score.

Derived: Meads developed out of, transformed from, acquired from, adapted from, etc.

Dermatitis: Refers to any inflammation of the skin. Several types are known and generally associated with specific causes, but according to many authorities psychosomatic factors lead to a predisposition and exacerbation of many forms.

Dermatographia: Skin writing; the appearance of raised welts on the skin upon being lightly stroked. It is believed to be because of hyperirritability of the dermal capillaries.

Descriptive psychiatry: Refers to any system of psychiatric diagnosis that is used on the relatively straightforward description of overt, observable symptoms.

Desensitization: Means lessened reactivity, or a decreased emotional sensitivity with respect to a personal defect or social problem after counselling.

Desexualization: Refers to any procedure which results in the "removal" of sexual significance from something.

Design: Refers to a plan involving forethought, I or a graphic or schematic representation.

Desire: Refers to a conscious longing or want, or a conscious wish to be rid of an unpleasant or aversive stimulus or situation.

Detached affect: Refers to affect that has been removed ("detached") from the painful, anxiety-producing idea or thought with which it was originally associated.

Deterioration index: It is a way of estimating the degree of deterioration of mental functioning. The index is based on the .observation that certain abilities that the test measures decline with age.

Deterioration: Refers to a progressive impairment or loss of function.. The deteriorative psychoses are those in which the predominant system pattern is one of loss of judgment, emotional, and intellectual deterioration, and progressive loss of memory.

Determinant: Refers to a cause or antecedent condition, or a factor that is decisive or final in a cause-and-effect relation.

Determiner: Refers to a cause, an antecedent condition that results in some particular outcome.

Determinism: Refers to the doctrine that for every effect there is a cause. According to determinism, given a complete knowledge of the individual's past and of present environmental conditions, his behaviour could be predicted precisely.

Determinism: The doctrine that for every effect there is a cause. It is assumed that all behavior is a function of causal factors either in the individual's environment or within himself.

According to determinism, given a complete knowledge of the individual's past and of present environmental conditions, his behavior could. be predicted precisely. Some degree of determinism is postulated by all schools of psychology. *Contr.* Free will. *Hard determinism* is a strict deterministic point of view allowing no room for freedom of choice or indeterminism.

Classical psychoanalysis exemplifies such a point of view. *Soft determinism* allows for a limited freedom of choice. The soft determinist believes that, within the limitations of one's constitution and past, it is possible to choose one's future programs of action. Contemporary existential psychologists take a position of soft determinism.

Detour problem: Refers to an experimental setting which requires subjects initially to move away from a goal so as to obtain it eventually. The problem was first introduced by the Gestalt psychologists under the German term Umweg Problem.

Detoxification: It is the process of treatment making use of rest, fluids and changes in diet to restore proper physiological functioning following disruption by overuse of drugs.

Detraction: Refers to the lessening of attention without loss of the local point of what one attending to.

Deuteranomaly: It is a visual condition wherein there is a slight diminution in sensitivity to green, wavelengths. A deuteranomalope will need more green light to achieve colour , matching than one with normal vision.

Deuteranopia: It is a form or red-greed blindness wherein weakness for green is the predominant symptom. Shades of gray are seen in place of red and green, but the relative brightness value of the spectral colours remains unchanged.

Development: Refers to the progressive and continuous change in the organism from -birth to death.

Developmental age: It is a measure of development stated in age units, or a combined index of all developmental estimates or scores

Developmental level: Refers to a division of the span of life according to arbitrarily fixed chronological ranges. The period of infancy lasts from birth to, approximately one year; childhood from 1 to 12 years; adolescence, from 12 to 21 years; maturity from 21 to 65 years; and old age from 65 years to death.

Developmental norm: It is a norm that is based on the representative performance to be expected of children at a given age or developmental level.

Developmental psychology: That branch of psychology that studies the processes of pre- and post-natal growth and the maturation of behavior. The developmental psychologist is interested in the various stages of development, the principles or laws of maturation, and the effects of early experience and later practice on development. In its broadest sense, developmental psychology includes the periods of infancy, childhood, and adulthood.

Developmental quotient: It is equal to the developmental age, or any measure of development divided by the chronological age.

Developmental scale: It is an inventory of behaviour for the purpose of assessing the level of development reached by a child.

Developmental sequence: It is the order of appearance of maturational patterns characteristic of the species.

Developmental stage: Refers to any period of development during which certain characteristic behaviours appear.

Developmental tasks: Refers to

skills, levels of achievement, a social adjustment considered important at certain ages for the successful adjustment of the individual.

Developmental unit: Refers to an interval in a scale of measurement that is equal or approximately equal at different ages.

Developmental zero: It is the hypothetical point where development start; the point of fertilization of the ovum.

Deviance: Refers to any pattern of behaviour which is markedly different from the accepted standards within a society.

Deviate: Refers to one who differs markedly from normal, or whose standards of conduct and attitudes are sharply in conflict with accepted standard, a sexual pervert.

Deviation IQ: Refers to a standard score on an intelligence test like the Stanford-Binet. The interpretation of the deviation IQ is similar to that of the conventional IQ.

Deviation score: A value giving the degree to which any single Score deviates from the mean of all the scores in a sample. Generally denoted as x or d.

Device: Any instrument, piece of apparatus or cognitive procedure used for some specific purpose.

Dexterity test: Refers to a test which requires both speed and accuracy in manual operations. Such tests utilize peg boards and simple assembling operations.

Diachisis: Refers to a temporary increase in the threshold for excitability in a nerve center.

Dialectic (al) psychology: It argues that conflict and change are the basic principles of life-Dialectics had its origins in Heraclitus and was further developed in philosophical and political forms by Hegel and Marx respectively. On this position, man transforms his environment by action which, in turn, changes him.

Dialysis: It is the process of purifying a liquid by passing it I through a membrane.

Dichotomy: It is a division in two classes according to some pre-, determined criterion.

Dichromacy: Refers to any of several kinds of colour-vision deficiencies. Two forms of dichromacy involve weakness in the perception of reds and greens two others involve blues and yellows synonyms for dichromacy are, dichromatism, dichromatopsia, dichromopsia, dichromia and dichromasy.

Dichromat: Refers to an individual having any of the various forms of dichromacy.

Diet: Means way of living. Thus

Food substances and liquids normally consumed in day-to-day living.

Differential aptitude test: A battery of eight tests primarily for use in educational and vocational guidance in grades 8 through 12. There are tests of verbal reasoning, number ability, abstract reasoning, clerical speed and accuracy, and language usage.

Differential conditioning: Refers to the establishment of a conditioned response to one of two or more stimuli by selectively reinforcing thc desired conditioning stimulus and not reinforcing the rest.

Differential diagnosis: It is the process of distinguishing between two similar diseases or abnormalities by discovering a critical symptom that is present in one but not in the other.

Differential extinction: Refers to selective extinction of responding by withholding reinforcement for that response while continuing to reinforce other responses.

Differential growth: Refers to growth or development of an organ at a rate different from that of other organs in the same organism.

Differential inhibition: Describes the gradual elimination of responding to stimuli that are similar to, but, discriminably different from, the original, conditioned stimulus.

Differential psychology: Refers to study of psychology which focuses on individual differences in behaviour.

Differential psychology: The branch of psychology that investigates individual differences, their consequences, causation and magnitude among groups.

Differential reinforcement: Refers to the application of reinforcement to one of two alternative responses. For example, if an animal is responding to both a tone of 260 Hz and one of 290 Hz, rewarding only the 260 Hz tone would be differential reinforcement leading to a discriminated response.

Differential reinforcement: The application of reinforcement to one of two alternative responses. For example, if an animal is responding to both a tone of 256 Hz and one of 280 Hz, rewarding only the 256 Hz tone would be differential reinforcement leading to a discriminated response.

Differential response: Any response that is elicited by a particular stimulus among many possible different stimuli. For example, an animal may be trained to salivate to a tuning fork of 256 Hz by selective reinforcement and not to forks of closely related frequencies.

Differential response: Refers to any response that is elicited by a particular stimulus among many possible different stimuli.

Differential scoring: The scoring of a test battery in several ways in order to obtain measures of several different variables. The Strong Interest Blank, for example, is scored along more than thirty dimensions in order to obtain the individual's relative interests in that number of different occupations.

Differential threshold: Refers to the minimally effective stimulus difference which is reported correctly as a difference 75 Per cent of the time.

Differential: Pertaining to factors or features that make one thing different from another.

Differentiation of life space: Refers to the organization of the life space into different regions, like the past, the present, and the future, and oil the levels of reality and unreality.

Differentiation: Refers to a biological process whereby a group of initially similar cells generates a number of different kinds of cell or a mathematical process of carrying out a differential or in sociology, refers to the process by which groups, roles, statuses, etc. develop within a society. In psychology proper there are two distinct uses. In conditioning studies, whenever an organism must learn to make two or more different responses to two or more similar stimuli.

Difficulty scale: Refers to a test whose items are arranged and graded in the order of difficulty.

Difficulty value: it is a measure of the discriminating power of a test item in terms of the percentage of individuals who passed the item.

Diffraction grating: Refers to a polished surface ruled 'by 'fine lines that is used for producing a spectrum.

Diffraction: It is the process of bending of light or sound waves around the edges of some object in the path of the wave.

Diffuse: Means lacking in specificity or coordination like the diffuse responses in infants which show a lack of goal direction and coordination.

Diffusion: It is the spread of cultural traits from' one group to another or the spread of a stimulus through cutaneous tissues or the scattering of light in the eye because -of spherical aberration.

Digit- span test: Refers to a test of immediate recall wherein the subject repeats a random series of digits following a single presentation.

Digital: Pertaining to the

numbers in any given numbering system; e.g., 0—9 in the decimal system, 1—2 in the binary, etc. or The fingers and toes.

Diglottic: Refers to the simultaneous stimulation of two areas of the tongue with the same substance.

Digraph: Refers to any 2 letters in a word which are pronounced as a single phonetic unit; e.g., the ch's in church.

Dilemma: Refers to a situation wherein one is faced with two or more mutually exclusive or mutually incompatible alternatives from which to choose when none can be taken as truly satisfactory.

Dimension: Refers to three characteristics of physical space height, width and depth. Now a days one speaks of colour as having, three dimensions (brightness, hue, saturation) or of a pure tone as having three (amplitude, frequency, phase).

Dimming: Refers to the enhancement of an afterimage by reducing the intensity of the area wherein the image is projected.

Dimorphism: Means having two forms of manifestations. Refers to species of which there are two distinguishable forms, as in juvenile and adult or male and female.

DIN colour system: Refers to colour classification system used widely in Europe. It is based on the three primary dimensions of hue, brightness and saturation.

Dingdong theory of language: The hypothesis that language origi-nates in the mimicry of natural sounds.

Diopter: A unit of measurement applied to the power of a lens to bring light rays toa focal point. The measure for any lens is the quotient obtained by dividing unity by the focal distance of the lens.

Diphenylbutyl piperidines: Refers to group of major tranquillizers classified as antipsychotic drugs and used primarily in the treatment of schizophrenia.

Diphthong: Refers to speech sound produced by gliding from one vowel to another.

Diplacusis: Refers to an auditory disorder wherein a tone is heard as two tones differing slightly in pitch in the two cars.

Diploid: Characterizing the two sets of chromosomes present in all cells except the gametes. .

Direct association: Refers to memory bonds between items with out intermediary connections.

Direct reflex: Refers to any reflex where the receptor and effector involved are homolateral, or on the same side of the body.

Directions test: Refers to a series

of ordered tasks given to examinees as items on an intelligence test assuming that the ability, to carry out verbal instructions is one indication of intelligence.

Directive counseling: Counseling in which positive advice and interpretation are given and where the counselor suggests the area of personality to be explored.

Dis: A prefix meaning apart, away from, lack of, separation from, reversal.

Disability: Refers to a severe, handicapping, loss, or impairment of a bodily organ, with corresponding functional loss.

Disambiguation: Refers to the act of determining the contextually appropriate meaning(s) of an ambiguous word, phrase, sentence, or other situation.

Discharge: Means the firing of a stimulated neuron or the release of pent-up tensions or the flowing away of a bodily secretion or the secretion itself.

Discontinuity theory of learning: The assumption that in learning that involves discrimination, the required discrimination cannot be learned until the organism relates it to the problem as a whole.

Discriminating range: Refers to the spread of scores at which a test separates or measures subjects on the dimension measured.

Discrimination: Refers to the process of distinguishing between, two objects or the process of distinguishing differences between stimuli.

Discussion leader: In small groups, refers to one whose function is to promote discussion.

Disease: Refers to an abnormal condition within the body, involving a serious impairment of function.

Disgust: Refers to the emotional feeling accompanying attitudes for repulsion, rejection, and withdrawal.

Disinhibition: Means the temporary removal of inhibition by introducing an outside or irrelevant stimulus or a loss of self-control upon overindulgence in alcohol or while under the influence of drugs.

Disjunctive concept: A concept that contains at least one element from a larger class of elements. For example, a strike in baseball has the common element of being a pitch that (1) is in a certain zone, (2) is struck at and missed, (3) results in a foul ball provided there are not two strikes against the batter, or is an unsuccessful bunt after two strikes.

Disjunctive concept: Refers to concept that can be defined by the presence of any one of 2 or more aspects.

Disorder: Refers to a disease or lick of organization or meaningful relations among phenomena.

Disorganized behaviour: Characteristic of extreme emotional conditions where the individual's behaviour lacks harmony and may show unintelligible relationships with environmental conditions, such as occurs in hysterical laughter induced by a tragic loss or disaster.

Disorganized: Refers to that which has lost or half disrupted its previous structure and functioning.

Disorientation: Refers to inability to orient oneself with regard to spatial, temporal and contextual aspects to the environment.

Disparation: Refers to the doubling of images nearer or farther than the point of fixation.

Dispersion circle: Refers to the circle of light seen when looking at a single point source.

Dispersion: Refers to the scatter of a group of scores plotted in a frequency distribution or on a scatter diagram.

Displaced aggression: An attack against a person or object other than the source of frustration. Displaced aggression occurs when the actual source of frustration is unavailable or is likely to retaliate.

Displaced vision: Refers to the research on perceptual experiences produced by Various modifications of the visual field brought about by wearing special lenses that alter incoming light.

Displacement: Refers to the distortion of an eidetic image wherein there is inversion and reversal of the image or the transference of an affect or emotional attachment from its proper object to a substitute.

Disposition rigidity: The tendency to maintain a response or pattern of behavior beyond the point of its adaptive utility.

Disposition: Refers to the organized totality of the individual's psychophysical tendencies to react in a particular way.

Dissonance: Refers to the harsh, unpleasant effect produced by two notes sounded simultaneously which do not blend or fuse.

Distal effects: Refers to responses which alter the environment in some manner.

Distal response: Any response that alters the environment beyond the manipulative boundaries of the organism. For example, throwing a brick through a window.

Distance receptor: Refers to any receptor or receptor system which responds to stimuli arising some distance from the body.

Distance vision: Refers to the visual discrimination of objects more than twenty feet distant from the observer.

Distance: It is the distance between a source of stimulation and the organism or on graphic rating scales, the linear distance between two data points.

Distorted room: It is a room constructed in a way such that the subject perceives it as rectilinear when, in reality it is not.

Distortion: Refers to any twisting or contorting that changes the shape of something so that it no longer surely represents the object. In psychoanalysis as a defense mechanism which functions to alter or "disguise" dream content that would be unacceptable in nondistorted form.

Distractibility: Refers to tendency to be drawn away from that to which one is attending.

Distractor technique: In short-term memory, the interpolation of material in order to prevent rehearsal between presentation and recall.

Distress-relief quotient: The number of verbal expressions of distress or discomfort divided by the number of statements expressive of relief. The distress-relief quotient is utilized in therapy and counseling situations as an index of improvement.

Distributed practice: The spacing of periods of practice over a period of time rather than massing the practice in one long learning session. Distributed practice is usually found to be more efficient than massed practice, in relation to learning time for most tasks.

Distribution, probability: It is similar to frequency distribution except that instead of pairing each class or category with the, frequency with which it occurred it is paired with its probability of occurrence.

Distribution, sampling: Refers to any distribution which results from taking samples of specified size from a population.

Distribution: A tableor graph of the frequency of scores plotted against their appropriate numerical values. The sores are typically plotted on the horizontal axis, the frequencies on the vertical axis.

Distribution: It is a table or graph of the frequency of scores plotted against their appropriate numerical values.

Disulfram: It is a drug that is used for treatment of alcoholism. It causes acetaldehyde, a breakdown product of alcohol, to accumulate in the blood resulting in a variety of most unpleasant experiences including dizziness, nausea, vomiting, sweating and a throbbing headache. Its success rate in treating alcoholism is not high and one likely reason for the failure is that the alcohol is not the unusual or novel stimulus that the conditioned aversion response needs for effective learning.

Disuse, law of: Refers to the Assumption that responses or associations which are not practised will weaken and disappear.

Diuretic: Refers to a substance that causes increased secretion and passage of urine.

Divagation: Refers to a tendency to distress and ramble while speaking confused thought.

Divergence: Refers to the property of moving away from a central point or of lying in different directions.

Dizygotic twins: Refers to fraternal twins, or twins arising from two separate eggs.

Dizziness: Refers to the sensation of falling or whirling generally accompanied by nausea.

Doctrine: Refers to a teaching ; a set of beliefs, generally without adequate supporting evidence but with the implication that given further research adequate supportive evidence will be forthcoming,

Dogmatism scale: It is a questionnaire designed to measure rigidity and inflexibility in thinking.

Dominance hierarchy: A series of behaviours or responses that occur in the form of a rack order of importance or dominance.

Dominance need: Refers to the need to control others or to lead or dictate to others.

Dominance: 1. The trait of desiring to be on top. *Contr.* SUBMISSION. 2. prepotency; the relative strength that causes one response to win out in a conflict of responses. Foe example, flexion of the limb in withdrawal to a painful stimulus is dominant over an extension reflex. 3. in genetics, the capacity of one trait to suppress a recessive trait. 4. the preferential use of one hand or one side of the body over the other. 5. the tendency for one side of the brain to be more important than the other in the control of the body.

Dominant wavelength: Refers to the spectral wavelength which when mixed with white, will match a sample hue.

Dominator: Refers to a retinal ganglion cell which responds over, the entire visible spectrum Such cells do so in a nonuniform fashion and display peak sensitivity a particular wavelength.

Donders' law: Refers to a

principle of visual fixation which states that regardless of how an ocular position is reached, every position of the line of fixation corresponds to a definite, invariable angle of torsion of the eyes.

Door-in-the-face technique: It is device used for obtaining compliance wherein the individual initially requests something very large, so large that it will surely be denied and than de-escalates to a more modest request.

Dopamine: Refers to one of the catecholomines important in neural transmission. Also used in the treatment of depression and in Parkinson's disease.

Dopaminergic: Pertaining to pathways, fibers or neurons wherein dopamine is a neurotra-nsmitter.

Doppler effect: It is the shit in hue or pitch when a source of light or sound is moving rapidly in reference to an observer.

Dorsoventral: Refers to the axis extending from the back to the ventral side of the body.

Dosage: It is the amount of a medicine or other preparation prescribed to be given.

Dotting test: It is a paper-and-pencil test of mechanical ability wherein the subject is asked either to make as many dots as possible (tapping test), or to put dots in small circles as quickly as possible (aiming test).

Double bind: Refers to the situation faced by a person who is receiving contradictory messages from another, powerful person.

Double images: 1. The duplication of images on the retina as a result of optical defects. 2. the doubling of images in the distance when fixating on near objects or of near images when fixating on far objects.

Doubtful judgment: In psychophysical experiments refers to a judgment of difference between stimuli of which the subject is uncertain.

Dowsing: Means locating underground sources of water or minerals by prospecting with a divining rod of forked twig held, by the two branches in the two hands. When the rod or twig dips toward the earth, the dowser takes this as a sign of success. Psychologists generally account for the phenomenon as unconscious muscle movements.

Dramatization: Refers to the transformation of repressed wishes or impulses into symbolic forms, as in dreams.

Dream analysis: Refers in psychoanalysis to the contents of dreams that are analysed for underlying of disguised motivations, symbolic meanings or evidence of symbolic representations.

Dream determinant: Refers to any factor in the environment which plays a part in the causation of a particular dream and lends it is particular flavour.

Dream interpretation: It is the process of deciphering the meaning of a dream. The procedure used by psychoanalysts is, to have the patient free-associate around the dream content until its wish-fulfilment nature has become apparent.

Dream interpretation: The process of deciphering the meaning of a dream. The procedure employed by psychoanalysts is to have the patient free-associate around the dream content until its wish-fulfillment nature has become apparent. Considerable use is also made of dream-symbol interpretation. Some symbols are held to be universal and immediately interpretable, such as pointed objects, which are phallic symbols, and running water, which symbolizes birth. Many other symbols are peculiar to the individual dreamer and must be interpreted by the process of free association.

Dream symbolism: Refers to the disguised expressions in dreams in which one thing is a "stand-in" or a symbol for something.

Dream wish: Refers to the symbolic representation of a repressed or unconscious wish in a dream.

Dream, ego: Refers to a separate component of the ego which was considered to be responsible for dreaming.

Drill: Refers to practice by systematic repetition to the point of mastery.

Drive arousal: Refers to the activation of a drive by an internal or external condition, or, by a combination of both.

Drive displacement: Refers to the arousal of behaviour appropriate to one-drive upon the frustration of another.

Drive specificity: Refers to the assumed relationship between drive stimuli and the responses which satisfy the drive.

Drive state: It is the hypothetical intraorganic state which gives rise to drive behaviour. Such states are considered to reach a certain critical level before initiating goal-seeking behaviour.

Drive stimuli: Refers to the afferent nervous impulses which, are considered to arise in organs in a drive state.

Drive: It is an around goal-directed tendency of an

organism that is based on a change in organic processes.

Drug addiction: Refers to the habitual use of drugs, with psychological and physiological dependence.

Drug effect: Refers to any change in behaviour or in a psychological state which is systematically related to drug dosage.

Drug interaction: Refers to the effects of two (or move) drugs taken together, when their combined effects are different from what would be produced by only one of them taken alone. For example alcohol And a sedative where the interaction produces central nervous depression far greater than either drug alone would yield.

DSM (I, II, III): Refers to Diagnostic and Statistical Manual. Having been revised twice in recent years the three versions are denoted as I, II and III.

Dual memory theory: The assumption that there are two fundamental types of memory short-term memory (q.v.) and long-term memory (q.v.).

Dual personality: A multiple personality consisting of two components.

Dual-code hypothesis: Refers to the belief that human memory is made up of two coding systems one based on a visual-imagery process and one on a verbal-coding process.

Dualism: 1. A philosophical position whose chief exponent was Plato Dualism holds that there are two fundamentally different substances in the universe, mind and matter. 2. the psychological position that mind and body are separate processes. In psychological dualism, differences in the nature of mind and bodymay or may not be implied.

Ductless gland: One of the endocrine glands whose products are poured directly into the bloodstream.

Dull normal: It is a category for persons having 'IQ's between 70 and 90.

Duplicity theory: The theory-now considered as-established fact-that there are separate visual receptors for brightness vision (rods) and for colour vision (cones).

Dura mater: It is the tough, outermost membrane covering the brain and spinal cord. Below it lie the arachnid layer and the pia mater.

Dural sinus: It is the space between layers of the dura mater, or hard outer covering of the brain, that carries blood from the cerebral veins into the neck.

Durance: It is an interval of time

during which a life activity takes place.

Dvorine test: It is a test used for defective colour vision it is similar to the Ishihara test.

Dyad; diad: Refers to a social group made up of two persons or a chord composed of two tones.

Dynamic equilibrium: A generally stable organization of forces or energy. Changes in one part of a system in dynamic equilibrium are reflected by a rearrangement of the energy distribution in the whole, and are further characterized by constant change and activity. The concept of dynamic equilibrium has been applied by Gestalt psychologists to the cerebral cortex.

Dynamic psychology: Any system of psychology, such as field theory or psychoanalysis, emphasizing the search for cause-and-effect relationships in motives and drives.

Dynamic subsidiation: Refers to a sequence of subgoals, leading to a final goal.

Dynamic subsidization: A sequence of subgoals leading to a final goal.

Dynamic system: A system in which the parts are interrelated in such a way that a change in one part will influence the entire system. A dynamic system is analogous to a field of force that, if disturbed at any point, reflects that disturbance throughout. A static system, by way of contrast, does not necessarily reflect changes in all parts. A telephone switchboard is a type of static system.

Dynamic system: A term applicable to, any system in which the several, elements are all interwoven or interrelated so that changes in one sector of the's system have systematic effects on the rest of the system.

Dynamic theory: The theory that the brain's action is characterized by constant changes of energy and that there is no fixed point-for-point correspon-dence between events in the cerebral cortex and environmental stimuli.

Dynamic trait: It is a trait which has motivating characteristics or is manifested in goal-directed behaviour.

Dynamics: In field theory refers to the forces which act upon a psychological field.

Dynamism: Refers to a mechanism of adjustment. Whose primary function is to fulfil drives and motives and to protect oneself from stress and discomfort.

Dynamogenesis; dynamogen: Refers to the initiation of motor responses due to sensory stimulation or the correlation of effector responses with receptor activities.

Dynamometer: It is an instrument used for measuring strength of muscular response, usually hand-grip.

Dyne: A unit of force defined as the force needed to accelerate 1 gram of matter through 1 centimetre per second.

Dysacousia: Refers to a psychological condition in which ordinary noise causes discomfort.

Dyschiria: Refers to inability to tell which side of one's body has been touched.

Dyschronism: Refers to disturbed time sense, specially one caused, by flight across 5 to 10 time zones, which maximally disrupts biological rhythms.

Dyseneia: Refers to defective articulation of words, due to deafness.

Dysgenic: Pertaining to influences detrimental to heredity or biologically deficient.

Dyshomophilla: A psychosexual disorder wherein, the sufferer is severely distressed and rendered highly anxious by his or her sexually, arousing fantasies about homosexuality.

Dyslexia: Refers to inability to read; impairment of the reading function.

Dyslogia: Refers to a deficiency in the ability to express ideas verbally.

Dyspareunia: Refers to painful sexual intercourse. Considered as a functional disorder not associated with Any physical or matomical dysfunction.

Dysphasia, aphasia: Refers to impairment of inability in any of the language functions.

Dysphoria: Depression accompanied by anxiety.

Dysphrasia: Impairment in writing or speaking because of mental disorders.

Dysphrenia: An old term for mental disorders.

Dysplasia: Abnormal growth because of an abnormal physique.

Dysplasio: Abnormal growth resulting in an abnormal physique.

Dysplastic type: An irregular body build difficult or impossible to classify according to one of the type theories.

Dyspraxia: Impairment in coordination; inability to carry out skilled movements.

E

Ear: The organ that contains the receptors for hearing. It is divided into three main parts the outer, middle, and inner ears. The outer ear consists of the pinna and the external auditory canal, which terminates in the eardrum, or tympanic membrane. The middle ear consists of three auditory ossicles—the hammer, anvil, and stapes—the third of which articulates with the cochlea at the oval window.

The eustachian tube, a pressure equalizer, enters into the middle ear from the mouth. The inner ear consists of the cochlea, which contains the receptors for hearing and the organs connected with the static sense and the sense of movement. The cochlea consists of three canals: the scala tympani, the cochlear canal, and the scala vestibuli. The organ of Corti, containing the receptor cells for hearing, rests on the basilar membrane.

Economic: It is thoroughly equivalent to or pertaining to energy. Hence, the so-called economic *concepts* are those pertaining to the origin, distribution, transfer and use of psychic energy or libido.

Ectomorphy: It is a one of the three Primary dimensions of body type. An ectomorph is one whose physique is dominated by the embryonic ectodermal component, the outer skin and the nervous system:

Ectomy: Combining form meaning removal, particularly surgical removal.

Ectoplasm: It is the outermost layer of cell protoplasm. In Parapsychology, a hypothesized psychic substance believed to emanate from the body of a medium in a trance during a seance.

Eczema: Refers to any of several forms of chronic dermatitis. Some cases are caused by irritating substance of hers are considered to be due to psychological factors and are considered as psychosomatic.

Edge: It is a line in the visual

field at which there is a detectable difference in some aspect of the stimulus on one side of it as compared with the other.

Educational psychology: A branch of psychology that deals with theories and problems in education. It *includes* the application of principles of learning to the classroom, curriculum development and reform testing and evaluation of aptitudes and abilities, socialisation processes and their interaction with cognitive functioning, teacher training, etc.

E-F scale: A scale from the Minnesota Multiphasic Personality Inventory (MMPI) consisting of 30 items and designed to measure attitudes toward ethnocentricity and authoritarianism.

Effectance motive: An over-all motive embracing all specific intrinsic motives. The biological significance of the effectance motive is to attain competence in dealing with the environment.

Effectance: It is the capacity to cope with the environment to be competent. An effectance motive is that which functions by making a child feel a strong need to become competent in order to overcome feelings of inadequacy or inferiority.

Effeminate: Means female-like. Refers to a biological male whose behaviour patterns are more closely associated with females.

Efferent: Means carry away from. Hence, in neurophysiology it refers to the conduction of nerve impulses from the central nervous system outward toward the periphery (muscles, glands). Efferent neurons and neural pathway§ carry information to effectors and are commonly known as motor neurons or pathways.

Efficacy: Refers to a very primitive cognitive experience by which the young child's emotions and feelings are considered to be responsible for events in the world.

Effort: Refers to the work required to perform some action. In psychology, the subjective sense of the amount of work needed to perform some action.

Ego analysis: A psychoanalytic term, for a relatively short form of analysis that focuses on the integrative, positive ego functions rather than on the deeply repressed id functions.

Ego anxiety: In psychoanalytic theory refers: to any reaction because of threats to the ego; the anxiety caused by conflicts between id, ego and superego.

Ego boundary: A concept according to which part of the normal ego development consists in establishing a boundary separating self from others.

Ego cathexis: A channelling or

focusing of libido on an object within the domain of the reality-oriented ego.

Ego failure: Refers to "break-down" in ego function, particularly a failure to restrain id impulses so that they conform with the strictures of the superego.

Ego function: Refers to the primary role of the ego—to mediate between the id and the superego in ways which are responsive to society and self-protection.

Ego integrity: The final of Erikson's stages of man. Full egg integrity in this conception allows the acceptance of old age and one's ultimate death without despair.

Ego neurosis: A classification in psychoanalysis which includes neuroses like paralyses, hysteria, memory loss, etc., which are hypothesized because of disruption of ego functions.

Ego psychology: Refers to the psychology of the ego. That is the examination of those developing structures and processes that are considered as being within the purview of the ego.

Ego resistance: Refers to resistance on the part of the patient to give up neurotic patterns of behaviour, to recognize repressed impulses and to abandon defence mechanisms.

Ego structure: Refers to the pattern and organization of ego traits functions, etc. Just what "structure" the ego "has" depends entirely upon the theorist under consideration.

Ego trip: Refers to any pattern of behaviour engaged in primarily for the purpose of boosting one's sense of self.

Egopathy: Refers to the tendency to bolster one's own ego by inappropriate hostility and aggression toward others.

Egotisation: Refers to the process whereby some mental process becomes part of the ego or self; *e.i.*, the process whereby it comes to be freed from id-based impulses, of aggression and sexuality and becomes structured and reality-oriented.

Egotism: Refers to the tendency to consider oneself very highly, particularly to the point of having an annoyingly overblown opinion of self.

Ejaculatory incompetence: Refers to the inability to ejaculate within the vagina during intercourse; in a sense, the reverse of premature ejaculation.

Ekphorize: In psychiatry refers to bring back the effect of a specific psychological experience.

Elaborated code: Refer's to the speech mode adopted when one is speaking with person's from different bankgrounds from oneself. Under such conditions the discourse is relatively slow, words and phrases are carefully selected, the speech is relatively unpredictable and elaborately planned.

Elberfeld horses: Refers to a group of superbly trained horses in Germany popular during the early part of the century. The most startling was "der kluge" Hans who could seemingly perform complex mathematical problems, answer factual questions, spell, etc.

Elective mutism: Means refusal to speak, psychiatrically it is considered a childhood disorder and generally associated with any of a number of other factors like abnormalities of articulation, extreme shyness, emotional trauma, social isolation, compulsiveness and functional enuresis.

Electrical Brain Stimulation (EBS): Refers to the application of a weak electrical current to a specific locale in the brain. It is used in a number of contexts from neurosurgical procedures wherein it helps the surgeon, determine the areas of the brain that need to be surgically removed and those that need to be protected, to experimental studies of the relationship between various cerebral structures and the functions they control.

Electrocardiogram (ECG or EKG): It is a record of the activity of the heart obtained by recording the spreading electrical potential generated by the heart beat and, putting it in graphic form. It has been used as a measure of emotional arousal, of physical exertion, etc., and so has served the role of dependent variable in studies of conditioning, of emotionality etc.

Electroconvulsive Shock (ECS): Refers to a brief electrical shock applied to the head which produces full-body seizure, convulsions and mostly loss of consciousness. It, is used in two ways: (a) As a research tool to study the neurophysiology 'of memory and (b) As a therapeutic procedure for psychiatric disorders.

Electroencephalogram (ECG): It is a device used for measuring eye movements by recording the electrical potentials of the muscles that control the eye movements.

Element: It represent the basic unit of consciousness, in a way analogous with its usage in chemistry. That is, the contents of consciousness were thought to consist of combinations of a finite number of basic mental elements, in the same way as physical matter consisted of combinations of a finite number of chemical elements.

Elementarism: Refers to any

atomistic philosophical position that considers that complex phenomena can be understood only by reducing them down to their most primitive -parts.

Elicit: Means to draw forth, draw out. It refers to behaviour which is not spontaneously produced by an organism but is "drawn out" by the presentation of the appropriate stimulus.

Ellipsis: Refers to the omission of a word or words from a spoken or written message where the missing words are predictable or determinable from the structure of the sentence or from context.

Elsthesiometer: It is a device used for measuring sensitivity to touch, specifically a compass-like instrument for determining the two-point threshold on the skin.

Embryo: Refers to an organism in the earliest stages 'of prenatal development. In mammals, the organism during that period before it develops physical similarity to its mature form. In man, the organism, during the period of about six weeks during which internal and external organs become differentiated.

The embryonic period follows the *germinal,* that itself lasts about two weeks, during which time the fertilized ovum grows into a hollow sphere of approximately 5 mm. After the embryonic stage the term fetus is used.

Emit: Means to produce, to send out. It is used to refer to behaviour which is generated or produced by an organism within the context of an appropriate stimulus.

Emmetropia: Normal vision in the sense that when the eye is at rest the light is refracted so that the focus is directly on the retina.

Emotion: Variously defined by psychologists of different theoretical orientations, but with general agreement that the emotional state is a complex reaction involving a high level of activation and visceral changes, and accompanies by strong feelings, or affective states. *Feeling* are conscious experiences activated either by external stimuli or by various bodily states. We smell a rose and experience a pleasant feeling. The taste of sugar is pleasant. Similarly, many sensory stimuli are intrinsically pleasant.

Many, on the other hand, are unpleasant. Organic and kinesthetic stimuli arising from the organs and muscles can also give rise to feelings of pleasantness and unpleasantness. There are the common pleasant feelings associated with a good dinner, milk exercise, sexual satisfaction. Commonly experienced unpleasant feelings are associated with such conditions as illness, fatigue, and ingestion of certain chemicals. *Emotions* may be defined as an aroused state of the organism involving conscious, visceral, and behavioral changes. Emotions are therefore more intense than simple feelings, and involve the organism as a whole. Where a mild feeling of anger or annoyance may go unobserved by another, rage is accompanied by such profound visceral, expressive, and other behavioral changes as to be clearly distinguishable even to a casual observer.

Although the early psychologists put a great deal of effort into their attempts tolerate feelings to nervous and organic processes and, at the same time, into discussions of the differences between feeling and emotion, contemporary psychologists treat the two as aspects of the same fundamental process.

Feelings are always a part of emotions. Both involve visceral and conscious changes, and , in the last analysis, the two are primarily distinguishable on the basis of the greater intensity of emotional states. It might also be added that in recent research more attention has been given to emotions that has been given to feelings, largely because the bodily changes accompanying the emotions are more readily observable and therefore lend themselves to laboratory investigation. A problem of definition that has loomed large in recent psychological discussion of the emotions is that of the relationship between feeling and emotion on the one hand and motivation on the other. Common experience tells us that when we are motivated we are also emotionally aroused. A strong desire to escape is accompanies by fear.

A motion to destroy or attack, by anger or rage. The sexual goal, too, has its characteristic emotional state. Indeed, so close is the relationship between motives and emotions that some psychologists believe we do not need both terms. Although we need not become involved in what is still a controversial theoretical issue, there can be no disagreement that emotions, once aroused, impel us to activity.

One psychologist has, in fact, suggested an *activation theory* of emotion that stresses the high level of neural activity in the reticular system and cerebral cortex during strong emotional states. Using the electro-encephalograph to record brain waves, he compared the low level of nervous excitation in sleep, coma, and drowsiness with the relatively high level of arousal in rage, pain, and excitement. Activation, as it is used to describe such states, is almost synonyms with motivation.

However, if we change our frame of reference, several differences between motives and emotions may be pointed out, demonstrating that although emotional and motivational processes are closely related, there are, nevertheless, differences. To begin with, the primary motives or drives are cyclic in their appearance, dependent as they are upon changing psysiological rhythms.

Emotions, on the other hand, are likely to be more dependent on stimulus situations and their personal significance for the individual. The normal person does not show periodic outbursts of anger, rage, love, grief without revocation. Rather, the arousal of these emotions depends upon outside circumstances—what others say or do, how our work goes, what happens to our finances, and so on.

Secondly, drives and motives are geared to habitual patterns of satisfaction. Emotional reactions, on the other hand, are more typically aroused by situations for which we have no ready-made pattern of response. Thirst, hunger, and sex, for example, are usually satisfied by learned patterns of behavior that become more or less habitual in the normal adult. But should we lose a loved one, inherit a fortune, or meet a bear while strolling in the woods, we have no habitual modes of reacting to enable us to cope with such situations in a sterieotyped, semiautomatic fashion.

Finally, emotional behaviour is frequently disorganized and disturbed, whereas motivated behavior is typically goal-directed. In the more acute, emergency like states of rage, terror, wild grief, and the like, the individual's behavior becomes completely disorganized by extreme behavioral reactions. Non-emotional motivated behaviour, on the other hand, is well organized, is goal-directed, and shows a level of arousal commensurate with he task in hand.

The chief problems in arriving at an agreed-upon definition of the motions are those of associating emotions are those of associating emotional with other types of behavior and of distinguishing between emotional and other types of behaviour. High activation levels, strong visceral responses, and conscious states of feeling may separately and in combination enter into other processes and behavior patterns.

In general, few psychologists would disagree that such traditional emotions as fear, rage, love, joy, disgust, grief, and the like are phenomena to be explained. The problem is how to relate them to the organic and conscious changes in a meaningful way and one that is operationally valid.

Emotional blocking: Refers to an individual's inability to perform complex mental 'tasks due to a highly intense emotional state.

Emotional instability: Refers to all tendency to be emotionally labile, to display inappropriately abrupt and unpredictably extreme emotionality.

Emotional maturity: A state or condition of having reached an adult level of emotional development and therefore no longer displaying emotional patterns appropriate to children. The term emotional maturity often carries with it the implication of emotional control. Most adults experience the same emotions as children but suppress or control them better, particularly in social situations.

Emotional: 1. Pertaining to the expression of the emotions or the visceral changes that accompany the emotions. 2. characterizing idividuals who are readily stimulated to emotional behavior.

Empirical: Refers to experience in general or Descriptive of procedures carried out without explicit regard to any theory.

Empty organism: Refers to the system's unwillingness to make inferences about internal states or to posit hypothetical conducts.

Enantiodromia: Refers to the view that eventually all things becomes transformed into their opposites.

Encapsulation, psychological: Refers to behaviour that avoids a person from experiencing a painful situation, like refusing to read newspaper accounts of massacres or covering one's eyes when an accident is imminent.

Endocrine: Refers to glands which secrete hormones internally that is, there secretions are distributed through the body by the bloodstream, the glands are ductless.

Endoderm: It is the inner layer of embryonic cellular structures which develops into the digestive tract and the viscera.

Engineering psychology: It is branch of *industrial/organizational* psychology which focuses on the "man-machine interface". That is, study of the behaviour of individuals using tools, working with machines, etc.

Engram: A postulated, biochemical change due to external stimulation. The engram is hypothesized to be the biochemical manifestation of memory, the permanent alteration of neural tissue which represents what has been learned.

Engulfment: It is a form of anxiety which is experienced by insecure persons who view relationships with others as threats to their identify.

Enrichment: Refers to some theories of perceptual learning which assume that perceptual processes go beyond a direct representing of the various aspects of the stimulus field.

Enuresis: Incontinence, the involuntary passing of urine. It is equated with bed-wetting, particularly when it takes place in young children.

Environmental psychology: The branch of psychology concerned with the relationship between behaviour and the environment in which it occurs, with special emphasis on the variables of space, architecture, crowing, and noise.

Environmentalism: A general term for a class of theoretical and philosophical school which stresses the role of the environment in determining behaviour.

Enzyme: Biological catalysts which produce chemical changes another substances without being changed themselves. Enzymes are complex proteins found in degestive process which break down complex food substances into simpler compounds.

Epidemiology: A branch of science dealing with psychological, sociological, demographic and medical aspects that deals with, the study of diseases, their distributions in populations and their environmental impact.

Epigenesis: Refers to the belief that during development the complex morphological properties of an organism develop gradually out of an interaction between the prenatal environment and intracellular process.

Epiglottis: It is a thing valve-like structure of cartilage which covers the *glottis* and stops food and drink from entering the larynx.

Epilepsy: Refers to a number of disorders characterised by different combinations of the following: periodic motor or sensory seizures with or without actual convulsions, clouding of or loss of consciousness, motor, sensory or cognitive malfunctions and accompanied by an abnormal encephalogram (EEG).

Epileptic equivalent: Refers to any episodic sensory or motor symptom that an epileptic may experience instead of convulsive seizures.

Epileptogenic: Refers to those factors which cause epilepsy or circumstances that produce seizures in individuals with epilepsy.

Epinephrine: It is a hormone of the adrenal medulla whose effects are similar to those brought about by stimulation of the sympathetic division of the autonomic nervous system, *e.g.,* cardiac stimulation, vasoconstriction, arousal.

Epiphenomenon: Refers to any event which takes place in the presence of or incidentally accompanies some other process or event but in fact plays on part in that process or event.

Epiphysis: In the developing infant and child refers to a bone-forming (ossification) centre attached to another bone by cartilage. The degree of ossification can be used as a measure of growth.

Epithelium: Refers to a thin layer of tissue which covers the surface or lines the cavity of an organ. Generally performs a secreting or protective function.

Equated scores: Refers to any two sets of scores from different tests or from different parts of the same test that have been reduced to a common scale.

Equation, empirical: It is any mathematical equation which is used to fit observed data. Empirical equations are after-the fact attempts to characterize quantitatively a set of observations, and the value of such an equation is given by the closeness of the "fit" between it and the data.

Equation, rational: It is a Logical or mathematical expression which is based on (rational) assumptions about processes. Such equations differ from *empirical equations* in that their parameters are derived by deduction from theoretical assumptions and not simply from attempts to fit data.

Equilibrium: It is a synonym of *balance,* with several special usages. 1. In physiology it is the point at which opposing biochemical reactions are stable, homeostasis. 2. In perception it is a point where the body maintains a stable upright posture with respect to its center of gravity also called the *equilibrium sense* or *static sense.* 3. In social psychology refers to the theoretical tendency for a social system or bring about corrective changes to maintain itself as a functionally integrated unit.

Equipotentiality of cues: Refers to the hypothesis according to which in a perceptual situation one sensory cue may substitute for another.

Equity theory: Refers to a class of broad social psychological theorise which seek to explain behaviour by reference to the concept of equity, *i.e.,* those conditions wherein the rewards to individuals in a group are in proportion to their efforts on behalf of the group.

Equivalence coefficient: The correlation coefficient between two equivalent forms of the same test given to the same group. High coefficients of equivalence are taken as evidence of reliability.

Equivalence test: A test to determine which aspects of a stimulus pattern may be altered without destroying the equality of the pattern. Patterns that elicit the same response are considered equivalent.

Equivalence: Refers to a relationships between two "things" such Mat one may be substituted for the other in a particular setting and not alter significantly the situation.

Equivalent form: An alternate form of a test constructed with similar items so as to render the two forms as nearly the same in function as possible. Equivalent forms are useful in test-retest situations where it is desired to avoid practice effects.

Equivalent groups: Two or more groups that are matched with respect to all known variables. Within narrow limits, the means, standard deviations, and range of scores should be the same. Equivalent groups are used in experiments where an experimental group or groups will be compared with a control group. The groups must, therefore, be equivalent on all variables except the experimental variable.

Erg: It is the work done by a force of 1 dyne acting through a displacement of 1 centimetre in the direction of the force. In psychology it is used in various combinations that are metaphoric and relate to energy, force purpose or dynamic qualities.

Ergodic: In probability theory, refers to any stochastic process wherein every sequence of events is statistically the same and therefore may be taken as representative of the whole.

Ergograph: Refers to device used for measuring the amount of work accomplished by a muscle or muscle group.

Ergonomics: It is the science of the "fit" between jobs and Persons it deals with the study of the relationship between an individual's anatomy, Physiology and psychology and the demands of particular forms of work

Erikson's Ego Psychology: Erikson's theory of personality development is similar to Freud's (q.v.); however, he has cast his theory into a psychosocial form, added a number of stages, and emphasizes the ego rather than the id. Stage one is the oral-sensory stage during which the child leans basic trust or mistrust depending on the success of the first encounter with the parents. In stage two, the muscular anal stage, the child leans autonomy if successful, or shame and doubt if unsuccessful. The locomotor-genital stage is the third, and the child's learning is initiative or guilt. The fourth stage is the latency stage, during which industry and inferiority are the alternative modes of development. In puberty and adolescence, the fifth stage, they are identity versus role confusion. In young adulthood, which is the sixth stage, intimacy or isolation will be the result of the crisis in development. The seventh stage is adulthood and presents the alternatives of generativity versus stagnation. In the final, eighth stage, maturity, ego-integrity, and despair are the alternatives. In each of these stages are crises that must be coped with either successfully or unsuccessfully. Each represents an encounter between the child and the demands of society. Of particular importance for a successful, healthy adult personality is the successful resolution of the identity crisis during puberty and adolescence.

Erogenous zones: Those areas of the body whose stimulation gives rise to erotic or sexual sensation. Sometimes called erotogenic zones.

Eros: The Greek god of love. In Freudian theory, Eros refers to the whole complex of life-preservative instincts. Included among them, are the sexual instincts.

Erotic: Generally, sexual of libidinal, it may pertain to: 1. Feelings arising from the genitals particularly. 2. A more general sense of sexual arousal. 3. The stimuli that give rise to sexual arousal. 4. Any motive or need that has sexual components. 5. Love in any of its manifestations.

Eroticism: Means sexual arousal or a greater than average disposition for the sexual, a tendency to be easily aroused sexually or Sexual excitement arising from areas other than those specifically sexual, other than genitals.

Error, chance: Refers to an error that arises from chance factors. Since such errors are in principle random and unbiased they tend to cancel each other out and' the sum of chance errors, when a sufficiently large number of cases in considered, approaches zero.

Error, constant: An error due to some factors that affects all observations similarly so that the errors are always in one direction and do not cancel each out. 'Usually such an error can be detected and corrected for during statistical analysis.

Error, experimental: Refers to a class of possible errors whose origins lie in One inadequacy of an experimental design or procedure. The history of psychology is well salted with legendary experimental errors due to improper control of some important factor. The most common are failures to control for practice effects, time errors, observer differences, experimenter biases, physiological and species differences and the abiquitious Sampling error.

Error, sampling: Refers to the difference between the true value of a statistic within a population and the estimated value of that statistic derived from a sample of that population.

Error, subjective: Refers to a systematic error introduced into, observation or interpretation because of individual's biases or prejudices.

EST: Abbreviation for *electroshock therapy*. A form of psychotherapy based on the "theories" of Werner Erhard. The procedure consists of large group sessions of rather extraordinary intensity. For up to 60 hours several hundred people are gathered in a large hall and subjected to physical privation, guided meditation and fervent diatribes on the EST way to "get in touch" with one's inner sense of personal responsibility.

Estimate: It is a reasonable guess about the value of some factor. In statistics, it refers to a "best guess" of the value of some variable or statistic based on refined computational procedures that provide both the estimated value as well as a measure of the likelihood which that value falls within ascertainable limits of the true value.

Estradiol: The most biologically potent of the naturally occurring *estrogens.* It is produced primarily by the ovaries and, in small amounts, by the adrenal cortices.

Estrogen: Refers to a group of related steroid hormones produced chiefly by the ovaries, but also by the adrenal cortices and, in very small amounts, by the testes. It include are *estradiol, estrone* and their metabolic product, *estriol.* Estrogens, are responsible for the development of most of the female secondary sex characteristics, breast development, maturation of the genitalia, deposition of body fat-but not auxiliary and public hair.

Estrus cycle: The ovarian cycle in female sub-primate mammals. It has four stages: proestrus, estrus, matestrus and diestrus. The second stage, *estrus,* is that associated with ovulation, swelling of the vulva, various uterine processes and receptivity copulation.

Ethics: It is a branch of philosophy that deals with that which is deemed acceptable in human, behaviour, with what is good or bad, right or wrong with human conduct' in pursuit of goals and aims.

Evocative therapy: Any form of

therapy in which the primary technique involves the interpretation of the patient's verbal productions.

Evolution: Refers to loosely, orderly development. More specifically, the process by which plant and animal forms developed by descent, with modification, from earlier existing forms.

Exceptional child: Refers to both extremely talented and gifted children as well as to those having low intelligence or other learning disabilities.

Excitation: In physiology refers to a process by which some stimulus energy pattern sets up a change or pattern of changes in a receptor. In the study of learning refers to a general high level of activity in the whole nervous system. In social psychology refers to an increase in psychological tension.

Executive area: In neurophysiology refers to any cortical area that serves integrative, organizing functions.

Exhaustion delirium: Refers to acute delirium occasionally observed under conditions of extreme exhaustion brought about by intense extended physical effort or by other debilitating conditions like high fever.

Exhaustion: It is a physiological a state wherein the metabolic process has been depleted, producing fatigue, weariness and a general lack of responsiveness.

Existential psychology: 1. The school of psychology, primarily championed by Wundt in Europe and Tichener in America, that held that the subject matter of psychology was conscious content to be investigated by the method of introspection. 2. the system of psychology associated with the philosophical position of existentialism. Its adherents oppose what they term the abstractions of both academic psychology and classical psychoanalysis and emphasize instead that existence takes precedence over essence; that freedom of choice is paramount over determinism.

Existential psychotherapy: Existential psychotherapy is not a unified set of procedures or techniques for helping the individual find a better way of living. Some existential therapists favor a modification of the analytic technique of free association; some utilize the client-centered or face-to-face approach. Others have developed their own specialized techniques. Moreover, those who practice existential therapy are not agreed upon a systematic body of theory out of which clinical practice evolves. Rather, there are certain more or less commonly accepted existential themes that form the basis of therapy. Because the most basic of all existential themes is that of *being,* therapy must deal with the problems of being or being-in-the-world. The patient's relationship to the world of things, to other people, and to his own internal world of consciousness must be explored. Being, it is emphasized, is conscious *existence* that is never fixed but always becoming. Existence is therefore free to determine the future.

Non-being is essence that is fixed the without freedom to determine its future. Because existence is free to choose, anxiety arises. The individual without choice has no reason to fear. Those who must face alternatives and take risks experience fear. To escape anxiety the individual may adopt in authentic modes of existence such as becoming detached or alienated, pursuing pleasure, or losing the self in conformity to the demands of society. It follows that an essential goal of therapy is to examine being in all its manifestations and particularly to explore the patient's inauthentic modes of living.

Anxiety and inauthentic modes of being can be overcome by commitment, not to egotistical goals, but to those that favor humankind. Existential psychotherapy rejects the unconscious determi nism of classical; psychoanalysis. The individual who is living a maladaptive mode is not forever determined to do so because of his past. The goal of therapy is not merely to make him more comfortable with his disability, but to show him that he can choose a new mode of being and free himself from the past. Therefore emphasis in therapy is on the present and the future and not on the past. Fulfillment, not the resolution of conflicts, is the model for personality.

Ultimately the patient must experience a transformation in the meaning and valucs that he attaches to living. He does this through the analysis of his own being and his relationship and commitment to his fellowman.

Existential therapy: It is a form of psychotherapy which based upon the philosophical doctrine of existentialism. It is highly subjective and focuses on the immediate situation. It differs from most other therapies in that there is a strict avoidance of intellectual explanation and interpretation; the focus is on the immediate reality shared by client and therapist.

Existentialism: An important 20th-century philosophical movement that carved out a domain for itself between rationalistic idealism and totally objective materialism. The emphasis is upon personal decision to be made in a world without reason and without purpose. It emphasizes subjectivity, free will and individuality and has acted as a philosophical 'counterbalance to ' theories that stress the role of society and social groups.

Experimental control: The application of the principle that all conditions and variables in an experiment must be known and regulated in such a manner that the influence of the independent variable will be unambiguous. This involves excluding or holding constant any variable or environmental conditions that might influence the dependent variable. Some experimental conditions call for the use of control groups.

Experimental group: A group of subjects who are subjected to the independent or experimental variable in an experiment. The experimental group is matched in all respects with the control group, which is treated in the same manner as the experimental group except for the application of the experimental variable.

Experimental psychology: A branch of psychology that, deals with the study of psychological issues using experimental procedures.

Extinguish: Means to carry out the procedure of experimental extinction, or to diminish the responsiveness of an organism by running experimental extinction.

Extirpation: Refers to removal of an organ or bodily structure Generally surgical removal. When only part of the organ of structure is removed the term *ablation is* used.

Extrapolate: Means to estimate from a series of known values, the values of a variable that are higher or lower than the known range.

Extrapunitive: Refers to the tendency to react to frustration by showing anger toward and investing blame in others.

Extrapyramidal motor system: Refers to set of complex, diffuse neural structures both cortical and subcortical including the basal ganglia, cerebellum, parts of the reticular formation and their connections with the motor neurons of the spinal cord and nuclei of the cranial nerves.

Extrasensory perception (ESP or psi): Perception without the mediation of sensation. There are two main classes of phenomena included under the general heading of extrasensory perception: (1) *extrasensory perception* that in turn includes (a) *telepathy*, or direct thought transference from one individual to another without the intervention of any known exchange of physical energy, (b) *clairvoyance,* or the ability to know objects and objective events by some means other than the sense, and (c) *precognition,* or knowledge of future events; (2) *psycho-kinesis* (PK) or the ability to influence objects by direct mental manipulation.

Telephathy is typically investigated by means of an experimental arrangement involving two people, one of whom (the sender) attempts to send a message is a symbol from a pack of ESP (Zener) cards consisting of 25 cards, the face of each marked with one of the following symbols: star, cross, circle, square, wavy lines. Since each pack has 5 cards bearing each of the 5 symbols, the percipient could only get 5 correct by chance. If on many runs the subject scores consistently above chance, the result is attributed to ESP. Great care must be taken to avoid inadvertent sensory cues (preferably by isolating the sender and percipient in different buildings) and errors of recording by having independent checkers. In clairvoyance experiments no sender is involved.

Instead the subject attempts to guess the sequence of a pack of cards that lies facedown on the table. A record of the subject's guesses is made before the cards are examined. In precognition experiments the percipient attempts to guess what is *going* to be sent on the *next* trial. In psychokinesis experiments the subject attempts to influence the throw of dice. In all of these procedures standard statistical methods are employed to evaluate the significance of the results.

On the average only small differences are found between observed guesses and chance expectations. However, such differences are statistically significant if a large number of runs is involved. Nevertheless, most psychologists remain skeptical of ESP because of the lack of consistency in subjects (even the best subjects appear to lose their ability after a number of runs), the finding that the tighter the experimental controls the less evidence of ESP, and the fact that the evidence for such phenomena is based only on statistical inference involving very large numbers of run.

Extraspectral hue: Any hue which cannot be characterized by a single wavelength e.g., Purple, that requires a mixture of long wavelengths (red) and short wavelengths (blue).

Extraversion: In personality theory refers to the tendency to direct one's energies outward, to be concerned with and derive gratification from the physical and social environment.

Extrinsic motivation: Motivation not inherent in the behavior itself. Engaging in activities for the material rewards they bring is *extrinsic* motivation, engaging in activities because one enjoys them in *intrinsic motivation*.

Eyewitness testimony: Basically a legal term for the use of the eyewitness to a crime to provide testimony in court about the identity of the perpetrator.

F

Field structure: 1. The patterning of relations among the various parts of the psychological field. 2. the hierarchy of parts that lends rigidity and stability to the psychological field.

Field theory: A systematic point of view in psychology developed by Kurt Lewin (q.v.), an associate of Wertheimer and Kohler at the University of Berlin. Lewin was completely dissatisfied with traditional associational and structuralistic psychology and became attracted to the Gestalt point of view.

However, he found the strong interests of Wertheimer and Koffka in perceptual theory, and Kohler's interests in brain theory, insufficient to develop a system that would take into account motivational factors in behavior. Field theory can, therefore, be considered a close relative of Gestalt psychology, but a system in which motivational and social factors are considered of paramount importance. The psychological field is the individual's life space, or the space containing the individual and his environment.

Psychologically, the environment is the environment only as perceived by the individual in relation to his needs, goals, and purposes. His perception is therefore highly selective. Some objects and persons will be ignored, some considered of little importance, and others of great importance. If an object is of importance to the individual it will have positive valence, that is, it will be attractive; if it has negative valence, the object is one that the individual will avoid if possible.

The individual is shown in the life space as directed toward or away from objects by means of vectors, or directed lines. A vector tends to produce movement toward or away from objects or persons, but it is sometimes impeded by a barrier, particularly in conflict situations. Lewin used the rudiments of topology for mapping the life space—showing the individual, his goals, and the routes tot he goal. Vector analysis was brought into the system in order to represent needs, motives, tensions, or, in general, motivational state. Lewin's use of the mathematics of topology and vector analysis has been controversial. However, his work and that of his associates on such problems as level of aspiration, regressive behavior at barriers, democratic versus authoritarian atmospheres, conflict, and the tensions associated with interrupted tasks, have proved challenging to psychologists of every theoretical point of view.

Fields of psychology: Divisions or branches of psychology in which psychologists specialize. There are eight main fields of psychology: *Abnormal psychology* is concerned with mental disorders, their causes, treatment, and prevention.

Child psychology specializes in the development of children and of immature animals; the child psychologist is particularly interested in discovering the principles that govern changes in the behavior of immature forms as they develop. *Comparative psychology* and *physiological psychology* are two closely related specialties; the comparative psychologist studies animals, striving to discover principles of behavior that apply to all animals, including man, and the physiological psychologist is interested in the relationship between behavior and the nervous system and endocrine glands.

Clinical psychology is concerned with the diagnosis, treatment, and prevention of adjustmental problems. *Educational psychology* applies tne principles of psychology to educational problems.

General experimental psychology is concerned with the establishment of general laws of behavior. *Industrial psychology* applied the principles of psychology to industrial and military problems.

Figural aftereffect: A perceptual phenomenon illustrating the principle that there is a tendency to maintain stability in the figureground relationship. An inspection figure is fixated to a test figure. The test figure will be distorted, due to the aftereffect of the inspection figure.

Figural cohesion: The tendency of all parts of a figure to maintain mutual attractiveness and to "hang together" perceptually. Thus, a disjointed picture or cartoon is perceived as a recognizable whole despite the fact that it is no more than a collection of broken lines.

G

General psychology: 1. The broad branch of psychology that seeks to discover the laws and principles that apply to persons in general, as opposed to differential psychology, which seeks to discover the ways in which people differ. 2. the broad synthesis of all findings and theories in the field as typified by an introductory textbook or course.

Gestalt psychology: The school or systematic position within the field, to the effect that the proper subject matter for psychology is behaviour and experience studied as wholes. Some degree of analysis is permissible but should be of the phenomenological variety, since molecular or elemental analysis would destroy the unitary quality of that which is undergoing analysis. Similarly, conscious experience cannot be meaningfully resolved into structuralistic elements, nor can behavior be reduced to combinations of reflexes or conditioned responses and still retain its uniqueness and meaningfulness. The Gestalt psychologists also object to treating the nervous system as a static, machinelike structure capable only of responding piecemeal to incoming stimuli.

Rather, the cerebral cortex is viewed as analogous to a field of force in active equilibrium and in which each incoming stimulus affects the entire field. Cortical events, moreover, are isomorphic to external events. That is, there is a point-for-point correspondence between cortical events and objects in the environment, but the correspondence does not represent an identity. Instead, the two are related in the same manner in which a road map is related to a highway. The map distorts the landscape and the twists and turns in the road are smoothed out for simplicity, but the essential relations remain valid. The best-known of the Gestalt contributions are in the field of perception and learning. The perceptual concept of figure and ground, the laws of primitive organization of perception—proximity, contrast, similarly, and contiguity—the principles of transposition, closure, good figure, and *Pragnanz,* are all contributions of the school. In learning, the Gestalt psychologists are noted for their studies of insight in apes and the extension of their theories into productive thinking in human subjects.

Gestalt therapy: Psychotherapy in which there is emphasis on the principles of Gestalt psychology (q.v.) as applied to the treatment of behavioural disorders. Healthy personality functioning is seen as the patient's perception of experiences as meaningful wholes, with fluid relationships existing between focal or figural experiences and background experiences. Emphasis is placed on attention, self-awareness, spontaneity of perception, involvement in experiences, overcoming gaps or distortions in experience believed to produce anxiety, compulsive behavior, and loss of zest.

H

H sealing: Refers to the utilization of several items, of equal acceptability as if they were, one item, so at to increase reliability.

Haab's pupillary reflex: The process of contraction of both irises when the gaze is directed toward a source of light in a darkened room.

Habit family hierarchy: (*Hull*) the arrangement in a preferential order of alternate routes to a goal. When the most preferred route or response is blocked, a less favored one will appear.

Habit hierarchy: the organization into a hierarchical form of a number of simpler habits into progressively higher-order systems. Used by learning theorists to explain plateaus in learning curves for complex sensorimotor tasks, such as typewriting.

Habit interference: a conflict of two or more incompatible responses that results in mutual weakening or the eventual domination of one response over the other.

Habitat: Refers to the geographical area in which conditions are well suited to the life of a particular species.

Habituation: Refers to the elimination, with practice of useless emotional responses in animal learning.

Hair cells: A type of cell which acts as a receptor like the hair cells in the organ of Corti in the inner ear.

Halfway house: Refers to a self-governing facility for discharged mental patients who no longer need hospitalization but do reed the support of a restricted social community to assist them in the transition back to society.

Hallucinatory image: Refers to a mental image that is taken for reality.

Hallucinogen: Refers to any of group of psychoactive chemical pounds capable or producing hallucinations.

Halo effect: Refers to the tendency to allowing impression of a person or ones outstanding trait to influence rating of that person.

Hampton court maze: The famous English garden maze which was used as a model for many early maze-learning studies with animals.

Handicapped: A person having less than normal ability or having an anatomical or functional defect which makes it difficult for him to compete with his peers.

Haphalgesia: Refers to a sensation of pain when the skin is touched by a normally nonirritating stimulus.

Hard drug: Refers to any drug which produces *physiological* **dependence* Generally used for opium-based narcotics.

Hardness: A perceptual quality. In vision, it characterises colour high in saturation and brightness.

Harmonic: Refers to an overtone, or partial, whose frequency is a multiple of the fundamental one.

Harria: It is a factor trait that is characterised by toughness, decisiveness, assertiveness and realism in outlook.

Harshness: It is an unpleasant quality of sounds arising out of aperiodic or irregular have forms.

Hate: Refers to a strongly aversive attitude involving anger, ill will; and the desire to inflic injury on the object of hatred.

Hawthrone effect: It is the tendency of people to work harder when experiencing a sense of participation in something new and special.

Healy picture completion test: A performance test which needs the assembling of incomplete pictures by selecting, the correct parts from a large number o possibilities.

Herbartian psychology; A system of educational psychology formulated by J.F. Herbart in 1825 and based on the assumption tha ideas are competitive in thei struggle to arrive in the center o consciousness. Its central doctrine is the doctrine of apperception which holds that new sense impression striving for recognition has to be related to the body o previously acquired ideas (the apperceptive mass) before it can become meaningful. The doctrine of apperception was taken over by Wundt and the structuralists.

Hereditarianism: Refers to any position stressing the role o heredity in the determination o behaviour.

Heredity: the totality o characteristics transmitted from the parents to the offspring. The transmission of geneti characteristics is a function of the CHROMOSOMES and GENES (q.q.v.). The exact mechanism of hereditary transmission was not known until the discovery of deoxyribonucleic acid (DNA) and ribonucleic acid (RNA). It is now believed that the molecules of DNA serve as a kind of code whose built-in program influences the developing tissues through the agency of RNA, which serves in turn as a messenger for DNA. However, the concept of the gene as a determiner remains useful in describing dominant, recessive, and sex-linked characteristics.

Dominart characteristics are those that will appear in the offspring as actual or manifest traits. Recessive characteristics may be present but do not appear in the offspring unless both parents are the carriers of recessive genes. Sex-linked characteristics are those transmitted by the sex-determining chromosomes and may only appear in the presence of the male sex hormone.

Color blindness and baldness in men are examples of such sex-linked characteristics. These traits are carried by women but do not become manifest except in the presence of relatively high levels of the male sex hormone. In general, heredity interacts with environment to produce the individual; all traits are a product of the combined interaction of the two factors.

Heritability: Refers to that portion of the total variability in a trait which can be attributed to genetic differences.

Heritage: Refers to transmission from generation to generation. May refer to either biological heredity or to social transmission of customs and traditions.

Heroin: It is a morphine derivative which is one of the most widely used of the addictive drugs. It has a narcotic effect.

Hertz (Hz): One cycle per second. It is the standard international term now in used, and has replaced *cps* (or cycles per second).

Heterozygous: Referring to an organism possessing a triat whose genetic makeup is made up of both-dominant and recessive genes.

Heuristic: A method of discovery, a procedure for solving a problem, a technique that operates as a vehicle for creative formulation. Essentially, it is any sophisticated, directed procedure which functions by reducing the range of possible solutions to a problem or the number of possible answers to a question.

Hidden observer: Refers to a hypothesized concealed consciousness which is inferred to experience events differently from the hypnotized consciousness.

Hidden-cue test or situation.

Refers to a task wherein the learner must discover the feature of a stimulus situation which will lead to the reward.

Higher-order conditioning: Classical conditioning wherein a conditioned stimulus (CS) from an original conditioning series is used as the unconditioned stimulas CS in a new experimental setting.

Hindbrain: During embryonic development the brain evolves three separate portions, the hindbrain, midrain and forebrain. The hindbrain is evolutionarily the oldest; it differentiates into the metencephalon and the myelencephalon. The metencephalon gives rise to the cerebellum and the pons, the myelencephalon to the medulla.

Hippocampus: A curved nerve tract make up of gray matter in the floor of the inferior horn of the lateral ventricle. Its shape resembles a sea hours. The hippocampus is considered to function in olfactory, visceral processes and short term memory.

Histogram: It is a graphic form of the frequency distribution wherein the number of cases within each-class is represented by a Vertical bar whose height is proportional to the number of cases within the class.

Hodology: Refers to the geometry of vectors, paths, and the space wherein they Occur Hodology is used as a model of behaviour. Vectors, or directed lines are used to represent, motivation-and tensions, paths are the routes on which behaviour taken place in moving from one space to another; and the concept of hodological space is used in the sense of dynamic space having its psychological properties.

Holergasia: Refers to any psychiatric disorder which affects the entire emotional, cognitive and behavioural repertoire of an individual.

Holmgren test: It is a test of colour blindness wherein the testee must sort a number of skeins of coloured wool into three basic piles in accordance with a sample set. The test has has been used as a test of abstracting ability.

Homogamy: Refers to inbreeding among members of a genetically isolated group which results in the development of similar traits among the various members.

Homologous organs: Refers to those organs which have the same essential structure but different function-for example, the fin of a fish and the band of a man.

Hope: Refers to an attitude which is characterised by an expectation of the favourable, outcome of an event.

Horizontal growth: It is the

increase in the number of activities' or skills on the-same level of difficulty attained by the subject.

Hormic psychology: a system of psychology advocated by William McDougall, whose fundamental assumption was that behavior is characterized by purpose, or a tendency to seek goals.

Basically, goal-seeking behavior is motivated by propensities that are instincts or sentiments. Instincts are innate propensities, such as flight, curiosity, pugnacity, reproduction, acquisition, and self-assertion.

All instincts are describable in terms of their three fundamental characteristics or attributes—*cognitive*, *affective*, and *conative*. That is, all instincts have a sensory, a motivational, and an emotional component. Instincts may be modified into sentiments, such as love, jealousy, or patriotism, which are combinations of instincts and, through experience, become associated with complex stimulus situations.

Hospice: A 'specialized nursing home meant for terminally ill patients- Here patients can live out their final days in dignity.

House-tree-person test: A projective test wherein the subject is asked to draw a house, a tree and a person. The drawings made' are then interpreted according to a more or less standardized set of criteria.

Human engineering: It is an applied branch of psychology and engineering that deals with problems of machine, design, working conditions, skills, learning ability and efficiency.

Human factors: Refers to the name of the professional speciality which studies the *man-machine interface*. Its main focus is on problems of perception, psycho-physics, decision-making and other aspects of information processing.

Humanistic psychology: a theoretical and therapeutic system of psychology that emphasizes particularly human processes—the uniqueness of the individual, the validity of subjective experience, freedom of choice, and the tendency for each individual to strive to realize his potential. Humanistic psychology grew out of the work of ABRAHAM MASLOW, a personality, theorist, and the clinical practice of CARL ROGERS.

Humm-wadsworth temperament scale: Refers to a personality questionnaire used to measure relative standing on paranoid, hysteric, manie-deprpssive, and schizoid tendencies.

Hunger pangs: Refers to the sensation associated with Strong' hunger contractions in the stomach.

Huntington's chorea: Refers to a neurological disorder which [is characterised by progressively more serious loss of coordination spasmodic, jerky movements, and mental deterioration. The disease is hereditary.

Hypercathexis: Means investing psychic energy in one process for the purposes of furthering or facilitating another.

Hypergasia: Refers to overactivity which is characteristic of the manic phase of bipolar disorder.

Hypermnesia: Refers to unusual ability to remember. Hypermnesia may take place under hypnotic states or during free association.

Hyperopia: Farsightedness a condition wherein the rays of light entering the eye come to a focal point behind the retina due to shortness of the eyeball.

Hyperplasia: Refers to increase in the size of an organ due to some abnormal increase in the number of cells.

Hyperpolarisation: An increase in polarization; in neurophysiology refers to the increase in the membrane potential of a neuron.

Hyperprosexia: Refers to any exaggerated fixating on some idea to the exclusion of others.

Hypertelorism: It is an eye disease which is characterised by increased interpupillary distance.

Hyperthyroidism: It is a condition of excessive secretion by the thyroid gland. It is associated with an elevated metabolic rate, restlessness, excessive motility, and apprehension. If neglected, the condition is fatal.

Hypoglossal nerve: Refers to the twelfth cranial nerve. Its chief component is motor to the muscles of the tongue.

Hypolexia: Refers to retarded reading ability, *dyslexia,* which is the more common used term here.

Hypologia: Refers to a lack of capacity for speech due to neurological or functional disorders.

Hypoplasia: Refers to a detective development of tissue producing a structurally diminished organ or organ part.

Hypotension: Refers to diminished tension or tonus in a muscle or organ or a condition that is marked by an abnormally low blood pressure.

I

Iatrotropic stimulus: Refers to the event or symptom which causes a person to seek medical attention.

Icarus complex: Refers to a syndrome that is characterised by fascination with fire, a history of bedwetting a desire to be immortal, narcissism and lofty but fragile ambition.

Ideal observer: An observer whose sensory and perceptum systems operate without error and devoid of bias.

Idealism: It is a philosophical doctrine which holds that the, ultimate reality is mental and that this mental representation forms the basis of all experience and knowledge.

Idealization: It is a defense mechanism wherein an object about which one is ambivalent is consciously split into two conceptual representations.

Ideal-self sort: A form of sort designed to evaluate the difference between and individual's real, objective sense of self and his or her idealized sense of self.

Id-ego: In psychoanalytic theory it is the primitive unit from which the separate id and ego become differentiated.

Identical retinal points: Refers to any two points, use on each retina, that receive stimulation from the same objective point at infinite distance.

Identity crisis: Refers to a lack of the normal feeling of one's historical continuity.

Identity formation: Refers to the point of view that mature identity formation emerges when various early, more primitive identifications and influences are rejected.

Ideographic: Refers to or deals with the concrete, the individual, the unique. A psychological system or theory with this orientation is labeled an idiographic approach.

Idiom: An expression having a special meaning which cannot be determined from the meanings of its component parts.

Idiopathic: Refers to a primary pathological condition. That arises within the affected organ and not as a result of external dysfunctions.

Imaginary companion: Refers to an "invisible" friend, created by a young child and treated as real.

Imago: In biology refers to an adult, sexually mature insect or the mature stage of insect life. In Psychology refers to unconscious representations of other persons, typically a parent with whom one identifies closely.

Impairment: Refers to any loss of or decrement in function. When such loss or decrement is due to injury or disease.

Imperative: Refers to speech act wherein the speaker directly commands or orders the listener to do something..

Implantation: In placental mammals, refers to the attaching of the embryo to the uterine wall.

Impotence, orgasmic: Refers to the inability to achieve satisfactory coitus. An orgasmically impotent person is not impotent in the sense of being incapable of coitus.

Impulse-control disorder: A disorder marked by failure to resist an impulse or temptation to engage in some act which ultimately proves harmful to oneself.

Impulsion: Refers to state of great urgency wherein one is highly susceptible to performing an impulsive act.

Inaccessibility: Refers to a state of psychological remoteness wherein one is unresponsive to ordinary social stimuli.

Incidence: It is the Frequency of occurrence of an event or a condition in relation to the population under examination.

Inclusive fitness: In evaluationary biology refers to the total measure of various strategies which an organism may use to ensure genetic success.

Incommensurable: Refers to two variables which have no common measure or standard of comparison.

Indissociation: In Piaget's theory refers to a very early stage of development wherein cognitive and perceptual systems are relatively undifferentiated.

Individual differences: Refers an approach to psychological phenomena which focuses on characteristics or traits along which individual organisms may be shown to differ.

Individual psychology of alfred adler: A system of psychology founded by Alfred Adler, whose aim is the understanding, prevention, and treatment of mental disorders. As an early associate of Freud's, Adler became dissatisfied with the former's emphasis on sexuality in the development of personality and the neuroses, and he emphasized the childhood weakness and helplessness that lead to feelings of inferiority and, in severe cases, to an inferiority complex.

Feelings of inferiority are greatly accentuated if the child has either a real or imagined organic inferiority, is a member of the female sex, or is a member of a minority group. Such accentuated feeling of inferiority lead to compensatory activity and a style of life characterized by active striving to overcome the minus situation of inferiority by achieving a plus situation of superiority.

Compensatory behaviour is likely to lead to over compensation with attempts to dominate others, to generate hostility toward competitors, and to develop asocial or antisocial attitudes such as are characteristic of the delinquent, criminal, or withdrawn individual.

Individuals suffering from excessive feelings of inferiority are also driven by an exaggerated notion of their own worth, which takes the form of an unreasonable guiding fiction toward which they strive and that dominates their style of life. The great gap between the reality of the individual's life and the idealized guiding fiction creates anxiety, further striving, and more over compensation, and so a vicious circle is generated.

Adler laid great emphasis on the family constellation as the chief factor in the development of the life-style. The oldest child is particularly vulnerable to developing feelings of inferiority if another child comes along and dethrones him from his position of preeminence. The mother, who holds the critical position as the first social contact the child experiences, must be on guard against either inadvertently or consciously rejecting the older child in favor of a younger.

Equally important, she must avoid pampering the child and thus preventing him from developing an independent, self-reliant spirit. In treating a patient, Adler first sought to determine the patient's style of life, to determine the cause of his going astray and discover where the patient began to seek to dominate people instead of mastering his inferiority feelings in a socially constructive manner.

Of considerable importance in arriving at a diagnosis is the individual's earliest memory, which reveals the first attempts to solve problems. Adler also accepted dream analysis but, unlike Freud, did not emphasize the sexual nature of dreams; instead he interpreted them as another instance of the individual's attempts at problem solving.

Adler strove to help the patient realize his mistaken style of life and to seek sound, socially satisfying adjustments in the marital, vocational, and social aspects of living. Adler's system of Individual Psychology became popular in the years immediately after its founding, the Adler attracted a number of followers who helped him in the establishment of centers for the practice of Individual Psychology. With his death the system went into an eclipse in the spreading shadow of Freudian psycho-analysis.

But Alderian concepts of personality formation, the causation of the neuroses, and therapeutic theory and practice have been enjoying a rebirth in recent years and are found with increasing frequency in the literature on these subjects.

Individual psychology: Differential psychology associated with the personality theory of Alfred Adler.

Individual response: Refers to any unusual, idiosyncratic response that is given in a word-association test.

Individuality: Refers to all those characteristics which distinguish an individual from all others.

Induced colour: A perceived colour or colour change which is determined by stimulation In other parts of the visual field;

Induction test: Refers to any test wherein the, subject is asked to induce a coherent general principle on the basis of a fixed set of exemplars

Industrial psychology: That branch of psychology concerned with applying the methods and findings of psychology to the solution of industrial problems. Areas of concern are employment and personnel practices, working conditions, fatigue, morale, rewards for work, and efficiency. In its broadest sense, industrial psychology is extended to include the areas of business, advertising, and the military.

Infantile autism: A serious developmental disorder of infancy, childhood, and adolescence. It is characterized by an almost total lack of responsiveness to others, with gross impairment of linguistic development, bizarre behaviour involving repetitive movements, and self-abusive behaviour such as head banging. The disorder is relatively rare, involving 2-4 children per 10,000 and about three times more prevalent in males than females. The identification of the disorder occurs when the parents discover that the child appears cold and unresponsive, does not smile, and fails to begin to speak at the normal age.

Such children may play with the same toy for hours, make irrelevant and repetitive movements such as hand clapping, head banging, or turning light switches on and off endlessly. The appear disturbed if their routines are changed, and seem to prefer being left alone. As they grow into adolescence and adult-hood, only 15 to 20 percent make an adequate adjustment. Most remain totally dependent on others and many are institutionalized.

The causes of infantile autism are unknown. Originally believed to be associated with cold, unresponsive mothers, it is now thought to be due to other factors, such many autistic children have warm, caring mothers.

The psychoanalytic school has emphasized a failure to develop through the oral, anal, and early genital stages with consequent inability to establish contact with reality and the lack of ego development. Others have suggested that the disorder is an early form of schizophrenia. Some investigators have argued that it has an organic basis but have been unable to demonstrate precisely where the physiological deficit lies. Treatment has taken the form of attempting to provide an intensely warm, high contact environment in order to encourage the child to emerge from his inner world.

Recent behavioral techniques involving reinforcement of positive social responses have been tried with some success. However, the overall success of treatment programs remains poor.

Infantile sexuality: In Freudian psychoanalytic theory, it refers to the capacity for sexual desire and experience in the infant particularly as manifested by passage through a series of stages beginning with the oral and moving through the anal and early genital.

Infantilism: It is a condition of an older child or adult who, for certain reasons, still displays cognitive and emotional behaviours which are characteristic of infancy.

Inference: Any logical judgement made on the basis of sample of evidence, previously made judgements, prior conclusions, etc., rather than on direct observation.

Information processing theory: Deals with the input, processing, storage, and retrieval of information in men and machines. Stimulated by the invention of computers and other devices for processing data efficiently, information processing theory attracted the attention of psychologists who believe that an analysis of the problems involved in developing machines that simulate sensing, memory, learning, and problem solving in human beings can be of help in understanding how the brain can carry out these functions.

On the input, side, the brain is dependent upon the sense organs for detecting information from environmental stimuli and transducing it into nervous impulses. The sensory nerves and their pathways through the spinal cord and subcortical centers are analogous to channels in machines and, like the machine, have a limited channel capacity. This capacity is described in information processing theory as bits of information.

Ordinarily the individual can detect only 5-9 bits of information of a random nature, such as the correct number of dots scattered on a sheet of paper or random digits pronounced orally to be repeated immediately. If, however, bits are combined into chunks, channel capacity is greatly increased. For example, if sixteen dots re arranged in random order the correct number cannot be apprehended in a single act of perceiving. The same dots arranged in chunks of four are readily apprehended. The brain, like the digital computer, can recognize, select, or reject information on the basis of certain distinctive features. One type of detection system is template matching, a technique widely used in processing bank checks. Special numbers are printed on the checks which the computer can be programmed to recognize by means of determining whether they fit the correct template or pattern.

Human memory is organized in such a manner that the individual can instantly recognize information presented to the "memory banks" in the brain. Psychologists are not yet read to suggest that the brain makes use of template matching in retrieving information.

The process is undoubtedly far more complex. The greater complexity of the human organism is revealed in the fact that we can recognize information presented in unusual ways. Numbers and letters can be set in all kinds of type and still be recognizable. The machine, however, can recognize only special stylized type. Moreover, we can keep track of several streams of incoming information at the same time. This is known as parallel processing—an ability not possessed by machines that can deal only with one channel of information at a given time. This is called sequential processing. Machines have been constructed that are capable of learning in the sense of modifying the sequence of processing on the basis of experience. Moreover, machines can solve problems by techniques known as algorithmic and heuristic processing. In algorithmic processing every possible solution to the problem is tried out an rejected until the correct solution is found.

In making a possible chess move to counteract an opponent's, the machine might be programmed to run through every possible move before "deciding" on the most appropriate. By contrast, in heuristic problem solving the machine is programmed to try out certain predetermined combinations that are likely to be successful.

The latter technique is clearly more effective than the former which for relatively simple problems can involve an astronomical number of possible combinations of choices.

Machines have been built that can play checkers and chess, solve mathematical equations, make crude or literalistic translations of foreign languages, and simulate various aspects of human learning and thinking. In developing such programs for machines, psychologists have arrived at a better knowledge of our input system, our processing systems, and our retrieval (memory) system.

Information test: A test that samples the individual's knowledge in a given area or number of areas. The information sampled is usually of the incidental type, which theoretically should be common to everyone.

Information theory: A branch of science and engineering dealing with the transmission of information and its measurable characteristics. Quantities of information are measured in units called *bits*. A bit tells which of two equally probable events has taken place. Information is analyzed in terms of signals and their characteristics and in terms of the effect of the structure of informational form on the reliability of communication.

Informed consent: Refers, to permission to carry out a research or medical procedure where the subject is given information such as (a) the nature of the procedures; (b) potential known risks and benefits any other alternative procedures which are available; and (d) acknowledgement that such consent if voluntary.

Infrared: Pertaining to electromagnetic radiation ("light") whose wavelength is longer than that of the light to which normal human eye responds, above roughly 700 nm.

Inherent: Meaning *sticking to* or *in,* characterising a property or attribute of something or someone which is inseparable and permanent.

Inherit: Means to receive from one's predecessors. In biology' refers to the process of genetic transmission.

Inkblot test: Refers to any of the several projective tests which make use of inkblots e.g., the Rorschach Test; Barron Movement Threshold Inkblot Test and the Holtzman`Inkblot. Test.

Inner-directed: Refers to a tendency to react according to an internalized set of goals or values.

Innervation reciprocal: Refers to innervation of a pair of antagonistic muscles through which, neural impulses induce flexion in one and extension in the other.

Inoculate: Means to introduce a microorganism or other substance into the body generally by means of an injection.

Inoculation hypothesis: Refers to the hypothesis that ones belief is some point of view can be strengthened if we present weak and refutable counterarguments.

Input: Refers to any stimulus that is some form of energy that enters some system (an organism). Particularly a signal fed to an electrical circuit, a message which acts on a receiver, etc.

Insanity defense: A legal concept according to which person cannot be convicted to a crime if it can be shown that he or she lacked "criminal responsibility," that he or she was (legally) insane.

Insensible: Means without sensibility. Refers to an organism, in a state of unresponsiveness e.g., one who is unconscious or in a coma.

Inset ear: It is the innermost component of the ear containing the cochlea and the organs of balance.

Insomnia, rebound: Refers to insomnia taking place after withdrawal from drugs taken to relieve insomnia.

Instant: A duration so brief that two or more (perhaps) sequential events are perceived as simultaneous.

Instigation therapy: It is a form of therapy wherein the therapist sets up positive models for the client and actively reinforces progress toward them.

Instinct, closed: Refers to innate species-specific behaviour patterns that are rigid and inflexible.

Institution, total: Refers to institutions where life style is sharply restricted, formalized and under the control of special staff.

Institutionalize: Refers to the process of institutionalization of a person by either indoctrination into a system of social roles or physical placement in an institution such as a prison or a mental hospital.

Instrumental behaviour: Refers to behaviour or act which is goal directed, a means to some end.

Insulin shock: Refers to Hypoglycemic state produced by excess insulin, because of a lowering in blood sugar and a comatose state.

Integrate: Means to bring into a harmonious or coordinated whole by rearranging, organizing and some times adding or deleting elements or parts.

Integration cultural: The blending of cultural traits, that were conflicting, to form a modified, integrated system.

Integration, behavioural: Means the blending, chaining or combining of many separate behaviours into a coordinated whole.

Intellectualisation: A defense mechanism by which problems are analysed in remote, intellectual terms.

Intelligence test: An intelligence test consists of a series of tasks of graded difficulty that have been standardized on a representative sample of the population. Tests are of two types individual tests, which must be administered to a single subject by a trained psychologist; and group tests, which may be administered to large numbers of individuals simultaneously. However, the results of group tests should be interpreted and utilized only by trained individuals.

Intelligence, coefficient of: It is an index of intelligence obtained by forming a ratio between the score obtained by an individual on an intelligence test and the norms for that person's age.

Intelligence, concrete: Refers to the ability to function effectively with concrete problems.

Intention: Refers to any desire, plan, purpose, aim or belief which is oriented toward some goal, some end state.

Interaction variance: In statistics it is the proportion of the total -variance which is not related to the action of single variables but because of the interaction between them.

Interaural differences: These are differences in the sound arriving at the two ears.

Interest inventory: Refers to an instrument designed to evaluate a person's interests in or preferences for a variety of activities.

Interface: Refers to the circuitry

in computers which connects the central processing core of a computer and is peripheral parts.

Intermediate needs: Just like physiological needs inter mediate needs are presumed to be activated by deficiencies. Such needs are safety, belongingness, self-esteem, security, etc.

Internal consistency: It indicates the degree to which the different parts of a test or other instrument measure the same variables.

International Phonetic Alphabet (IPA): A phonetic alphabet of approximately 95 phones. It is rich and flexible enough for all of the phonemes of the world's languages to be represented.

Interneuron: A connecting neuron, which lies between sensory and motor neurons. It is found within the central nervous system and also known as *internuncial neuron* or association *neuron..*

Interocular distance: It is the distance between the pupils when the eyes are in normal position while viewing, distant objects, i.e., focused on infinity.

Interpretative therapy: Refers to any form of psychotherapy wherein the therapist interprets the significance and underlying symbolic meaning of the client's statements.

Interquartile range: Refers to the range between the first and third quartiles (i.e., between the 25th and 75th percentiles) of a distribution.

Interresponse Time (IRT): Refers to the time that elapses between responses. It is used in evaluating operant behaviour.

Intersexuality: It is the condition in which both male and female characteristics are present specially the secondary sex characteristics.

Interval of uncertainty: In psychophysics it is the interval between the upper and lower thresholds.

Interview: It is a mode of directed conversation, In psychology, interviews aim at information-gathering or therapeutic purposes.

Intimacy disorder: Refers to the, inability to become intimate with others, to share emotions, trust others.

Intonation: Refers to the modulations of the voice, the shifts patterns, and the rise and fall in pitch while speaking.

Intraception: Refers to an outlook on life that is subjective, internally motivated, imaginative.

Intrafusal fibers: Refers to muscle fibres that function as stretch receptors. They are arranged in parallel with *extrafusal* *fibers* and detect the length of a muscle.

Intramural: Means within the walls; thus it pertains to events taking place inside the boundaries of an institution.

Intraocular modification: Refers to any change in the visual signal because of the characteristics of the eye.

Intrinsic: Meaning *inwardly* or *inward.* Refers to a property of , something that reflects the nature of the thing.

Introjection: Refers to the process whereby aspects of the external world are absorbed into or incorporated within the self, the internal representation then taking over the psychological functions of the external objects.

Intropunitive: Refers to the tendency to react to frustration by directing anger and blame toward oneself, the internally focused emotions generally being experienced as guilt or shame.

Intrusion response (or Error): Refers to any response in an ordered experiment that either *(a)* was not in the original list or (b) took place in the wrong position in the list.

Invented-U curve (or distribution): Refers to any distribution the curve of which is shaped like an inverted letter U, with high frequency for moderate values and low frequency for both very low and very high values.

Inversion or affect: Refers to sudden switching between two emotions which are at opposite poles 'on a continum, love and hatred.

Inversion, sexual: Previously used for hermaphroditism or Transvestism of homosexuality.

Inversion: It is a process of turning inside out or upside down, or the result of such a process.

Irresponsibility: In forensic psychiatry and legal parlance it, refers to the principle that an individual is not to be adjudged guilty of a crime if it can be determined that the normal conditions under which one could be held to be responsible for his or her actions do, in fact, not pertain.

Isometric contraction (or twitch): Refers to muscle contraction which causes tension but no movement.

Isomorphism: In mathematics refers to a point-by-point relation ship between two systems. In psychology it is the hypothesis that there is such a relationship between excitatory fields in the cortex and conscious experience.

Itch: Itching is, source of much interest and confusion. It is, a rather attention-demanding

J

J Curve: A curve describing the frequency of, compliance with a rule or standard. A commonly cited example has been the manner in which automobile drivers comply with a stop sign. ;Some stop completely, some not at all, and some slow down to Varying degrees. The curve representing the various degrees of compliance approximates the capital letter J in shape.

Jackson's law: Pertains to the manner in which memory functions are affected in mentally disturbed persons, recollection for events immediately preceding the onset being lost first.

Jacksonian epilepsy: A form of epilepsy which is characterised by, localized convulsions that are usually limited to one limb. The cause of the disorder gets localized irritation of the cerebral cortex.

James lange theory of the emotions: A formulation that tries to integrate the conscious and behavioural aspects of the emotions. Lange, a Danish physiologist, had argued that emotional processes have been—identical with changes in the circulatory system. James took this aspect of Lange's theory and incorporated it into his own theory, which holds that the emotional, experience is the result of the visceral changes arising from the individual's reacting to an emotion-provoking experience. The essence of the theory has been contained in the famous argument offered by James that upon meeting a bear in the woods we do not run because we are afraid, but are afraid because we run; that is, running stirs up a visceral reaction and this is the emotion.

Jealousy: An attitude of envy toward another due to the affection that individual shows to a third person.

Job analysis: An investigation of the ability requirements, working conditions, pay, opportunities for promotion, etc., that go with a particular job.

Job analysis: An investigation of the ability requirements, working conditions, pay, opportunities for promotion, etc., that, go with a particular job. Job analyses have been helpful in employee selection programs.

Job placement: The term used for the assignment of an individual to a job, on the basis of his abilities, experience, interests, and the requirements of the position.

Job specification: A description of a job and the requisite abilities which are needed for success in the work involved.

Jordan curve: A closed, nonoverlapping curve which is used to represent various aspects of the life space.

Jost's law: The principle that given two associations of equal strength but unequal age, practice will be of more benefit to the older. The law has been based on the empirical finding that older associations lose strength less rapidly with the passage of time.

Joy: A highly pleasant emotion which is associated with accomplishment, satisfaction, and gratification.

Judgment: Cognitive activity of bringing two ideas into an affirmation of similarity or difference, as in judging weights, lines, pictures, and the like.

Just-noticeable-differences method: A psychophysical technique for determining the just-noticeable difference. A standard stimulus has been presented along with a variable stimulus whose magnitude is gradually increased on some trials and decreased on other trials until the just-perceptible differences is reported by the subject. The average of the ascending and descending series has been taken, and the threshold has been calculated at that point where the difference can be recognized 50 per cent of the time.

Just-world hypothesis: The belief that people get what they deserve, and so could be held accountable for their behaviour.

Juvenile, delinquent: From the standpoint of psychology and sociology, a youth who has been brought before police officials or presented in court the charges having been sustained by the evidence.

K

K complex: Refers to a cortical response evoked by an auditory stimulus during sleep as revealed by the electroencephalogram.

K scale: A special scoring key for the Minnesota Multiphasic Inventory of Personality that detects malingering.

Kallikak: Refers to a family with two lines of descendents; one of normal and superior people, the other of delinquents, psychotics, and mental defectives.

Kappa effect: Change in the apparent interstimulus interval when the distance between two successively presented stimuli is changed.

Katasexual: Characteristic of sexuality wherein dead partners are the sexual goals.

Kelly's psychology of personal Constructs: Kelly's theory of personality takes as its point of departure the assumption that ordinary people, like scientists, attempt to predict and control events. Toward this goal the individual construes events or interprets them on the basis of personal experience. This result in the individual constructing hierarchial organizations to explain the way he conceptualizes the world.

Kelly's constant process: It is a psychophysical method used for fitting data for the normal ogive making use of the standard deviation instead of h. The latter measures the steepness of a distribution, where as the former measures its scatter or spread.

Kent-Rosanoff test: It is a standardized free association test and was devised by Grace Kent and A.J. Rosanoff. It is made up of 100 stimulus words and tables of relative frequency for responses to those words by 1,000 subjects. The results of an individual case can: be compared with the tabular material for common, unusual, and doubtful responses.

Key: It is a list of the correct answers used in scoring a test or a devise for coding or decoding information.

Kinephantom: An illusion of movement, specially in a shadow movement, like that which takes place when the shadows of the spokes of a wheel are seen moving in the opposite direction from that of the wheel.

Kinesics: Refers to the study of bodily language or communications by gestures and bodily positions and movements.

Kinesimeter: It is a device used for measuring the threshold of the sensation for movement.

Kinesthesis: Refers to the muscle, tendon and joint sense. This combination of senses provides information about the position of the limbs and body in space. The receptors for the muscle sense are known as muscle spindles, that take the form of microscopic fibrils which wrap around muscle fibers.

Kinesthetic method: It is a technique used for treating speech and writing disabilities by having the patient attend to the muscular sensations involved.

Kinesthetic response: It is a response category for projecting action into the blots.

Kinetic information: Refers to gestures, expressive movements, posture, and tension patterns which are used in making judgements about persons.

Kjersted-Robinson law: According to this principle the amount of material learned during equal portions of the learning time is relatively constant for different lengths of material.

Kleptomania: Refers to an obsessive impulse or compulsion to steal.

Klinefelder's syndrome: Refers to a genetic abnormality where the sex chromosome pattern is XXY. It is characterized by retarded gonadal development, mental retardation, and a tendency toward femininity.

Kluver-bucy syndrome: It is a behaviour pattern observed in those monkeys whose temporal regions have been removed with involvement of the tissues deep in the frontolateral region. They display "psychic blindness," or the inability to recognize objects, are aggressive, and suffer from hypersexuality.

Knee-jerk reflex: Refers to the reflexive extension of the lower leg upon a sharp tap to the tendon just below the patella, or kneecap.

Knowledge of results: Refers to any information given to a subject about the correctness of his response.

Knox cube test: It is a performance test wherein the subject, must tap a series of four cubes in different sequences according to a pattern presented by the experimenter.

Kohs block design test: It is a performance test of intelligence and makes use of a set of one-inch coloured cubes whose sides are painted red, blue, yellow, white, yellow and blue, and red and white respectively. Coloured designs presented to the subject on seventeen test cards must be reproduced using the blocks. It is a part of the Arthur Performance Scale.

Korsakov's Refers to a mental disorder brought on by alcoholism and marked by neural irritation, disturbances of memory and orientation.

Korte's law: Laws of apparent movement which state for the optimal movement of phi: (1) if intensity is held constant, the time interval for optimal movement changes directly with the distance between stimuli; (2) if time is held constant, the distance for optimal movement changes directly with intensity: and (3) if distance between, stimuli is held constant, then intensity for optimal movement changes inversely with time interval.

Krause end bulb: Refers to an encapsulated neuronal ending considered by some authorities to be a receptor for cold.

Kuder occupational interest survey: Grades 11- 12 and adults. An interest inventory which yields 114 occupational scores reported in terms of the relationship between the examinee's responses and those of successful groups in the occupations, recorded.

Kuder preference record—vocational: An early interest inventory which gives the subject's relative standing on ten broad areas of vocational interest, like social service, science, art, etc.

Kuder-Richardson coefficient of equivalence: Formulas used to estimate the correlation between comparable forms of a test on the basis of one administration.

Kuhlmanu-Auderson test: It consists of a series of tests of general intelligence ranging from kindergarten to adulthood.

Kundt's rule: According to this principle the divided or graduated lines or distances appear greater than nongraduated or undivided distances.

Kurtosis: Refers to the degree of flatness or peakedness of a frequency curve in the region of the mode.

Kwashiorkor: Refers to a Protein deficiency disease of infants and children that is characterized by edema, pot belly, and skin lesions. Found chiefly in Africa.

Kymograph: It is an instrument used for tracing records of temporal variations in any variable on a smoked or lightly waxed drum.

Some constructs are superordinate, containing other or subordinate constructs. Some, such as strong biases or radical positions, are preemptive constructs that prohibit any other constructs from becoming part of their elements. Others are constellatory constructs or powerful determinants of the way in which other concepts may be applied. Prejudices and stereotypes exemplify constella-tory constructs.

Propositional concepts, by contrast, are open to change and can, therefore, be modified by experience. Constructs, like scientific theories, have a focus and a range of convenience or applicability. For example, Sigmund Freud's psychoanalytic theory had a wide range of applicability but its focus was on sexuality. Similarly, an individual's construct system about good and bad will tend to have wide applicability but may focus on sexual or moral behaviour. Constructs may be verbal or preverbal. Most of our constructs can be verbalized, but those of young children often cannot be expressed in words. This same limitation also applies to the constructs of persons with serious behavioral problems. In formu-lating the distinction between preverbal and verbal constructs, Kelly allows for processes comparable to those regarded as conscious or subconscious by the psychoanalytic and related schools. For the purpose of diagnosis and therapy, Kelly assesses the individual by means of the REP test (Role Construction Reportry Test), a special technique devised by him to evaluate the individu-al's important constructs in relation to significant others-parents, siblings, teachers, close friends, those in authoritative positions, and sought-after and rejected individuals.

Persons with behavior problems are likely to have poorly verbalized and submerged constructs that are narrow in range. Such individuals are also beset by anxiety and defensive-ness about their constructs as a way of maintaining a restricted, and therefore "safe", way of interpreting events. Therapy consists in assigning the individual roles to play. Much as an actor plays a role to play, much as an actor plays a role that may be quite different from his behavior in real life. The therapeutic role is carefully constructed to provide new modes of reacting to others and to encourage more effective ways of constructing experiences.

L

L data: Stands for life record data that is obtained by rating the individual as he reacts to life situations.

L_1, L_2: In the study of bi- and multilingualism, L_1 is used to denote the first language learned, L_2 the second, etc.

Labia majora: Refers to the outer fatty folds which surround the vulva.

Labia minora: Refers to the inner, richly vascular folds that surround the vulva.

Labial: Refers to lips in general, but most commonly with reference to the oral lips.

Labiodental: It is h class of speech sounds which are produced by using the lower lip and the upper teeth; e.g., f and v in five.

Labyrinth: Refers to the portion of the inner ear. It contains the receptors for hearing and those for the static sense.

Lacrimal gland: The tear gland that lies beneath the upper eyelid and secretes tears than moisten the cornea.

Lactate: Means to produce milk. It also refers to salt of lactic acid.

LAD (or LAS): An acronym for language-acquisition device. The status of LAD is highly equivocal and most psycholinguists And cognitive psychologists find the idea fascinating but doubtful.

Ladder scale: It is a self-anchoring scale used to measure the individual's attitude toward the real world as contrasted with his attitude toward his ideal world.

Ladd-Franklin theory: A theory of colour vision which is not generally accepted now a days, that assumes a complex photosensitive molecule which responds differentially to red, green, blue and yellow light by releasing substances which stimulate respective nerve endings.

Lag: Refers to a time delay between stimulus and response or a brief period after the removal of a stimulus, when it is still perceived.

Laissez faire atmosphere: Refers to general socio-political climate established when the nominal leader of a group maintains a "hands off" policy and there is little or no guidance or direction imposed.

Laissez faire: It is a kind or leadership wherein a minimum of control is exerted.

Lalia: Combining form used in reference to speech, specifically disorders of speech.

Laloplegia: It is the inability to speak because of paralysis of all those muscles which are used for speech except the tongue.

Lamarckism; lamarckianism: According to this theory structural changes acquired by an organism through use or disuse can be transmitted to the offspring.

Lamaze method: It is a method of psychological preparation for childbirth wherein the expectant mother is trained in breathing exercises and muscle relaxation techniques which facilitate delivery.

Lambert: A unit of luminance or brightness. It is equal to the brightness of a perfectly diffusing surface emitting one lumen per square centimetre.

Lambert's law: This law states the interrelation of incidence, emission, and reflection of light, to the effect that these factors change directly as the cosine of the angle of the rays perpendicular to the surface.

Land effect: This effect produces the perception of colour from black and white photographs.

Landolt circles: These are the circles having gaps of different degree and are used in the determination of visual acuity.

Landolt ring(s): Refers to doughnut-shaped figure having an opening in it which-is used for measuring visual acuity.

Language acquisition devicc (LAD): The innate mechanism common to all human children which operates on linguistic data supplied by parents to produce a given language structure.

Language Acquisition Device (LAD): The Innate mechanism which operates on linguistic data supplied by parents to produce a given language structure.

Language behaviour: Refers to behaviour that involves the use of language whether oral, written, or in the form of gestures.

Language centers: A number of areas of the cerebral cortex that function in various aspects of spoken and written language and in music. Brook's area, or the speech center, is the best known of the language centers.

Language: 1. Any form of communication among people, whether verbal or gestural. 2. verbal behavior, either oral or written . 3. the symbols used in communication.

Language centers: A number of areas of the cerebral cortex which function in different aspects of spoken and written language and in music.

Lanugo hair: Delicate, downy hair that appears briefly during the later months of fetal development

Lanugo: Refers to fine, infant-like hair, or such fine hair which briefly covers the body of the fetus during the later stage of gestation.

Lapse: Means a slip or error or a brief period of forgetfulness.

Laryngeal reflex: Refers to coughing that is caused by irritation of the larynx.

Lary·x: It is a cartilaginous structure which sits atop the windpipe. It has a "valve" made up of a double set of muscular folds which is covered with a layer of mucous membrane.

Lashley jumping stand: Refers to a device used for experimenting on small animals. The animal is placed on a stand and must jump toward one of two or more stimuli placed in front of it. The device finds wide use in studies of discrimination and choice behaviour.

Latah syndrome: Refers to psychiatric syndrome that is characterized by symptoms of excitement, echolalia, echopraxia, coprolalia and often fugue and hallucinations.

Latency period: In classical psychoanalytic theory it is the period from roughly age 4 or 5 to the beginning of puberty during which sexual interest is considered to be sublimated.

Latency, response: It is the time between the onset of a stimulus and the occurrence of the overt response to that stimulus.

Latency: Refers to a condition of inactivity between the application of a stimulus and the onset of a response.

Latent content: (*Psychoan*) Type hidden content of a dream that must be brought out during analysis by means of free association. Presumably, some impulses and ideas are so incompatible with the individuals evaluation of himself that they must be hidden or disguised even in dreams.

Latent learning: Learning that is not manifested in performance. For example, nonhungry rats were allowed to explore a maze for ten days. On the eleventh day they were made hungry and found a food reward at the end of the maze. Within a day or two their performance was as good as that of the control group, which had been regularly rewarded. Evidently, then, learning had gone on during the ten-day interval but was latent until activated by a drive-reward situation.

Latent learning: Refers to learning which is not manifested in performance.

Latent period: It is a time interval between the reception of a stimulus and the onset of a response.

Latent process: Refers to a process that is latent. Generally in psychoanalytic theory, an infant's ego processes are said to be latent.

Latent social identity: Refers to social role which, though not a factor in functioning in-a-society, but has significant Impact upon an individual's behaviour in a social organization.

Latent traits: Refers to those genetically determined traits which do not manifest themselves in the phenotype of an individual but which can be passed on to future generations.

Latent: Means hidden; not manifest. Sexual behaviour in young children may be said to be latent in this sense.

Lateral fissure: Refers to a deep fissure in the temporal cortex that divides the temporal lobe from the parietal and frontal lobes.

Lateral inhibition: Refers to a set of conditions established when two or more neural cells are interconnected in such a way that excitation of one produces inhibition in the other.

Lateral lemniscus: Refers to a bundle of nerve fibers in the medulla and pons that carry auditory impulses.

Lateral thalamic nucleus: Refers to a large mass of cell bodies on the lateral aspect of the thalamus.

Lateral thinking: Refers to heuristic for solving problems wherein the individual attempts to took at the problem from many angles instead of making a search for a direct, head on solution.

Laterality: Refers to any preference for one side of the body over the other, like having a preferred hand or eye.

Lateralization: It is the process whereby different functions and processes become associated with one or the other side of the brain.

Latin square: it is a type of experimental design which provides for as many trials as there are experimental conditions.

Latitude of acceptance: Characteri-zing the range of attitudes or opinions about an issue that an individual is willing to accept.

Latitude of rejection: Characteri-zing the range of attitudes or opinions about an issue that an individual finds objectionable.

Law: Refers to a statement of a uniformity found in nature. Scientific laws are broad generalizations which describe cause and effect relations among variables and their antecedent conditions.

Law analysis: Refers to psychoanalysis as practised by some one who does not possess a medical degree but who has undergone special training in the theory and technique of psychoanalysis.

Law, empirical: Refers to principle or generalization which relates variables to each other and based on observations or experimental findings.

Lax: In phonetics, a distinctive feature descriptive of speech sounds produced when the vocal tract is in-its normal resting position.

Lay analyst: Refers to one who has received psychoanalytic training and is recognized to practice but who has not taken a degree in medicine.

Layman: Refers to an individual who is not professionally trained in a given area.

Leader: Refers to one who guides, directs, or controls the actions of others or one who possesses the personality traits and other qualifications for leadership.

Leadership: 1. The exercise of authority; the control, guidance, and direction of the conduct of others. 2. the qualities of personality and training that make for success in guiding and controlling the conduct of others.

Leadership: Means the exercise of the authority; the control, the guidance and direction of the conduct of others or the qualities of personality and training that make for success in guiding and controlling the conduct of others.

Leading eye: Refers to the eye which first turns toward an object of attention.

Learned helplessness: Refers to a condition that follow a number of bad experiences, where the individual thinks he is helpless to control events.

Learning: 1. Acquisition of any relatively permanent change in behaviour as a result of practice or experience. 2. process of acquiring responses as a result of special practice. Psychologists interested in the investigation of learning use a number of different procedures. In studying learning through conditioning, two models are available, *classical conditioning* and *operant conditioning*. In classical *conditioning* the essential process involved is the paired repetition of a conditioned (to be learned) stimulus and an unconditioned stimulus and an unconditioned stimulus (also referred to as the reinforcement). Thus Pavlov utilized a bell or a tuning fork as a conditioned stimulus, which he paired with a puff of meat powder in the mouth eventually to train the animal to salivate to the sound of the bell.

The process of salivation to food in the mouth is the unconditioned response; salivation to the sounding of a bell or any arbitrary stimulus is the conditioned response. In *operant conditioning* the animal is allowed to emit a response, which is then reinforced. Thus a rat might be put in a cage with a kind of slot-machine arrangement so that when he presses a bar, a pellet of food is delivered.

The animal's rate of bar pressing is the measure of learning. Classical conditioning has been utilized to study the acquisition of simple habits and autonomic responses. Operant conditioning is utilized in a wide variety of investigations involving both simple habits such as learning machines, a form of operant-conditioning situation.

Psychologists also utilize various types of puzzle boxes and mazes to study animal skills and place learning, and a large part of this research has been developed to the investigation of the laws of learning. In studying human learning, psychologists utilize various types of mechanical puzzles, mazes, and verbal materials ranging from nonsense syllables to meaningful connected discourser.

Performance in verbal learning has been found to be a function of the type of material learned, the conditions of practice, and the personal characteristics of the learne·. **Learning curve:** A graphic ı·presentation of the course of learning with practice. Learning curves can be plotted with gains or errors on the vertical axis and trials on the horizontal axis. Curves may be individual or group; they may represent each trial plotted separately or they may be based on successive fractions of the total learning

Learning set: Means an intention to learn or the acquisition of a certain method or approach in learning.

Learning theory: Formulation of laws and conditions of learning tasks through practice at learning practice at learning. some psyshologists believe that learning to learn can account for behavior formerly classified under insight learning.

Learning to learn: Refers to the fact that with successive presentations of problems of a similar form the subjects become increasingly successful in learning how to solve them.

Learning, laws of: Three are the principles that attempt to formulate the conditions under which learning takes place.

Learning, S-R: Stands for stimulus-response learning. It refers to any and all kinds of learning which are assumed to be fundamentally governed by the forming of some link or bond between a particular stimulus and a specific response.

Least- effort principle: Refers to the generalization that an animal tends to follow that route to a goal which involves a minimum of effort.

Least preferred co-worker test: It is a test used to measure if a leader is people-centered or task-centered.

Least square law of: It is the assumption that the best estimate of a value is that for which the sum of the squares of the deviations is at a minimum.

Leboyer method: It is a natural childbirth method developed around the assumption that child bearing can be made less "violent" for the infant. Delivery takes place in a darkened room, the infant is bathed in warm water and then placed on the mother's abdomen and the severing of the umbilical, cord is delayed.

Legend: Refers to a traditional belief about a person, place, or important event which is not supported by adequate historical evidence.

Leiter international performance test: It is a nonverbal test of intelligence and makes use of matching pictures and forms, colour designs, number series, and concealed figures.

Lemma: In logic refers to a proposition which is accepted as true for use in the proof of another proposition.

Lemniscal system: It is a polysynaptic pathway which ascends through the reticular formation. It is made up of the lateral lemniscus, that runs rostrally through the medulla and pons carrying fibers of the auditory system.

Lens: Refers to the transparent structure attached to the body of the eye by the ciliary muscle. The lens is capable of accommodation or adjustment for near and far vision and so it makes focusing possible.

Lentiform or lenticular nucleus: It is the outermost of two large nuclei of the corpus stratum.

Lerema: Refers to the tendency of some types of psychotics to be talkative.

Lesbianism: Homosexuality among women.

Lesion: Refers to an injury to tissue from disease or surgical procedures.

Lethargy: Drowsiness. It is on apathetic condition of extremely low motivation and activity level.

Lethologica: Refers to temporary inability to recall a proper noun or a name.

Level: Refers to a position or rank attained on a test or a mental age or point score that all persons of a given chronological age should reach.

Level of aspiration: A self-imposed standard against which a person judges his own performance. Level of aspiration is an index of confidence and varies with the pattern of success or failure.

Level of confidence: In the test (q.v), an expression of the assurance with which the null hypothesis (q.v) can be rejected, often expressed as a percentage. If the desired result could occur by chance one in 20 times, the level of confidence is 5 percent; if one in 10 times, 10 percent.

Level of intelligence: The degree of tested intelligence on a standardized intelligence test. Generally speaking, when the term level is employed, it is implied that the test in question is of the mental-age type. 2. the functional level of intelligence as revealed in performance in everyday life.

Level of significancy: In the test(q.v), an expression of the confidence with which the null hypothesis (q.v) can be rejected, usually expressed as a faction. If the desired result could occur by chance in 20 times, the level of significance is 05.

Leveling effect: The tendency for repeated series of measurements to group or cluster about the mean, due to the reduction of extreme differences because of practice effects.

Leveling: In memory, the tendency to reduce irregularities, to make drawings or stories less sharp, to leave out details. Concomitantly may occur with leveling to cause considerable distortion in the memory trace.

Levelling effect: Refers to the tendency for repeated series of measurements to group or cluster about the mean, because of the reduction of extreme differences due to practice effects.

Levelling: In memory refers to the tendency to reduce irregularities to make drawings or stories less sharp, to leave out details.

Lexicon: Refers to an alphabetic listing of the words of a language, a dictionary.

Lexicostatistics: It is a technique for estimating the historical connection between two languages.

Libidinal development: Refers to the growth and differentiation of the libido through different infantile Stages of oral, anal, and early genital eroticism

Libidinal object: Refers to the object (person or thing) wherein libido is invested.

Libidinal: Relating to the sexual energy obtained from the id; highly sexual.

Libidinization: It is the process of becoming the object of libidinal attachment.

Libido: Refers to the sex instinct or erotic desire or erotic pleasure or more generally, the combination of the life instincts (eros) and death instincts (thanatos).

Library: In cognitive psychology, refers to the totality of information about the world which a person carries about.

Life: It is the collective total of those properties that differentiate the living from the nonliving.

Lie detector: Refers to a collection of instruments used to measure minute changes in emotionality which accompany the telling of lies.

Life age: It Is the age of the individual since birth; chronological age; calendar age.

Life cycle: Refers to the typical pattern of birth, development, maturity, reproduction, and death which characterizes a given species.

Life goal: Refers to the fundamental aim of achieving the particular form of superiority which will allow one to compensate for one's primary, felt inferiority.

Life lie: Refers to the individual's rationalization that he cannot succeed due to obstacles or personal defects.

Life plan: Refers to the individual's style of life, including his guiding fiction, his attempts to achieve superiority, and to rationalize or explain failures.

Life span: It is the actual duration of life of an individual organism from inception to death.

Light reflex: Refers to the pupillary response; it includes both dilation when light levels drop and constriction when they are raised.

Light: The radiant energy that constitutes the stimulus to vision. Light is measured in nanometers (NM) or billionths of a meter. With various salient wavelengths are correlated certain primary or salient colors, such as red, approximately 700 nanometers; yellow, approximatley 600 nanometers; green, approximately 480 nanometers. Other colors are related to intermediate wavelengths, and white is a mixture of all wavelengths, and white is a mixture of all wavelengths. The blacks, whites, and grays from the achromatic series.

Light: The stimulus for vision, electromagnetic radiation of wavelengths between approximately 400 and 700 nanometers. Light may be either particle or wave; the latter is most useful for Work in psychology.

Lightness: Refers to that attribute of an object colour which allows it to be classified along the series of grays which runs from black to white.

Likert scale: It is a type of attitude, scale where on the subject is asked to indicate his degree of agreement or disagreement with stated attitudes on a three or five-point scale.

Limbic system: It is a complex set of evolutionarily old structures of the forebrain lying in an area below the corpus callosum. The individual structures probably are involved in behaviours which are emotional and motivational.

Liminal stimulus: Refers to a stimulus that is just at the threshold or that barely evokes a response.

Limulus: The horseshoe crab. Important in psychology due to a very large compound eye which lends itself nicely to experimental study.

Linear perspective: Refers to the relative differences in size of an object at different distances from the eye.

Linear: Pertaining to a straight line or pertaining to continuous, as opposed to discrete, functions.

Lingual: Pertaining to the tongue, or pertaining to languages.

Linguistic relativity: The theory according to which cultural differences are created by linguistic differences; hence individuals in different cultures perceive and think about the world differently.

Linguistics: It is the study of the origins, evolution and structure of language(s).

Linkage: In genetics refers to two or more genes which are said to be linked if they tend to be passed from generation to generation as a unit.

Lip erotism: Refers to a tendency to seek sexual satisfaction through stimulation of the lips.

Lip key: It is a device used for measuring the reaction time of speaking as detected by up movements.

Lip reading: It is a technique used by the deaf to understand spoken speech by watching the speaker's lips.

Lisp: Refers to articulatory speech disorder wherein sibilant sounds (s, z, sh, ch) are mispronounced generally by substituting a th sound.

Lissajou's figures: Refers to revolving abstract designs which are produced either by reflections from vibrating mirrors or on an oscilloscope screen. When watched closely for a time the direction of apparent rotation reverses.

Listing's law: It is a principle of eye movement stating that if the eye moves from one primary position to another, the rotation of the eyeball in the new position is the same as if the eye had turned in a fixed axis that is at right angles to the initial and the final lines of regard.

Lithium carbonate: It is a compound of the element lithium which has been found useful in treating manic depressive disorders.

Load: Refers to a weight or factor loading or a caseload, or the number of patients or clients being cared for by a social worker or therapist.

Lobectomy: Refers to the surgical removal of the preforental region of the frontal lobes.

Location chart: Refers to reproductions of the Rorschach inkblots included in the record blank so that the examiner may record the location of the subject's response.

Locomotion: Refers to the movement of a person through his or her life space.

Locomotor behaviour: It is the behaviour involved in travelling from place to place.

Locus of control: It is the degree to which the individual attributes the cause of his behaviour to environmental factors or to his own decisions.

Logagnosia: Refers to a condition wherein the patient can see and read words but not identify them in terms of their meanings.

Logamnesia: Condition wherein the patient is unable to recognize spoken or written words.

Logic: It is a branch of philosophy that deals with the criteria of validity in thought, the canons of correct predication and the principles of reasoning and demonstration.

Logography: Refers to any writing system which is based on the use of signs to represent words or morphemes.

Logomania: It is a pathological state of volubility or incoherent wordiness. Characteristic of mental disorders.

Logorrhea: Refers to incoherent bursts of talking; pathological volubility.

Logotherapy: A system of psychotherapy, founded by Viktor

Frankl, based on existential principles. The goal of therapy is to help the patient overcome the "existential neurosis". to assume responsibility for his life and to reexamine his experiential, creative, and attitudinal values in order to achieve a more meaningful and productive style of living. Each patient must find his own solution to the problems of living, but each must do so in the context of his membership in society and responsibilities to one's fellowman.

Long-circuiting: (*R.B.Cattell*) The renunciation of immediate satisfactions in favour of attaining remote goals. Luminosity the relative brightness or intensity of a light as dependent upon its reflectance, conditions of illumination, etc. Thus, a white paper in a dimly lighted room is more luminous than a gray paper.

Long-Term Memory (LTM): Refers to permanent memory or memory which endures for long period may be for life.

Looking-glass self: Refers to a person's perception of himself or herself as a reflection of the perception which the person has of how he or she appears to others.

Looming: Refers to the complex of gradient transformations produced as one rapidly approaches some object, or vice-versa.

Loose construct: Refers to a construct which permits variable, even contradictory, predictions.

Loudness: It is the psychological attribute of an auditory stimulus corresponding to the physical dimension of intensity.

Love, romantic: Refers to that kind of love which is hypothesized to exist between opposite-sexed peers.

Low-grade defective: Refers to an individual of subnormal ability needing institutionalization and close supervision.

Lumen: The unit of luminous flux it is defined as the amount of light within a solid angle of a unit size originating from a source of one candlepower.

Luminance: It is the luminous flux emitted, reflected or transmitted by a surface and measured in foot-lamberts..

Luminous intensity: The luminous flux per unit solid angle emitted in a given direction from a source of light, usually one standard candle.

Luria technique: It is used in the measuring of emotional tensions. It this method the subject presses the fingers of one hand on a sensitive tremor recorder as he responds in a free association test

Luteiniziug Hormone (LH): A hormone which in the female, regulates Progesterone production during the latter stages of the menstrual cycle and, in the mate, regulates the production of androgen.

Lutenizing normone: It is a tropic hormone produced by the anterior pituitary that stimulates ovulation, the growth of the corpus luteum, and the testes to produce androgen.

Lux: A unit of illuminance which is equal to the amount of light falling on a surface 1 meter from a source of 1 international candle or candela.

Lymph: Refers to the alkaline fluid of the lymphatic vessels. Lymph differs from blood in that red corpuscles ire absent and the protein content is lower. It is found in tissue spaces all over the body ; it is gathered into small, vessels and carried centrally, eventually entering the blood stream at junctions with the large veins near the heart.

Lysergic Acid Diethylamide (LSD): It is one of a group of psychomimetic drugs which product psychological changes resembling a psychosis.

M

Machiavellianism: 1. A belief that people can be manipulated through flattery, threats, and deceit. 2. the attempt to manipulate through such techniques.

Machine theory: The point of view that behaviour or nervous processes may be treated as if they were the expressions of an elaborate machine. the general point of view is called *mechanism and* is often contrasted with a *dynamic, or field-theory,* view point.

Magical thinking: A stage in a child's thinking in which he believes he is the cause of physical phenomena. Said to be characteristic of children between one and six years of age.

Magnetropism: An orienting movement of the organism toward a magnetic field.

Magnitude: The characteristic of objects, spatial extents, temporal durations, etc., in respect to which one may be larger, longer, or otherwise greater than another.

Main score: *(Rorschach)* A score based on responses given during the test proper. Additional scores or with drawls are given for responses that occur after the completion of the test proper.

Mainstreaming: The practice of helping persons suffering from chronic mental disorders to adjust successfully to the community with the aid of support systems.

Maintaining stimulus: A stimulus that continues to elicit a response as long as it is present. In the case of the spider, the absence of a complete web is sufficient stimulus to maintain spinning until the web is completed.

Masked epilepsy: Epileptic equivalent, or a form of epilepsy in which the patient does not suffer true conclusive attacks but in which there is a substitute-a dreamy state of an out-burst of anger.

Masked obsession: *(Psychoan)* An obsessive idea or impulse that has been disguised: in particular, pain of psychogenic origin is said to mask impulses toward forbidden pleasure.

Masking: 1. The interference or block-age of one sensory stimulus by an other. 2. the partial or complete obscuring of one tone by another. Low notes mask high notes better than high notes mask low notes.

Maslow, Abraham H: American psychologist. Born in Brooklyn, New York, Maslow received his professional training at the University of Wisconsin, where he earned the Ph.D. degree in 1934. He taught at Wisconsin, Brooklyn College, and Brandies University, Maslow is known for his advocacy of humanistic psychology, his studies of self-actualizers, and his hierarchical theory of human motivation.

Maslow's theory of human motivation: Maslow rejected the dominant American schools of behaviourism and psychoanalysis as offering too narrow a conception of man, and championed a "third force" in psychology- humanism. As he conceived it. humanism concerns itself with higher human motives, and the need for self-realisation, knowing, understanding; and with aesthetic needs.

These Maslow characterized as abundancy needs in contrast to deficiency needs, which arise out of the physiological motives and feelings of insecurity and alienation. The highest development of the abundancy needs is found in self-actualizers: individuals who include both outstanding historical figures, such as Thoreau, Beethoven, and Einstein, and people who exhibit such characteristics as spontaneity in living, a problem- centered rather than a self-centered approach to life, and a tendency toward mysticism, nonconformity, and creativity. Such individuals enjoy "peak experiences" moments of great awe, understanding, and rapture.

Peak experiences may be creative periods or they may be of a contemplative nature a compassionate, nonactive, and noninterfering awareness. In his writing and lectures, Maslow urged people to recognize and encourage peak experiences for their value in healthy, happy living. Maslow's views are closely related to those of Alfred Adler, Erich Fromm, Rollo May, and Carl Rogers, who also espoused a humanistic psychology in contrast to psychoanalytic and behaviouristic views.

Membrane theory of conduction: A theoretical explanation of the propagation of the nervous impulse in terms of electromechanical events occurring on the surface of the neuronal membrane.

Memorizing: The process of

committing verbal material to memory by repetition.

Memory afterimage: A perceptual experience that consists of a vivid revival or prolongation of an experience after it has passed. For example, one may seem to hear the shout of "Fire!" hanging in the memory after shouting has cased.

Memory color: The color of an object as it is remember and as it influences the perception and as it influences the perception of a present color. The effect of the memory color is often surprisingly strong. the remembered grass is much greener than the actual grass, the remembered hair less gray than the present hair.

Memory: 1. The function involved in reliving past experiences. 2. the totality of past experiences that can be remembered. 3. a specific past experience.

The memory process is measured by recall, reproduction, recognition, and relearning. In *recall* the subject must demonstrate that he can remember what has been learned without the aid of stimulus cues. An easy examination measures recall. In *reproduction*, he must show, by a drawing or by rearranging objects in their original order, that he can remember what was originally learned or perceived. In *recognition*, the subject must demonstrate that he can remember which of several alternatives were originally learned when all are presented together. The multiplechoice examination draws upon this type of memory. In *relearning*, the amount of time or number of trials saved is measured for the relearning of a passage learned in the past.

Mental age: Level of mental development expressed in units of chronological age for which the mental development is judged normal. Mental age *(Abbr.MA)* is most effectively calculated for children up to the chronological age 15 and is ordinarily ascertained by the child's performance on an intelligence test. A child whose MA is significantly higher than CA (chronological age) is brighter than normal: one whose MA is significantly lower than his CA is duller than normal.

Mental analysis: 1. A list of the components of mind or its attributes. 2. psycho-analysis. 3. the discovery of the components, attributes, or relationships in an object or objective situation without overtly dealing with the object or situation. One who sits and analyzes a chess situation without actually moving the pieces is engaging in this type of mental analysis.

Mental chemistry viewpoint: The view that mind behaves like chemical compounds, that mind is possessed of elements compounded by association into more complex processes that may no longer resemble the elements from which they arose.

Mental disorder: Any serious maladjustment that is disabling in its effect. The disorder may be either psychogenic or organic in origin and includes both psychotic and the more serious neurotic reactions.

Mental element: A psychological process that cannot be resolved into anything simpler. the structuralists found by means of introspective analysis that the mental elements were sensations, images, and affective states. the concept is now chiefly of historic importance.

Mental evolution: The progressive changes in mental organization with increasingly higher levels of a complexity as we progress up the phylogenetic scale.

Mental examination: 1. A comprehensive examination of an individual's abilities, usually for establishing normalcy or abnormality. 2. a mental test, such as an intelligence test.

Mental growth curve: A graphic plot of mental age and chronological age that shows the rate of mental development. Mental age is plotted on the vertical axis and chronological age on the horizontal axis.

Mental healing: The healing of mental disorders and physical diseases by suggestion or faith.

Mental health: A state of good adjustment with a subjective state of well-being, zest for living, and the feeling that one is exercising his talents and abilities.

Mental hygienes: The investigation and application of those measures that prevent mental disorders that prevent mental disorders and promote mental health.

Mental illness: Any behavioural disorder, whether functional or organic, of such a degree of severity as to require professional help and (usually) hospitalization.

Mental image: A conscious representation of something that is not present to the senses.

Mental level: 1. The individual's standing on a standardized test of intellectual ability. 2. (Psychoan) one of the divisions of consciousness: conscious, preconscious, and unconscious. 3. *(Jung)* one of the three divisions of the psyche: the conscious, the personal unconscious, and the collective unconscious.

Mental retardation: Intellectual deficiency or subnormality of such degree as to seriously impair the individuals functioning in society. the most profound degree of mental retardation occurs in individuals whose Q's are below 20. these people show poor motor development, often are unable to talk, and cannot learn to read or write. They are unable to care for their own personal hygiene and are totally dependent upon others. For these reasons the profoundly retarded are institutionalized.

Severe retardation occurs where the IQ range is 20-35 and is characterized by the inability to profit from ordinary education or vocational training. Severe retarders show serious motor, speech and intellectual impairment.

Some can be trained in simple health care and self-maintenance habits but must be kept under close supervision and are therefore usually institutionalized. Moderate retardation (IQ range 36-50) offers the possibility of training in social and vocational skills, with some individuals completing the first two grades of schooling. Because many lack the skills for complete self-sufficiency, they are maintained in controlled or sheltered environments or are dependent upon their families for support.

Mild retardation characterizes persons whose Q range is approximatley 51-70. They are capable of profiting from elementary schooling and achieve sufficient levels of social and vocational skills to function in society with some guidance or assistance from family and friends. The causes of retardation lie in genetic abnormalities, brain damage during the gestation period or at birth, nutritional deficiencies, or severe environmental impoverishment during early childhood. Retardation may also result from certain infectious diseases such as rubella, or German measles; encephalitis; and syphilis.

Mentally handicapped: Educationally and vocationally retarded because of subnormal mentality.

Milieu therapy: Therapy that seeks improvement in a behavior disorder by providing a controlled and stimulating environment.

Military psychology: The branch of applied psychology that investigates the selection and assignment of military personnel, training procedures, morale, the design of equipment, and other problems bearing on life in the armed forces that may have psychological aspects.

Mind reading: The alleged ability of one individual to know what is passing in the mind of another without direct communication. Mind reading depends upon the interpretation of subtle muscular movements and other deliberate or inadvertent cues.

Mind: 1. The organized totality of psychological processes that enables the individual to interact with his environment. 2. *(Structuralism)* the totality of conscious experiences. 3. the totality of enduring structures employed to account for conscious experience and psychological activities. 4. the self or psyche. 5. the intellect or intelligence. 6. a characteristic mode of behavior or manner of thinking,such as the *American mind or the mind of a savage*. Although psychology has been traditionally defined as the science that deals with mental activities, there has been no commonly agreed upon definition of mind.

A canvass of a number of psychologists would turn up an equal number of definitions. Nevertheless, a large number-the majority-would associate mind with the *processes* of perceiving, thinking, remembering, and intelligent behaviour. Today most psychologists do not concern themselves with the ultimate nature of mind, nor do they concern themselves with the exact relationship between mind and body, a problem that was once a central issue in psychology.

Mind-body problem: An issue in philosophy and psychology that extends back to classical Greece and one that has been wrestled with by all modern systematic psychologists. The central problem is the exact relationship between body and mind. Are they separate substance? do they interact? Are they ultimately reducible to one? Traditionally, the view that mind and body are two separate substances with no interaction between then is called *dualistic*. Plato was the first dualist. the view that mind and body are of a different nature but interact is called *interactionistic* and is represented by Descartes's view that mind and body, though separate, interact at the site of the pineal gland.

Mind-dust theory: The assumption that mind is made of particles or atoms that exist everywhere in the universe and coalesce to form the individual mind.

Mind-twist hypothesis: The theory that mental disorders are functional in nature, or the result severe maladjustments, as opposed to the brain-spot hypothesis, which assumes that all mental disorders are organic.

Minority group: A population subgroup possessing social or religious interests that differ from those of the larger group. Minority groups are subjected to various kinds of segregation and unfavourable treatment that may be quasilegal, or purely social.

Mixed cerebral dominance: The failure of one side of the brain to be clearly dominant over the in motor control. The resulting conflict is held to be cause of speech disorders by disrupting the delicate motor control normally exercised by the side that control normally exercised by the side that controls handedness.

Motivation research: The study of consumer motivation by advertisers and specialists in the field of psychology who attempt to discover the motives that make people buy the way they do and who strive to modify buying habits by discovering more effective appeals and making changes in packaging, or in the product itself, that will meet with more favorable attitudes.

Motivational hierarchy: The theory proposed by Abraham Maslow that human motives from a hierarchy with the primary or physiological drives on the bottom; safety and security next then gregariousness, love and affection as the next highest category; prestige, power, and possession are immediately higher than gegariousness, love, and affection; self -actualization, the need for knowing, and aesthetic needs are the top of the hierarchy.

Motive: 1. A state of tension within the individual that arouses maintains, and directs behavior toward a goal. 2. the conscious reason the individual gives for his behaviour. 3. an unconscious reason for behaviour. 4. a drive,.

The term *drive* is used primarily to refer to the primary motives for which the bodily basis is known. 5. a set or attitude that guides behavior. Of the many intervening variables that psychologists use, the concept of motive (or motivation) is among the most controversial and least satisfactory. There seem to be as many different major definitions as there are major theories of motivation. Some of the more common usages are included above. The concept is also freighted with a number of subtle connotations from general English usage and with specialized denotations from the literature of psychology. Some of these are reflected in the following list of related terms.

Murray's personology: Murray's definition of personality treats it as a "continuity of functional forms and forces manifested through sequences of organized regnant processes and overt behaviors from birth to death". By *regnant processes*, Murray means *brain processes*, reflecting his view that behavior is functionally dependent upon the central nervous system. The definition also emphasizes the longitudinal continuity of personality and its enduring patterns of behavior.

Personality is also a dynamic process, as revealed by the many needs that play an important role in its organization and functioning.

Some of the more important needs given by Murray are needs for affiliation, deference, nurturance, succorance, harm avoidance; needs for avoiding inferiority feelings, blame, abasement; needs for passivity, seclusion, and inviolacy. There are, in addition, needs for aggression, autonomy, dominance, rejection, achievement, recognition, exhibition, sex, acquisition, cognizance, construction, and order.

Murray's list of human needs leans heavily on Freudian concepts, reflecting his lifelong interest in psycho-analysis. The needs are closely related to what Murray calls *perceptual press* (singular and plural), which reflects what significance an object or person has for the individual. Some of the more important press are absence or death of parent, danger or misfortune, birth of a sibling, dominance by another; exposure to sex, illness, and awareness of inferiority feelings. Needs and press are interrelated in Murray's theory in that press depend upon needs. Specifically, if there is no existing need, an environmental object or person has no significance for the individual and therefore cannot be a press. Personality is revealed in the *proceedings*, or concrete activities, of the individual over a period of time. Proceedings may be internal- thoughts, memories, fantasiesor external, comprising the individual's attempts to cope with environmental events.

The development of personality as it interacts with the environment and persons in the environment who have significance for the individual follows development envisaged by Freud. Murray accepts the ego, id, and superego, with some modifications. The concept of complexes is also taken from Freudian literature, with modifications and additions. Characteristic methods of study include the use of interviews, projective techniques, and psycho-analysis.

Muscle spindle: A type of receptor consisting of a specialized filament of an afferent neuron wrapped around a muscle fiber and which gives information about the contractions of the fiber. Muscle spindles are part of the kinesthetic system.

Muscle tonus: The slight degree of contraction muscles maintain when inactive. Tonus keeps muscles in good condition and makes it possible for them to respond more readily than would otherwise be possible.

N

Nail biting: It is a nervous habit, generally observed in children, wherein the fingernails are chewed down to the quick.

Nalorphine: Refers to narcotic antagonist which blocks the primary pharmacological effects of opium.-based drugs.

Narcissistic neurosis: Refers to a neurosis wherein the libido I regresses to a very early phase of development.

Narcissistic object-choice: Refers to the object which is chosen for narcissistic reasons. The choice is either the self or one very much like oneself.

Narcosis: Refers to a state of markedly reduced responsiveness, both in behaviour and in normal physiological functioning, induced by narcotic drugs.

Narcosynthesis: The interpretation of the patient's verbal productions obtained under the influence of narcotic drugs.

National character: Refers to characteristic behaviour patterns, attitudes, values, etc., that are found in a nation.

Nativism: According to this point of view the role of heredity is important as opposed to environment, in the development of mental and behavioural processes.

Naturalism: According to this point of view mental processes, attitudes, and other psychological processes are part of the system of natural phenomena and so interpretable according to natural laws.

Naturalistic observation: Refers to the collection of data by careful observation of events in their natural setting.

Natural law: Refers to a statement, generally in mathematical form, of a consistently observed and predictable phenomenon of nature.

Natural monism: According to this point of view all sciences are ultimately reducible to physics and chemistry. Thus, Psychology would be reducible to physiology, physiology to physics and chemistry.

Natural sciences: Those sciences which deal with physical and biological objects and processes. Psychology may be considered as a natural science or as a social science, depending upon the definer's point of view.

Nausea: Refers to a complex disturbance of the gastric, vasomotors, and sebaceous systems involving dizziness, sweating, a tendency toward vomiting, and feelings of weakness.

Necrosis: Refers to localized tissue death along with degeneration while still in contact with living tissue; e.g., as takes place at the site of a wound.

Need-drive-incentive model: A model of motivation which considers that basic, physiological needs are produced by states of deprivation, that such needs produce drives which are the true instigators of action and that the action is directed toward the incentive components of the goal state.

Negative: In mathematics, characteristic of a quantity less than' zero or pertaining to denials negation, disputatiousness, and attitudes or hostility.

Negative induction: Refers to the intensification of inhibition in a system due to the influence of preceding excitation.

Negative phase: Refers to any period that is marked by withdrawal of the individual or negativism during development or during the course of a disease.

Negative reward: Refers to a stimulus, situation, or verbal statement that leads to dissatisfaction, withdrawal or a decreased probability of response.

Negative transference: It is a state of hostility toward the psychoanalyst which commonly follows the stage of positive transference.

Neobehaviourism: A derivative of the older school of behaviourism, that retains the point of view that behavioural responses are the fundamental data of psychology but lacks the militant objections to certain molar concepts which are characteristic of the parent school and is more tolerant of verbal reports and the use of intervening variables.

Neo-freudian: Refers to a psychoanalyst who follows Freud's major doctrines but has added theoretical formulations which depart significantly, from Freud's original premises.

Nervous habit: Refers to an oft-repeated set of movements (*e.g.*, nailbiting, finger-tapping, facial and bodily mannerisms) which take place when one is under tension.

Nervousness: It is a state of restlessness with heightened emotionality and Visible signs of muscular tremor, tenseness, and overactivity.

Neural arc: Refers to any network or path of afferent, interneural and efferent neurous which forms a functional unit from a receptor through the central nervous system interconnections to an effector.

Neural crest: Refers to a band of cells arranged longitudinally along the *neural tube* of a vertebrate embryo which gives rise to the cells which form the cranial spinal and autonomic ganglia.

Neural discharge: Refers to the excitation and propagation of a localized disturbance in a neuron or nervous center.

Neural fold: Refers to one of two longitudinal elevations of the embryonic *neural plate,* that in vertebrates, unite to form the *neural tube.*

Neuralgia: It is a nervous disorder which is characterized by bursts of sharp pain generally localized to the field of innervation of one nerve.

Neural groove: It is the groove along the *neural plate* in the vertebrate embryo which ultimately forms the *neural tube.*

Neural tube: It is the tube produced by the fusing of the *neural* folds in the vertebrate embryo from which the central nervous system develops.

Neuraminic acid: An acid of unknown structure which can be isolated from the brain. It is said to be deficient in schizophrenics.

Neurasthenia: It is a form of psychoneurosis, that is characterized by excessive weakness, fatigue, complaints of visceral malfunction, and anxiety.

Neurilemma: Refers to the thin membraneous covering of *myelin sheath* of the axons of peripheral neurons. Neurilemma consists of *Schwann cells.*

Neurobiotaxis: It is the phenomenon in which the dendrites of neurons are stimulated to grow toward the axon endings of active neurons.

Neuroeffector junction: Refers to a junction between an efferent neurons and an effector like a smooth muscle or a gland.

Neurogenesis: Means growth and development of nerve tissue or growth and development of structures originating *from* nerve tissue.

Neurohumors: Refers to chemical agents, like acetylcholine or norepinephrine, which serve as mediators of nervous activity.

Neuroplexus: Refers to a network

of peripheral nerve fibbers. These common in the autonomic nervous system.

Neurosis: Refers to a benign mental disorder that is characterized by (a) incomplete insight into the nature of the difficulty; (b) conflicts; (c) anxiety reactions; (d) partial impairment of personality.

Neurotic: Pertaining to an individual suffering from a neurosis or characterizing behaviour or traits symptomatic of a neurosis.

Neurotic fiction: Refers to a guiding fiction far removed from the possibility of real accomplishment thus unachievable and to keep the individual pursuing unrealistic selfish goals.

Neutral gray: A gray which lies at the 'midpoint of the continuum of brightness, one which is intermediate between black and white.

Neutralization: In psychoanalysis it is the process whereby the sexual and aggressive impulses of infancy are softened.

Neutral Stimulus: Refers to a stimulus which produces an indifferent response; a stimulus which does not ordinarily elicit the response is made to elicit after conditioning, when it has become a conditioned stimulus.

Nigro-striatal bundle: Refers to an axon bundle that originate in the substantia nigra of the pons and terminate in the caudate nucleus and putamen.

Nihilistic delusion: Refers to the delusion that is characteristic of some psychotics that the existing order of things his disappeared.

Nit: It is a measure of luminance of a surface and is equal to lux times 1 *k*. Nit (symbol: nt) is a relatively new term in photometry. It has replaced the *meter-candle* ro *foot-candle*. Multiplying it by 0.292 gives *foot-lamberts*.

Nodal points: These are two points in an optical system which are located along the axis of a Ions in such a way that a ray of light sent through one will produce a parallel emergent ray through the other.

Nominating technique: Refers to a sociometric technique used for the exploration of the structure of a group wherein each member nominates the person who best satisfies some criterion.

Nomogram; nomograph: It is a, chart made up of three parallel line -representing values of related variables in such a way that a straight lines drawn through the first two will intercept the related third value.

Nonadjustive: Pertaining to

counselling or therapeutic procedures wherein a minimum of direction is given by the counsellor or therapuetician.

Nonverbal intelligence: Intelligence as measured by performance on tasks requiring minimal use of verbal materials. Such tests are called *performance tests* and utilize incomplete forms, block designs, picture completion tests, and so forth. Psychologists do not believe there is one kind of intelligence that is nonverbal and an other kind that is verbal. Rather, the nonverbal test is useful as a supplement to the verbal test. Particularly in cases where verbal tests might be unfair, such as in testing recent immigrants or children with sensory defects

Noradrenaline; norepinephrine: It is a hormone that is believed to be the chemical transmitter in some sympathetic synopses. Its action is similar to that of adrenaline or epinephrine.

Normal: Anything which does not deviate markedly from the average, or the norm. Some psychologists prefer the statistical definition. That is, the individual who does not differ widely from the norm or average is considered normal.

Norm line: It is a curve representing the mean (or median) scores of successive age groups. Such norm lines are generally furnished with group tests for use in school systems.

Nose: It is the structure containing the organs for olfaction. The receptors are high up inside the nose, in the olfactory epithelium.

Nuclear complex or conflict: Within a number of psychoanalytic or psychodynamic theories refers to a fundamental conflict taking place during infancy or early childhood which is considered to be a root cause of a number of psychoneurotic disorders which may only emerge later in life.

Nucleus: It is the central, dark-staining portion of a cell generally containing a nucleus, or small, darkened mass, or the central portion, or mass, around which material is gathered, or a mass of cell bodies within the brain.

Nucleic acids: It is a group of complex acids found in the cells of all living things. They are involved in the self-duplication mechanisms which are fundamental to life and form the core of the processes whereby hereditary characteristics are transmitted.

Null result: Refers to any experimental outcome which was not significant. Mostly null results tend not to be reported in the scientific literature-that is occasionally unfortunate because the knowledge that such and such an effect does not obtain is often of considerable importance.

Nurture: Environmental factors that influence the individual from the moment of conception onward.

Nystagmus: Refers to a rapid sideways snap of the eye followed by a slow return to normal fixation or rapid oscillatory movements. Nystagmus may take place in pursuit movements of the eye, as in following a moving target, in blindness, or after-rotation of the body.

O

Object: 1. Any part of the environment of which the individual is aware-a material thing, a person, or an abstraction. 2. an end or goal. 3. the person or thing eliciting an instinctive reaction.

Object attitude: In structuralistic psychology, the attitude in which the observer attends to the stimulus or object rather than to experience.

Object blindness: A disorder in which one is unable to recognize visually presented objects because of brain injury in the visual association areas.

Object constancy: The tendency for objects to remain perceptually invariable regardless of wide variation in the conditions of observation. Thus, a chair remains a chair, regardless of the observer's position and in spite of the fact that under certain special conditions it may be no more than a disjoined collection of sticks. It must be noted that object constancy is not perfect is not perfect. People appear "antlike" when viewed from the top of a building. However, object constancy holds over a remarkably wide range of conditions.

Objective psychology: A point of view in psychology that would restrict psychological observation to behavioral processes open to public inspection and would exclude introspective or subjective data.

Observation: 1. A purposive or international examination of something, particularly for the purpose of gathering facts.

Obstruction method: A technique for measuring the relative strength of animal drives by pitting one against another. For example, the animal may have to cross a charged grid in order to reach food. In this case the drive for food is pitted against the drive to avoid pain. Using the same technique, the thirst, sex, and maternal drives can then be studied and the number of crossings made to each within a given time period may be taken as indicative of the relative strength of the drives.

Occupational ability: The individual's aptitude for a certain vocation or profession as measured by a standard test. Such abilities are typically reported in the form of a profile or pattern.

Occupational hierarchy: 1. The arrangement of the various occupations according to the level of ability or competence required. 2. the serial arrangement of occupations according to their social status.

Occupational therapy: The treatment of mental disorders by giving the individual useful work to do.

Oedipus complex Edipus complex: *(Psychoan)* The child's repressed desires for sexual intercourse with the parent of the opposite sex. Originally, Freud used the term *Oedipus complex* to refer to the boy's desire for the mother, and the term *Electra complex* to refer to the corresponding desire of the girl for the father.

More recently, psychoanalysts use *Oedipus complex to* refer to both sexes. The Oedipus complex was named after a Greek tragedy by Sophocles in which the hero, Oedipus, unwittingly killed his father and married his mother. In his youth the hero had his feet pierced *(Oedipus means " swollen feet")* and was left to die on a mountain, but was saved by a shephered and fulfilled his fate.

Operant learning: A learning situation in which the organism is reinforced for making a certain response in order to increase the probability of that response on the next trial. By progressively reinforcing responses that are in the direction of a desired pattern of responses, highly complicated behaviour patterns can be learned.

Operation: *(Guilford)* One of three basic dimensions of intelligence, the other two being content and products. Operation involve how information or content is utilized.

Operational operations research: The identification and study of factors in any system with the purpose of discovering how that system can be made to operate more effectively.

Operationism: The generalization that the validity of a construct rests on the validity of the producers used to establish it. Thus, the concept of intelligence has no other meaning than the procedures utilized on a specific test designed to measure intelligence—memory for sentences, vocabulary, reasoning problems, etc. and is valid only to the extent that those procedures are valid. Thus, intelligence may be defined differently according to the test used.

The term *operationism* comes from the science of physics, where it was introduced by Percy Bridgman in order to divest physical concepts of spurious and surplus meanings. Thus, resistance has no meaning other than the procedures used to measure it. It is not an entity apart from those measures.

Marry psychologists believe that the concept of operationism is useful in psychology for divesting psychological terms of validity they do not, in fact, possess.

Order: 1. A temporal and/or spatial arrangement. 2. in biology, a group of organisms above the family and below the class. 3. a position on a scale of merit or in a quantitative series.

Order of magnitude: An arrangement of values in an array from the highest to the lowest degree.

Organismic autonomy: *(Angyal)* The power of the organism to maintain itself because of the presence of intrinsic self-regulating mechanisms.

Organismic psychology: The point of view held by psychologists such as A. Gelb, K. Goldstein, J. Kantor, and R. Wheeler, emphasizing that psychology is the study of the biological organism. Mind-body distinctions are typically rejected or ignored by organic psychologists. The general approach resembles that of the Gestalt school, in that organismic psychologists do not favor reductionistic analysis but instead tend to study behavior as molar.

Organization: 1. A structure or grouping composed of units that function in an interrelated manner so as to form a unified whole. 2. in Gestalt psychology, the process whereby excitations form a unified and stable field.

Organized play: Directed play planned in advance, supervised and carried out with regard to rules.

Orgasm: A pattern of involuntary movements of the genital organs and associated movements of the voluntary movements of the voluntary musculature, accompanied by intense pleasure and strong sexual feelings and culminating in the ejaculation of semen by the male.

Orgasm normally is the climax of coitus, but it may be induced in other ways, as through masturbation.

Orgone theory: The theory formulated by Wilhelm Reich that all space is filled with a specific form of energy called orgone energy, which accounts for life and living functions.

Orientation: 1. Knowledge of one's position in time and space. 2. the position that a cell, organ, or limb is in. 3. the active turning toward a source of stimulation, such as occurs in tropisms. 4. a point of view or frame of reference. 5. in personnel practice, assisting the individual to know his job and the regulations and rewards associated with it.

Orthopsychiatry: A branch of psychiatry emphasizing the early treatment and prevention of mental disorders. The discipline deals primarily with borderline cases and is closely allied to mental hygiene.

P

Pain: 1. Unpleasantness; the opposite of pleasure. 2. the sensation resulting from damage to tissue. 3. the stimulation of the free nerve ending receptors on the skin.

Pain sense: A sensory modality whose receptors are free nerve endings and is experienced both on the periphery and internal parts of the body.

Paradoxical sleep: A state of sleep characterized by an electroencephalographic pattern similar to that in light sleep. However, the individual is not easily awakened. Paradoxical sleep may be accompanied by rapid eye movements and dreaming.

Paralysis: A partial or complete loss of function in the voluntary musculature. Paralyses may be of two fundamental types, *spastic and flaccid*. Spastic paralyses involve destruction, of the upper motor neurons from the brain, while flaccid paralyses indicate involvement of the lower motor neurons that extend outward from the spinal cord to the muscle. Paralyses are also commonly classified in terms of the part of the spinal cord involved. *Paraplegia* results from complete sectioning of the cord, with paralysis of both lower limbs, *Hemiplegia*, or paralysis on one side, is the result of a destruction of one side of the cord; *diplegia* of both sides.

Parapsychology: The field of psychology that investigates all psychological phenomena that apparently cannot be explained in terms of natural scientific laws or principles. Parapsychology includes the study of clairvoyance, dowsing, telekinesis, mediumistic trances, poltergeists, etc.

Parathyroid glands: Four glands, each about the size of a pea, located in the neck in the region of the thyroid gland. The hormone secreted by the parathyroids is necessary in calcium metabolism.

Partial tone; partial: Any of the simple constituents that make up a tone. Any sounding body vibrates not only in its entirety but also in fractional parts (see illustration). The tone resulting from the first partial vibration of the body is called the fundamental tone. This is the loudest and lowest in pitch of all partials. The rest are called upper partials or overtones and become progressively weaker. Partial tones lend various instruments their characteristic sounds.

Part method of learning: Learning in which the material to be learned is broken up into parts for separate mastery. For example, in learning a poem, the stanzas would be memorized one at a time.

Pattern analysis: A technique for identifying test items that go together or measure a common variable. For example, interest test results are analyzed according to the results are analyzed according to the patterning of answers on certain items, all of which theoretically indicate a common core of attitudes and personality traits likely to make for success in a given occupation.

In contemporary psychology perception is commonly treated as an intervening variable dependent upon stimulus factors, learning sets, moods, and emotional and motivational factors. Thus, the meaning of an object or objective event is determined both by stimulus conditions and by organism factors. For this reason, perception of the world by different persons is different. Since each individual perceives in terms of those aspects of the situation that have special significance for him. In the decade following World War II, research emphasis in perception was on discovering the relationships between perception and the various O factors that influence the process. More recently, perceptual research has been heavily influenced by information processing theory (q.v) with the result that the perceptual processes are conceptualized in terms of input-processing-output systems.

The perceptual process begins with attention, which is the process of selectively observing . The important stimulus factors in attending are change, intensity, repetition, contrast, and movement. Important organism factors are interest and learned habits of attention . Perception, which is the second stage in observing out world, involves understanding and knowing objects and events. Perceptions are organized into figure and ground. Figures are characterized by good shape, definite contour, and clarity in attention. The ground is fuzzy, not well contoured, and poorly localized. Perceptions may also be organized by such stimulus factors as similarly, proximity of stimuli, and continuity of lines. Highly important in perception are the perceptual constancies that refer to the tendency to see objects as invariable, regardless of wide variations in viewing conditions.

The important constancies are color, size, shape, and brightness. Illusions are exceptions to the constancies and consist of distorted perceptions, which occur for a number of reasons, including complex stimulus patterns and sets from past experience.

Depth perception is possible through the utilization of such physiological cues as accommodation convergence, retinal disparity of the eyes, and because of learned cues of linear and aerial perspective, interposition, relative size of objects in juxtaposition, shadows, and texture gradients.

A great deal of research has been devoted to the question of whether our basic depth perceptions are learned, but the issue remains in doubt. Psychologists have found it difficult to design experiments where the relative roles of maturation and learned factors can be held constant. Studies of animals reared in darkness and of human patients who recover their sight as adults suggest that while primitive space perception may be inherent, complex interactions with objects in space are dependent upon learning.

Perceptual defense: Selectivity of perception so that unpleasant or anxiety producing stimuli are blocked from awareness. Experimentally, perceptual defense has been demonstrated where taboo words are presented rapidly and are misperceived. For example, *bitch* might be preceived as *bitch*.

Personality: 1. *(Allport)* "The dynamic organization within the individual of those psycho-physical systems that determine his characteristic behavior and thought". 2. *(R.B.Cattell)* "that which permits a prediction of what a person will do in a given (Murray) "the continuity of functional forms and forces manifested through sequences of organized regnant processes and (Freud) the integration of the id, the ego, and the superego. 5. (Adler) the individual's style of life, or characteristic manner of responding to life's problems, including life goals. 6. (Jung) the integration of the ego, the personal and collective unconscious, the complexes, the arche-types, the persona and the anima.

As the definitions given above show, personality has been defined in a number of different ways by various theorists. Other theorists have emphasized temperament as the core of personality. In popular usage, the social-stimulus value of the individual is equated with personality. The psychotherapist is likely to emphasize the individual's characteristic patterns of adjustment. Regardless of differences in emphasis, there is a core of agreement in considering personality as an integration of traits that can be investigated and described in order to render an account of the unique quality of the individual.

Personality disintegration: The breaking apart of the unified organization of traits that comprise personality. It may be accompanied by some degree of intellectual deterioration, demoralization, loss of motivation, and impaired judgement.

Personality disorder: A difficulty in social adjustment that is not as serious as neurosis or psychosis but includes inadequacies in motivational and emotional processes and may include schizoid, paranoid, and cyclothymic tendencies as well as the sociopathic or societal disturbance.

Personality dynamics: The study of the motivational and emotional components of personality.

Personality integration: The organization of the various trait systems that constitute personality into a harmonious whole, resulting in effective adjustment.

Personality inventory: A questionnaire-type device to be answered by the individual about himself. Typically, a series of statements is presented to which the individual responds with *Yes*, *No*, or *?*. Norms are provided fro the purpose of comparing a given individual's performance with that of the standardization group.

Personality problem: A persistent maladjustment without psychosis or neurosis that interferes with social relations and personal happiness. Feelings of inferiority and jealousy and excessive preoccupation with sex are examples of personality problems.

Personality reorganization: A fundamental change in personality with redirection of goals and values brought about by extensive psychotherapy.

Personality sphere: (R.B. Cattell) The range of measurable human personality.

Personality structure: The integration of traits and systems consisting the personality.

Personality syndrome: An acquired organization of traits in a given culture that resembles the personality organization of other individuals in that culture. The analogy is to a disease that, although it may vary from case to case, is a recognizable entity because of the common symptoms involved.

Personality test: Any instrument or technique used in the evaluation of personality or in the measurement of personality or character traits.

Personality type: A classification of the individual into one or two or more categories on the basis of how closely his pattern of traits corresponds to the type category.

Personal space: The area around an individual considered to belong to him and whose invasion is experienced as threatening or unpleasant. (Jung) that part of the unconscious unique to the individual and which develop as a result of the repression of individual experience.

Personification: 1. Attributing personal or human characteristics to abstractions, models, or objects. 2. attributing to another that are missing in oneself.

Personnel: 1. (noun) The total group of individuals employed in an organization. 2. (adj.) pertaining to human factors in industrial or business operation.

Personnel psychology: The branch of applied psychology that investigates employment procedures, selection techniques, placement, transfer, promotion, rewards for work, and that in some cases may include limited guidance and therapy.

Personology: 1. The study of personality. 2. the point of view that all behavior should be studied in relation to the central core of personality.

Perspective: 1. The representation of the relative position, size, and distance of objects on a surface. 2. a point of view or frame of reference from which parts or elements of an object or a problem are seen to better advantage or from a better organization.

Physiognomic: 1. Pertaining to physiogonomy (q.v). 2. a type of empathetic reaction in which affective or conative elements are added to congnitive experiences. For example, a dilapidated car is said to look tired, a fine tree, proud.

Physiognomy: 1. The art of judging personality or mental abilities from the structure and expression of the face and other bodily organs. 2. the expression of the face.

Physiological age: The individual's developmental level as estimated by the maturational status of his glands, muscles, nervous system etc.

Physiological psychology: The branch of psychology concerned with the interrelationships of the nervous system, receptors, and endocrine glands, and of behavior and the mental processes.

Physiological zero: The temperature on the skin at which an object feels neutral-neither warm nor cold. The physiological zero point varies with the part of the body tested, but on the exposed surfaces of the hands and face in an ordinary room it is a little over 32.

Play therapy: The utilization of play as a form of catharsis to enable the child to express feelings and emotions that, if allowed to build up, could cause maladjustment. Lay therapy may also be a useful technique for diagnosing the source of a child's difficulty.

Pressure sensation: A sense modality aroused by relatively intense mechanical deformation of the skin and by tension in muscles, tendons, and joints. The receptors are believed to be Pacinian corpuscles. Distinctions are sometimes made between light pressure and deep pressure. It is likely that contact or touch may sometimes be confused in the literature with light pressure, whereas the terms deep pressure and simply pressure imply relatively intense stimulation.

Pretest: 1. A practice test to allow subject to become familiar with the procedures to be used during an experiment. 2. a preliminary series of trials for the purpose of establishing a standard or baseline. The scores obtained after the experimental variable has been administered can then be subtracted from the results of thee pretest and the difference is the result of the independent variable.

Primal anxiety: (psychoan) The anxiety associated with the separation of the infant from the infant's immature nervous system with stimuli immediately after birth. According to Freud. primal anxiety is the basis of all other types of anxiety.

Primal trauma: (Psychoan) An event in the early life of the child that is extremely painful psychologically and impress permanent harm on the individual. The birth trauma is an example. Witnessing the parents perform intercourse is another example.

Primary: 1. First in time 2. first in importance. 3. fundamental, such as a primary color or taste quality.

Primary integration: (psychoan) The recognition by the child that his body is something distinct from the environment.

Primary mental abilities: The fundamental or basic abilities hat make up intelligence. The best-known list of primary abilities is that based on the factor analytic work of L. L. Thurstone. They are: Verbal (V); Word Fluency (WF); Numerical (N); Space(S); Memory (M); Perceptual (P); Reasoning (R). Each of these is defined under its appropriate entry.

Primary mental deficiency: Subnormality in intelligence resulting from genetic deficiencies.

Primary motivation: Motivation arising from unlearned bodily needs, such as the huger, thirst, and sex needs.

Primary motives are also defined as universal in the species and unlearned as to origin. However, they may be, and typically are, considerably modified by learning in respect to manner of satisfaction.

Primary narcissism: (*Psychoan*) In the early stage of development in which the infant's libido is directed toward his own body.

Primary need: A basic, unearned need that is biologically determined. Hunger and thirst exemplify such needs. However, it is recognized by psychologists that primary needs and the drives to which they give rise may be modified by learning.

Primary personality: The original personality as compared to the *secondary personality*, which is the split-off-aspect of a multiple personality.

Primary position: The position assumed by the eyes when the individual is standing with head erect and fixating on a point infinitely distant.

Primary process: (*Psychoan*) The process in the id by means of which direct satisfaction of libidinal or other instinctual wishes is obtained.

Primary quality: A fundamental or basic property indispensable to the perceptual existence of an object. this, the moon's yellowness is not primary, since the moon can exist in perception without it; but the moon's spatiality is basic, since without it the moon cold not exist. the philosopher John Locke was the fist to distinguish between primary and secondary qualities in formulating his empirical theory of perception.

Primary reinforcement: 1. Any stimulus that increases the probability of a response without the necessity of learning the value of the reinforcer. Thus, food is a primary reinforcer. By way of contrast, a poker chip may only if it is associated with the possibility of obtaining a learning. 2. the reduction of a primary-drive state: drive-stimulus reduction.

Primary repression: (*Psy-choan*) The denial or re-entry in to consciousness of any menta content that would arouse feelings of guilt and anxiety.

Proactive inhibition: The interference effect of earlier on retention of later learning on retention of later learning. The experimental test model to measure proactive inhibition is as follows.

Probabilism: The position that it is possible to make predictions on the basis of rational and empirical data. Probabilism does not assume a perfect determinism or one-to-one correspondence between cause and event, but rather assumes that within the limits of mathematical probability one may make valid predictions.

Probabilistic functionalism: The theoretical point of view that behaviour is best understood in terms of the probability our perceptual constancies depend on our having build up strong expectancies that objects have definite shapes, colors, size, etc.

Probability: 1. In mathematics, the event will occur in a certain way as opposed to other possible ways. Thus, the likelihood of picking one specific playing card out of a deck is one in 52.2 the quality or state of being probable or likely of occurrence. 3. the science of probability or probability theory.

Probability curve: 1. Any curve showing the expected frequency of occurrence of variable. 2. the normal probability curve.

Probability of response: The frequency of occurrence of a response relative to the theoretical of a response relative to the theoretical maximum frequently of occurrences of that response or class of responses under a given set of conditions.

Probability theory: That branch of mathematics dealing with probability. Probability theory is based on certain assumptions regarding the uniformity of nature, laws of change, equality of occurrence of certain events, and complementary errors canceling each other out if sufficient observations occur.

Probable error: An index of the reliability of an obtained measure in terms of he extent to which the obtained values deviate from the mean of the measure in question. Abbr. P.E. or PE. the probable error is equal to .6745 of the standard error. Inn a normal distribution, half of the deviations from the mean fall within ± I PE.

Probing technique: In short-term memory, the presentation of a series of items, one of which must be recalled. The subject does not know which item will be tested for recall when the initial presentation is made.

Projective technique: The utilization of vague, ambiguous, unstructured stimulus objects or situations in order to elicit the individual's characteristic modes of perceiving his world or of behaving in it. The most commonly used techniques are the Rorschach Ink Blot Test, consisting of ten ink blots the subject must interpret; the Murry Thermatic Apperception Test, which consists of series of pictures about which the subject must tell a story; and various forms of play in which the child's behaviour is observed as he plays with dolls, dollhouses, or other materials.

Prompting method: In verbal learning, a procedure in which the rate of learning is measured by the number of prompts necessary to achieve perfect mastery of a list. As the lists are gone through, the experimenter prompts the subject whenever he can't give the expected response.

Proportion: 1. The ratio of one magnitude or value to another. 2. balance, especially pleasing or artistic balance.

Proportionality: In factor analysis, the requirement that any two columns of correlation coefficients must be in direct proportion if a two-factor patterns is to assumed for that series of test.

Proprioceptor: Any receptor that mediates proprioceptive sense are (1) Pacinian corpuscles, responsive to deep pressure: (2) muscle spindles, responsive to muscle stretch, (3) Golgi tendon organs, responsive to muscle stretch; (4) the receptors of movement and balance in the nonauditory labyrinth.

Pseudo conditioning: The elicitation of a response to neutral stimulus by presenting that stimulus after a conditioning series involving a different conditioned stimulus. Apparently the conditioning series sensitizes the subject to respond. Some authorities consider it a process of reflex sensitization in case where reflexes are involved.

Pseudocyesis: False pregnancy belief on the part of a woman that she is pregnant when she is not.

Pseudopsychology: Any unscientific system, such as graphology, palmistry, or phrenology, that pretends to discover psychological information but whose means are unscientific or deliberately fraudulent.

Pseudoscope: An optical system for transposing the visual images to the eyes. The solidity of objects is also affected so that solid objects seem hollow and an incised figure appears to be a bas relief.

Psychiatric social worker: An individual with special training in the fields of sociology and psychology who, in close collaboration with psychiatrists, works with mental patients and their families.

Psychiatrist: A medical doctor with a specialty in abnormal psychology who is engaged in the diagnosis, treatment, and prevention of mental disorders.

Psychic: 1. Pertaining to mind 2.

pertaining to spiritualism or the mediums who practice spiritualism. 3. pertaining to disorders that are psychogenic or psychological in origin.

Psychic blindness: 1. An inability to see, because of functional or hysterical conditions. In this type of blindness the receptor system is normal. 2. inability to make simple discriminations, such as to discriminate food form nuts and bolts, because of severe lesions in the temporal lobes.

Psychic impotence 1. Impotence due to psychological factors. 2. temponary paralysis of the mental processes, resulting in an inability to perform acts ordinarily performed.

Psythic isolation: (Jung) Defense by withdrawal from social contacts. The individual is believed to be harboring a shameful or fearful secret he does not wish to reveal.

Psychic research: Investigation of psychological phenomena that apparently cannot be explained according to natural law.

Psychoacoustics: A joint field of physics and psychology that deals with the phenomena of sound as related o audition.

Psychoanalysis: A system of psychology directed toward the understanding, cure, and prevention of mental disorders. As conceived by Sigmund Freud, psychoanalysis is a dynamic system of psychology that seeks the roots of human behaviour in unconscious motivation and conflict. It takes as its point of departure the concept of the *libido,* which is defined basically as sexual energy, both in its original form and as it is modified during development in to all forms of love, affection, and the will to live. How sexual energy develops in the child-whether normal, or blocked and distorted in to unhealthy channels- is of great significance in the individual's overall development and ability to adjust to life's problems.

In the earliest stage the libido is said to be *polymorphous perverse,* since it is fixated on several parts of the body in turn, attachments, that, if they occur in the adult, are considered perversions. The first source of satisfaction is the oral region, with pleasure being obtained form sucking, chewing, and biting. Weaning eventually interferes with this source of satisfaction, and the infant's libido is next directed toward the anal region, with satisfaction being obtained from the activities of the lower bowel and from playing with feces, a stage of infantile development development known as the anal erotic stage. Anal eroticism is eventually frustrated by toilet training and the child progresses to the period of early genital eroticism, satisfaction being derived from masturbation. Fixations may occur during any of these stages, with resulting weakly developed character structure.

The child is also seeking an external object to satisfy his erotic desires and because of proximity and tenderness toward him, the parent of the opposite sex is chosen. In the boy, this complex of desires is called Oedipus complex; in the girl it is called Electra complex. Because the child fears retaliation on the part of the parent for his incestuous desires, he eventually represses them, and the considerable portion of the libidinal energy is directed toward socialization. The beginning of this stage of development marks the end of the infantile period and the beginning of the learnt period, which lasts until puberty. With the onset of puberty, the stage of adult genital sexuality is reached.

Freud's account of mind and personality follows a tripartite schema, which in the case of mind involves three levels of consciousness, and the conscious. The unconscious-the seat of the libido and of repressed memories-is considered by Freud to be the most important level of mind. Personality is considered to have developed out of the primitive, id, or the original, animalistic to deal with reality at the same time as it strives to allow the ideas many of its demands as possible. The ego is also under pressure from the superego-Freud's equivalent of the conscience-which originates from the internalization of parental prohibitions and restrictions and continues to be a kind of ideal aspect of the self that seeks to govern the id through its mediator, the ego. Thus, in Freudian theory, mind is a three-way battle ground. Neuroses occur when the ego becomes weakened through severe conflict with the id or with the environment. Normally the ego can withstand great stress but, if its energies have been depleted by maintaining for dealing with reality.

Psychoanalysis as a therapy attempts to overcome repressions and thereby release energy for healthy, normal living. This is largely accomplished by means of free association and dream analysis conducted over long resistances and get at the sources of the unconscious impulses.

Psychoanalysts are not in agreement as to the mechanisms of development or the form of therapy. The neo-Freudian psycho-analysts, like Karen Horney, Calara Thompson, and Harry Stack Sullivan, put much more emphasis on security and interpersonal relations in the development of personality and the causation of the neuroses than on sex. However, the technique of psychoanalysis has remained more or less unchanged since it was developed by Freud.

Psychobiology: The field of psychology from the biological point of view, stressing the investigation of the organism in relation to its adaptation to its environment as this is made possible by the nervous system, endocrine glands, receptors, etc.

Psychodiagnosis: Any technique for the study of personality that aims at discovering underlying traits, particularly a these dispose the individual toward mental disorders.

Psychodiagostics: The study of personality through the interpretation of behavioral signs, walking, gestures, facial expressions, voice, etc.

Psychodrama: A diagnostic and therapeutic technique developed by J. L. Moreno that consists of having the individual act out on a stage his relations with others around whom conflicts center. The performance is carried out in the presence of a psychiatrist and others. Other actors may also take part in a session.

Psychodynamic: 1. Pertaining to the branch of psychology that investigates motivation and emotional processes. 2. pertainng to psychoanalytic and related depth psychologies. 3. pertainng to processes undergoing change or development.

Psychogalvanometer: A highly sensitive galvanometer used for measuring electrical changes on the surface of the skin.

Psychogenesis: 1. The origin and developmental history of the mind or psyche. 2. the origin.

Psychogenic disorder: A functional disorder that has no know organic basis and is therefore likely to be due to conflict or emotional stress.

Psychogenetics: The investigation of the hereditary causation of psychological traits.

Psychognosis: 1. The study of the individual from anatomical signs. 2. the study of the individual by means of hypnosis.

Psychogram: 1. A profile of the individual's relatives standing on traits, test scores, etc; a psychograph.2. (Murray) representation of the thema, or manner in which needs and psychological press (events of significance for the individual) interct to poduce behaviour.

Psycholinguistics: The study of language and communication as related to the individuals who use language.

The study of morphology and syntax emphasizes the surface structure of language. Formerly linguistics was primarily concerned with syntax, the rules of phrasing, sentence phrasing, and correct grammatical usage. The difference between surface and deep structure is illustrated by ambiguous sentences such as "Some workers are automatons," Which may mean that some working men behave like machines or it may mean that some units in a production line are operated by manlike machines. Psycholinguists study the transformational rules that enable speakers to generate surface structures from deep structures.

The suggestion that children the world over may have a common language acquisition device (LAD) has generated considerable interest and controversy in recent years. Studies of language development reveal that regardless of their national or racial origin or the difficulty of their native tongue, children acquire a fully functional language in a surprisingly short time in the process all go through similar stages. These studies also present evidence to show that children do not acquire language through passive imitation of their elders, but utilize a kind of "telegraphese" with its own rules, out of which they can generate new combination of words. The characterization of the language of young children as telegraphese is intended to convey the fact that it utilizes mostly nouns and verbs, omitting adjectives and adverbs. Thus the child is likely to render the sentence "We are going for a ride in the car" as "Ride in car". Those who emphasize conditioning and learning in the developmental process take the position that language is learned through the reinforcement of those sounds, words, and combinations of words favored by the verbal community in which the child develops.

Among other recent interests of psycholinguists are the study of how language determines though, whether language and thought can develop independently, and to what extent animals can utilize language. Some investigations have suggested that language determines thought (Whorfian hypothesis), while others (notably Piaget's) suggest that thinking and language develop separately through interaction with objects, in the case of thinking and with people, in the case of language. Among the more popular developments in the study of animal communication are those concerned with the investigation of the complex sonar system of porpoises and the ability of the chimpanzee to acquire American Sing Language.

Psychological: 1. Pertaining to psychology. 2. characterizing any event as within the domain of psychology. 3. mental in origin.

Psychological environment:

Those aspect of the external world influencing the individual. The Gestalt psychologists and field theorists would include imagined or remembered aspects of the world under this category. See also LIFE SPACE.

Psychological field: (*Lewin*) The environment as perceived by the individual the individual's life space at any given moment.

Psychological freedom: The awareness of the absence of external influence in making decisions; the feeling that one is able to make his own decisions without undue influence.

Psychological me: The self or self-concept.

Psychological primary: In topological psychological, any differentiated division of the life space.

Psychological test: A general concept including mental-ability scales, achievement tests, various kinds of special-aptitude test.

Psychological time: Time estimated subjectively, without the aid of a lock or the position of the sun. Such factors the number of events that have occurred, their nature, and physiological rhythms are used in making such judgments.

Psychological type: Any scheme for classifying individuals according to a set of personality characteristics, such as extrovert and introvert.

Psychological warfare: A general concept referring to all attempts to weaken the enemy's ability to wage war by weakening his morale, with corresponding attempts to strengthen one's own war potential.

Psychological weaning: 1. The process of breaking away from dependence on the parents. 2. overcoming parental domination.

Psychologism: 1. The point of view that psychology is the basic science among all those science that deal with man. 2. the point of view that the normative sciences (ethics, logic, and aesthetics) rest on empirical facts.

Psychologist: An individual who, by means of a course of training at least through the level of the master's degree and in most cases through the doctorate, has made a specialized study of the science of psychology.

Psychologist's fallacy: Projecting into the mind or behavior of another individual what is actually in the mind of a psychologist or what he believes is logical and appropriate in the situation.

Psychology as a science: The science of human and animal behaviour; the study of the organism in all its variety and complexity as it responds to the flux and flow of the physical and social events that make up the environment.

Behavior is sometimes overt or public, as maneuvers of an astronaut at the control of a space vehicle. Sometimes behaviour is covert, or hidden, as exemplified by glandular secretions, muscular tensions, or stomach contractions, like the behaviour of a scientist engaged in a program of research, while other behaviour the behaviour of the psychotic-appears irrational, strange, and occasionally bizarre. All types of behaviour , whether overt or covert, simple or complex, rational o irrational, are studied by psychologists ultimately hopes to understand the nature of man-his desires, hopes, fears, abilities, and limitations. The psychologist attempts to discover why people do the understand man's unrivaled ability to adapt to his environment, the nature of his inner conflicts, his behaviour as a social animal-indeed, it might be said that psychology, broadly speaking, is a search for the answer to that age-old question, what is man?

Many sciences and disciplines study human behaviour. Anthropologists, political scientists, and others in related fields, seek to know the nature of man; and in this sense, psychology is but one among many behavioral sciences. Each of these disciplines focuses on certain aspects of human behaviour-the sociologist on man's institutional and group behaviour, the anthropologist on primitive races and cultures, the economist on behavior leading to the production and consumption of goods. The psychologist emphasizes the study of the individual. This is not to say that psychologists never study people in groups or are uninterested in political or economic behaviour. Rather, it means that for the psychologist the individual is the unit of study, whether that individual is alone or in a group. For the sociologist, the group or institution constitutes the unit; for the anthropologist, the primitive culture. However, there is considerable borrowing and cooperation among the behavioral sciences. They are neither rivals nor competitors, but all are engaged in unravelling the mystery of man, each in the light of its own special interest and point of view.

Behaviour as responding

The behaviour of a child reciting a poem or of a policeman arresting a criminal is easily observable. Such behaviour patterns are *responses* that can be observed without the aid of instruments. But many responses are not so readily observable. Some people feel anxious or frightened when they have to make a speech.

Unless they re trembling, their listeners. However, if such an individual is connected to a "lie detector" capable of measuring hidden emotional responses, the subtle bodily changes underlying his anxiety can be amplified by the apparatus and made publicity observable. From these bodily changes his state of anxiety can then be inferred by a psychologist.

Much of the same situation is true of most covert or hidden responses. Psychologists have discovered ways of detecting them by means of suitable instrumentation or by employing other experimental arrangements in which covert behavior can be made overt. For example, when an individual is angry, subtle changes occur in his digestive tract, his vascular system, and in his breathing. Indeed, the emotion of anger is, in part, these hidden bodily changes. In order to make them available for psychological study, special instruments must be employed.

Consciousness and unconscious Processes: It is a fundamental fact of existence that we are consciously aware of our own mental activities. Everyone knows what it is like to feel pain, hunger, thirst, cold, anger, and fear, or to sense colors, odors, tastes, and sounds. We are conscious of our own opinion, aspirations, imagines, regrets. This private world of experience is directly accessible only to the experiencing individual. But this does not mean that conscious experience must be totally inaccessible to psychological investigation. Traditionally, the *verbal-report* technique offers the possibility of studying another's conscious experience by having him verbalize his consciousness either as it is in progress or afterward. A subject might be asked to report an emotional experience by having him verbalize his consciousness either as it is in progress or afterward. A subject might be asked to report and emotional experience, describe a dream, or tell how he solved a difficult problem in mathematics. Clearly, such a verbal report is liable to subjective errors and mistakes in interpretation and for these reasons is considered by most psychologists to be less reliable than the more objective technique of observing the subject's responses. However, most psychologists would agree that the study of conscious experience had a place in psychology; consequently the verbal report is accepted in lieu of more objective behavioral responses whenever experimental conditions make this necessary.

Mental activities of which the individual is unaware are called *unconscious processes*. A friend forgets a dental appointment; a child is unreasonably afraid of enclosed places; a student habitually excuses failures by blaming his instructors for including ambiguous questions on examinations. In all these instances the individual is unaware of the reasons for his behavior, and it is sometimes said that his "subconscious" or "unconscious" is responsible for his actions. Strictly speaking, any such description that implies there is a part or segment of the mind that serves as a reservoir for all sorts of undesirable patterns of behavior is misleading. That the individual in question has *behaved* in a certain way is all that can be observed. Because of the nature of his behavior, the psychologist *infers* that he is unaware of the reasons for his actions. The problem here is the same as that which arises whenever the psychologist tries to go beyond the observable. For example, he sees a person stop and drink at a fountain in apart on a hot summer's day. He may infer that the individual is thirsty. In this instance he is inferring a *motive;* as it happens, a motive of which the individual is aware. But whether conscious or unconscious, motives re inferred from observed behavior, and it must be remembered that these represent underlying *processes* within the individual and are not mysterious entities. In the case of thirst it is a changing of physiological conditions; in the rationalizing student, it may be feelings of inadequacy in the face of life's problems which he is unable to admit and for which he has developed a system of defenses, the basis of which he is unaware. But in no instance is it proper to assume that behavior is the result of "forces" or "the unconscious mind," since these have no independent existence apart from behavior.

More generally, it is wise to consider personal attributes in terms of action. To possess intelligence means that one behaves intelligently. To have an emotion means that one is experiencing certain feelings and bodily changes. To have a motive is a short-hand way of saying that one is undergoing physiological changes that arose him to action or that learned habits are guiding his activities. By thinking of psychological concepts as *processes* rather than real *entities* we avoid the error of personification. It may be helpful to compare the psychologist's reasoning about his working concepts with that of a physicist. The latter speaks of a wire as having a certain "resistance." The physicist has no way of observing the wire's resistance apart from its behavior as a current is passed through it. In other words, resistance is a property inferred from the observed characteristics of wires in the same way that intelligence is an attribute inferred from a standard sample of a human subject's behavior called a *test*.

Varieties of behavior

Just as psychologists can describe some behavioral processes conscious and others as unconscious, behavior can be classified in many other ways. Some behavior is *voluntary*, such as getting up and opening a door, while other behavior is *involuntary*, like blinking one's eye to a puff of air.

Some of the behavior patterns in lower forms we describe as *instincts*, such as the wasp's nest building. Thus, there are levels of complexity in behavior ranging from simple, involuntary reflexes, such as eye blinking, to highly complicated forms of behavior, are found in creative writing or painting. Simpler reflex behavior patterns are sometimes called *molecular units*, while more complex behavior patterns are known as *molar units*.

The analogy here is, of course, to gases. The chemist may study the molecules (molecular behavior) that comprise a gas, or he may investigate the behavior of the gas as a whole (molar behavior). Psychologists study behavior at all levels of complexity. However, most psychologists are more interested in molar than in molecular behaviour, and even when they investigate behavior at the molecular level, it is usually in an attempt to cast light on more complex psychological processes.

Methods in psychology

Methodology in the behavioral sciences is closely allied to the particular research interests of the scientist. To lesser extent this is also true of the physical and biological sciences. The astronomer's star-gazing, which is naturalistic observation, is not the same as the chemist's active experimentation with chemical compounds.

Both are observing nature, but one is taking a more active, manipulative role that the other. Similarly, the psychologist observing children playing in a nursery school is using a different method than if he were experimenting on the effect of rewards on learning, or striving to help an emotionally disturbed child. In short, the nature of the psychologist's problem determines the method he will employ in a given instance.

Basically, the aim of psychology is the same as that of any other science—the ability to make accurate predictions about the phenomena with which it deals. Because the key to predicting behavior, the phenomena of psychology, lies in discovering the *antecedent conditions* that give rise to behavior, the psychologist attempts to discover those conditions by employing two basic methods: the experimental method and the method of naturalistic observation. Both of these procedures ultimately rely upon *observation*. In the first, the experimental method, the psychologist actively manipulates antecedent conditions and observes concomitant, or parallel, variations in behavior.

In the second, the method of naturalistic observation, he observes differences in behavior as they exist in nature, as these are related to antecedent conditions. It must be emphasized that the psychologist's observations are not the casual, incidental observations of everyday life, but instead are carefully designed to provide specific and meaningful information. The psychologist, in contrast to the casual observer, is *ready* to observe and is a *trained* observer. His attitude is *objective*, and he is careful to *record* his observations as they occur so as not to become a victim of the errors of his own memory. Finally, he records *negative instances*, or failures, as well as positive instances, something a biased every-day observer often fails to do.

When he employs the experimental method, the psychologist assumes an active role in controlling the antecedent conditions, his subject's behavior, and the conditions of observation. To accomplish this, he must first identify the several variables with which he will be working. The antecedent condition that the psychologist believes may be the cause of the behavior he has under study is called the *independent* (or *experimental*) *variable*. The *controlled variables* are all those extraneous conditions were allowed to influence the subject's reaction and which must, therefore, be held constant. If such conditions were allowed to influence the subject at the same time that the experimental variable is under investigation, he experimenter would not know which was responsible for the subject's reaction.

Psychological experiments are designed to assess the influence of stimuli in responses. However, because stimuli must act on something or someone, the formula for an experiment is often written "S-O-R" rather then "S-R" However, the only observables are the stimuli and the responses. The O-variables are of course, inferred from the subject's reaction. Psychologists call these O-factors *intervening variables*, since they intervene between stimuli and responses. From this point of view, psychology is the study of intervening variables within the organism that mediate between stimuli and responses. They are analogous to such terms as *resistance, energy, gravity,* and the like, which physicists employ to account for the behavior of physical system. None of these physical concepts has independent existence apart from the experimental operations employed in its measurement or demonstration. Precisely the same is true of intervening variables in psychology. The must be operationally defined in terms of Manipulable antecedent conditions. For example, intelligence has no independent existence apart from the tests used to measure it.

Psychologists, like other scientists, formulate their experimental questions about natural phenomena in the form of *hypotheses*. A hypothesis is a shrewd hunch about the outcome of an experiment and is based upon the psychologist's knowledge of the phenomenon under study. It is, there fore, not a wild guess, but an educated prediction. If the results of the experiment confirm his hunch, the hypothesis is proved and the investigator has achieved his aim of being able to predict behavior. He may then *generalize* his conclusions within reasonable limits and predict that whenever the same antecedent conditions occur the subject (or subjects) will react as predicted . Of course, if the results of the experiment fail to confirm his hypothesis, it must be discarded. Naturalistic observation, another widely used method in psychology, is the oldest of the scientific methods. Essentially, it consists of the observation of natural phenomena under carefully controlled conditions.

It differs from the experimental method in that the psychologist finds a situation in which he studies behavior without manipulating the subjects or the antecedent conditions that give rise to their behavior. Because the experimenter does not manipulate conditions, he has less control over them. Suppose, for example, that he is interested in discovering whether restricting infants' movements will significantly delay their walking. For ethical reasons he cannot restrain infants, since the experimental procedures involved might do permanent harm to the children. However, he can study Indian

Children who, as infants, are kept restricted by their mothers in cradle boards. Just as is true in the experimental method, the psychologist in this case needs a control group with which to compare the restricted group. Fortunately, some Indian mothers do not place their children in cradle boards, and the psychologist can select a control group similar in age, genetic makeup, and other relevant factors, with which he can compare the original group.

Naturalistic observation is useful whenever the psychologist may be unable for psychologist may be unable for practical or ethical reasons to use the more active experimental method. It is particularly useful in situation where there is a danger that experimental work might interface with the behavior under study, as is often true when young children, animals, social groups, and mentally disturbed individuals have been carried out with the aid of this technique.

The individual in psychology

The academic psychologist who carries out his research programs with the experimental method and the method and the method of naturalistic observation is primarily concerned with establishing general laws and principles by means of which he can predict and, ultimately, understand human behavior.

His aims are the aims of the "pure" as opposed to the "applied scientist' He is interested in the individual not as a person but as a representative not as a person but as a representative of people in general. From the study of many individuals, he hopes to discover the nature of the behavioral processes.

However, many psychologists focus their interests on the individual. This is particularly true of those who practice psychology as profession, among whom we may include the clinical psychologist, the industrial psychologist, the vocational counselor, and the educational psychologist. Their aims are those of the applied scientists who seeks to bring the knowledge and tools of theoretical science to bear upon the solutions of practical problems. In doing so, the applied scientist often improves the tools of his trade, uncovers new problems of theoretical importance, and contributes in many other ways to the progress of pure science.

Thus, in psychology, these two broad areas- pure and applied, or academic and professional-are neither mutually exclusive nor antagonistic but a cooperative endeavor whose various phases complement one another. The largest single field of professional psychology is that of clinical psychology, whose primary concern is with the development and application of diagnostic and therapeutic techniques for the identification and treatment of behavioral disorders. Notable among these are the *psychological test* and the *clinical interview* , both of which are also widely employed in vocational, industrial, and educational applications.

Psychological tests, are, in effect, real-life situations into which the testee is placed in order to compare his intellectual ability or his personality with that of others. Standardized tests must be developed under controlled conditions. The questions are chosen with care and are evaluated by special statistical tests. In their formative stages tests are administered to large, representative groups of subjects in order to establish standards of performance for future comparisons of any individual with the standardization group. The administration of the final form of the test to individual subjects for diagnostic purposes requires special training, as does the interpretation of the results. Tests are also used by psychologists as instruments of research in the areas of personality and intelligence. By analyzing the results of tests given to large samples of individuals the psychologist strives to arrive at a more complete understanding of the abilities that he is measuring.

The case history and interview have found wide usage in two main area: vocational selection and clinical situation. A case history is a collection of developmental data including test scores, the results of interviews, and, if appropriate, a diagnosis of prognosis of the person under study. Today, psychologists and psychiatrists may be assisted in the development of case histories by social workers with the result that the case history becomes a multi-dimensional analysis of the individual's assets and liabilities. Interviews may be directive or nondirective. The typical formal job interview is likely to be highly directive in that its primary purpose is to gather factual information about the applicant, such as a record of his education, job experience ,and personal background. The non-directive interview to talk freely while he strives to create a warm, permissive atmosphere in which the subject can both express himself fully and arrive at a better understanding of his problems.

Psychometric: 1. Pertaining to any form of mental testing. 2. pertaining to a psychophysical function, such as the equation representing the probability of greater or lesser judgments in a differential- threshold experiment.

Psychometric function: A mathematical expression of relationship between quantitative variations in a series of stimuli and the observer's judgments of those stimuli according to a predetermined criterion. For example, in the method of limits as applied to the problem of obtaining an absolute threshold, a psychometric function may be plotted with the stimulus values on the base line and the proportion of judgments of presence or absence of a sensation as reported by the subject on the vertical axis.

Psychometrician: 1. An individual who engages in the administration of mental tests. 2. a specialist in the statistical analysis of psychological data. particularly in the analysis of mental-test data.

Psychometrics: 1. The specialized branch of psychology dealing with mental tests. 2. the branch of psychology dealing with the development and application of statistical and other mathematical procedures to psychology.

Psychopathology: The branch of psychology concerned with the investigation of mental disorders and other abnormal phenomena.

Psychopathy: A mental disorder that may be unspecified or given a qualifying diagnostic mane.

Psychopedics: The branch of psychology concerned with the guidance and clinical treatment of children.

Psychopharmacology: The study of the effects of drugs on psychological processes.

Psychophysical dualism: The doctrine that mental processes have both a bodily and a mental aspect, that neither is the cause of the other, and that there is no interaction, between them.

Psychophysical function: Any mathematically expressed relationship between a stimulus and observed judgments about that stimulus.

Psychophysical methods: The standard methods used in the investigation of psychophysical problems. specifically, the method of average error, the method of limits, the method of equal-appearing intervals, and the constant methods.

Psychophysical parallelism: The doctrine that for every event of consciousness there is corresponding event in the nervous system. The doctrine of psychophysical parallelism is a form of dualism.

Dualism was first promulgated by Plato and took the form of the separation of mind and body as two different and noninteracting entities. Descartes denied the separation, postulating interactionism as a modified dualism in which mind and body, though separate substances, interact at the site of the pineal gland.

Wundt and Titchener subscribed to the doctrine of

psychophysical parallelism. arguing that conscious events have their neural counterparts but that three are no causal relations between mind and body.

Psychosensory: Pertaining to experiences, such as imagined experiences, that do not originate in the sense organs.

Psychosexual: 1. Pertaining to sexuality in its broadcast sense, including both mental and somantic aspects. 2. characterizing a mental process as originating in sexual development.

Psychosis: A severe mental disorder characterized by disorganization of the thought processes, disturbances in emotionality, disorientation as to time, space, and person, and in some cases, hallucinations and delusions.

Psychotherapy: The application of specialized techniques to the treatment of mental disorders or to the problems of everyday adjustment. In its strictest sense, the term includes only those techniques (psycho-analysis, nondirective counseling, psychodrama, etc.) utilized by specialists. More loosely, psychotherapy can include informal talks with ministers, faith cures and personal discussions with teachers or friends.

The major techniques employed by psychotherapists include depth interviews, conditioning, suggestion, and interpretation. Some authorities would also include under techniques of psychotherapy various medical techniques, such as psychosurgery, electroshock therapy, and chemotherapy. Regardless of their differences, all forms of psychotherapy utilizing psychological techniques have basic features in common.

All involve close communication between therapist and patient, in which the patient is encouraged to discuss his anxieties and most intimate experiences without moral judgment or criticism on the part of the therapist.

The therapist, in turn, exhibits a warm, understanding attitude toward the patient in order to encourage freedom of expression and to minimize embarrassment.

To some degree the goal of all psychotherapies is to encourage understanding of the problem on the part of the patient, whose lack of insight into the nature of the maladjustment arouses anxiety and makes it difficult for him to cope with the demands of everyday living.

Systems of therapy that emphasize insight and understanding are often classified as depth therapies in order to distinguish them from systems that minimize understanding and insight and stress symptom modification, such as behavior therapy. The goal of all forms of psychotherapy is modification of the patient's behavior in such a way as to bring about a more effective adjustment to his environment. Techniques such as psychoana-lysis, clientcentered therapy, and behavior therapy have proved most successful with milder forms of behavior disorders. Psychotic individuals are so disturbed or withdrawn that medical intervention in the form of electroshock treatments or chemotherapy is necessary before such patients are amenable to treatment by psychological techniques.

Q

Q data: Information, or data, obtained through questionnaires.

Q method: The use of questionnaires in collecting psychological data.

Q technique: The correlation of the scores of two persons on a series of tests. Q techniques are used to obtain a measure of the relatedness of the two persons in regard to the traits measured by the tests.

Quality: 1. A basic aspect of a sensation by means of which it is distinguished from all other sensations. Quality as used in this sense implies a difference in kind and not in degree. 2. the relative level of goodness or excellence of anything.

Quantum: 1. A specific or discrete amount of anything. 2. in physics, the elemental unit of energy, such as a quantum of light.

Quota sampling: The selecting of a certain proportion of elements from a set of subgroups that make up the population from which the sample is drawn.

R

Race: A large subdivision of man characterized by a common ancestry and a number of common characteristics. Particularly visible or somatic characteristics. The term race has become highly controversial because of exceptions to the rule of what constitutes any given race, since there are so many variations in skin color, etc., that it is very difficult to establish criteria with any degree of certainty.

Race differences: Physical or mental differences associated with race. It has been difficult to substantiate mental or intellectual differences between races, because of the lack of cross-cultural tests.

Racial memory: Those structures, ideas, feelings, and memory traces presumed to be inherited. Carl Jung was the chief exponent of the theory that memories in the form of a racial unconscious could be inherited from one's ancestors.

Racism: The social and political belief that utilities race as a basis for economic, political, and social segregation, denial of rights, and treatment of the disadvantaged group as inferior.

Randsome sample: A number of cases taken from the entire population of persons, values, scores, etc., in such a way as to much chance of being picked as any other and that the sample will be a valid representation of the entire population.

Range: 1. The interval between the highest and lowest score. 2. the value obtained by substracting the lowest score from the highest. 3. the interval between the limits of dispersion of a biological species. 4. any interval, such as range of audibility.

Range effect: In pursuit tracking the tendency on the part of the subject to make overly large movements when the movements of the target is small and overly small movements when the movement of the target is large.

Rational equation: A mathematical equation based on assumptions as to the nature of the psychological process in question. Rational equations attempt to predict psychological equations attempt to predict psychological phenomena by making careful assumptions as to the psychological nature of the parameters in the equation and the relationship between those parameters.

Rationalism: The philosophical position first emphasized by Plato in which reason is extolled as a means of arriving at the truth.

Rational psychology: Any system of psychology founded on philosophical or theological concepts.

Rational type: (jung) An individual whose behaviour is guided primarily by thinking and feeling in contrast to the irrational type, whose behaviour is governed by intuition and sensation.

Ratio reinforcement: In operant conditioning, the administration of a reinforcement only after the animal has made a certain predetermined number of responses.

Ratio scale: A type of scale on which the various increments are equal and can be added or divided. However, the scale does not have an absolute zero. The ratio scale is employed in psychophysical measurements and is obtained by taking a certain interval or fraction as a standard and constructing a scale of intervals by finding equal-appearing increments.

Reaction time: The minimum time between a stimulus and a response. In the typical experiment for measuring simple-reaction time, the subject is confronted with a stimulus, such as a small light and when it goes on, the is to release a reaction key which interrupts a highly sensitive timer that began running upon the presentation of the light.

The reaction time is the elapsed time between the onset of the stimulus and the release of the switch. If more than one stimulus is employed, the experiment is then called a discrimination reaction-time experiment. if more than one response is required for alternative stimulus possibilities, the experiment is called a choice reaction-time experiment. For example, in a discrimination experiment, the subject might be required to react only if a red light comes on and not if a green light appears. In a choice reaction, he might have to react with the right hand to a red light and with the felt hand to a red light and with the left hand when a green light appears.

Variations of the experiment employ reaction time to words, called association time to words, called association reaction time, and to colors in which the subject's task is to name a series of color patches as rapidly as possible.

Reaction type: 1. In reaction-time experiments, a phrase used to characterize a particular type of readiness or set-motor, sensory, or mixed. The subject is instructed to assume the desired set and to concentrate either on his musculature (motor set) or on the stimulus (sensory set) 2. a type of psychotic syndrome or symptom pattern, such as the paranoid reaction, schizophrenic reaction, or manic depressive reaction.

Reactive inhibition: (Hull) The tendency toward a lessened magnitude of response with increasing practice of fatigue. Reactive inhibition is dissipated by time and is independent of reinforcement. It is maximized in mass learning and minimized in distributed learning.

Reading: 1. The visual perception of words and their meaning. 2. the perception of Braille symbols. 4. the perception of gestures or lip movements 5. an interpretation given by a fortuneteller, palmist, or phrenologist.

Reading age: 1. An age score on a standardized reading test. 2. the age at which reading can be initiate approximately age six for the normal child.

Reading disability: A marked retardation in level of reading ability in comparison with what is normal for the child's chronological age.

Reading quotient: An index of the child's ability to read, a compared with the reading ability of other children of his age. It is obtained by dividing his reading age, as measured by a standardized reading test, by his chronological age.

Reading readliness: The developmental stage at which the child can profit by instruction in reading. A specific age for reading readiness is difficult to define, since reading readiness depends upon both maturation and experiential factors. The traditional rule of thumb held that children were not ready to read until they had reached a mental age of six. Recent experimental reading programs have encouraged children of two to three years of age to read.

Reciprocal inhibition: 1. The inhibition of one neuronal are by the simultaneous activity of another. 2. a form of behavior therapy developed by Joseph Wolpe in which classical conditioning is used to condition responses incompatible with a response to be eliminated. 3. an inability to recall one of two associations because of mutual interference.

Reciprocal innervation: The relationship between the members of any pair of neuronal arcs that mediate muscle reflexed such that when one is active, the other is inhibited. Reciprocal innervation makes possible the mutual working relationship between antagonistic muscle pairs.

Regression: 1. A retreating; a moving backward. 2. a return to earlier levels of development; the manifestation in older individuals of more primitive levels of behaviour. 3. in statistic, the relationship between two paired variables. The regression is expressed in the form of an equation such that for each value of there is a given value of y, and vice versa. 4. in genetics, the tendency for individual organisms to revert to the typical form. This, the children of very tall men tend not to be as tall as their fathers, 5. in conditioning, the fact that a previously extinguished conditioned response may reappear after punishment. Compare with (2) above. Occasionally, previously acquired conditioned responses may reappear without punishment.

Regression analysis: A statistical technique for predicting the value of a continuously quantitative variable form qualitative ratings, the technique is illustrated in industry when the worker's output is predicted on the basis of his foreman's ratings.

Relation ship therapy: Between client and therapist, a relationship in which the individual learn to modify his feelings and his behavior patterns and subsequently can transfer these newly acquired adjustments to situations outside the theoretic situation.

Relaxation therapy: A form of therapy in which emphasis is put on teaching the patient how to relax, on the assumption that muscular realization will help bring about a lessening of psychological tensions.

Relearning: 1. Learning again what one originally learned but has forgotten. 2. a procedure for studying retention by having the individual learn a list and then having him relearn it after an interval. The amount of retention is measured as the savings in time or trials on the second learning.

Release therapy: 1. A from of play therapy designed to permit the expression of deepseated emotional conflicts. 2 more generally, any type of psycho-therapy that enables the individual to release pent-up emotions, particularly hostile and destructive impulses.

Replication therapy: In behaviour therapy, a technique in which the therapist elicits and reinforces behaviour patterns similar to those in the patient's everyday environment.

Representation: Act of taking the place of, or symbolizing, something. The term is used a great deal by psychologists of the psychoanalytic school, who believe that many of our memories, dreams, and perceptions really represent unconscious impulses or repressed experiences. The term is also employed in perceptual psychology to indicate the fact that psychological processes do not mirror the external world but are only representative of it.

Representative design: 1. Combining experimental and statistical manipulation of variables in order to permit all relevant variables to influence the depend variable. 2. the inclusion of a representative or stratified sample of subject in an experiment.

Reproductive strength: In learning the summation of all factors favoring the probability that a response will be made a given occasion.

Retention: The persistence of a learned act or experience during an interval of no practice. The most widely used measures of retention ate; (a) recall, (b) recognition, (c) reproduction, (d) relearning.

The course of forgetting has been studied in terms of both quantitative and qualitative changes. The quantitative decay of retention depends upon the conditions of original learning (conditions favoring efficient learning also favor good retention): the nature of the materials learned)materials that are meaningful and lend themselves to good organization are better remembered): and attitudinal and motivational factors (things we desire to remember are more easily remembered, while indifference or lack of interest may make for more rapid forgetting). Qualitative changes are revealed as distortions in memory, such as occur in rumors or in pictorial materials transmitted from person to person or recalled only at intervals by a single individual. Details are either omitted or added, and sometimes the story or picture is made "better" than the original.

Theories of forgetting have been formulated in terms of retroactive and proactive inhibition effects, systematic distortions in memory, and motivational factors, Retroactive inhibition refers to a loss in retention as the result of new learning which acts back upon and inhibits the traces of older learning whereas proactive inhibition refers to similar inhibitory effects that occur when the interpolated material is placed ahead of the material to be learned. Systematic distortions in memory are assumed to occur because of the selective dropping of details and the tendency to accentuate certain features of remembered events. In general, such effects are presumed to follow the same principles that account for good organization in original perceptions.

Motivational factors include amnesia, which is the complete forgetting of one's personal past, and repression, which is the forgetting of material that is psychologically painful or inconsistent with the individual's evaluation of the self.

Retinal disparity: The difference between the image received one eye and that received by the other, caused by the separation of the eyes. if the foreigner is held directly in front of the face and fixated alternately with the two eyes, more of the fingernail will be seen with one eye than the other. Retrial disparity is a cue to depth perception.

Reger's self theory of personality:

Roger's theory of personality grew out of his work with client-centered or non-directive, therapy, which he developed during the postwar years at the University of Chicago. The technique consists in allowing the mal-adjusted individual to talk to a counselor in much the same manner as that of a client talking to his lawyer-seated, face-to face-with the therapist taking a minimal role in eliciting clinical material and attempting to develop a warm, permissive atmosphere in which the client will feel free to talk and, in taking, come to understand himself.

The therapist occasionally attempts to clarify statements made by the client by repeating them with emphasis or modifying them to bring out significant points, but interpretation in the ordinary sense is kept to an absolute minium. Thus, the patient, in a manner of speaking is his own therapist.

The assumption that the individual can come to understand himself given the proper conditions to do so grows out of Roger's conviction that distorted experiences and symbolizations of experiences are the cause of mal-adjustment.

Ordinarily, we may ignore some experience and make others, which we believe to be a significance, part of the self. But some experience are neither ignored nor fully integrated. Instead they are distorted or denied. Thus, the child who is constantly told be is a "bad boy" for teasing his little brother may eventually distort his true feelings in to the form " I don't like to tease my brother" (whereas in reality he does), because he fears losing his parents' approval.

Distorted or denied experience result in states of conflict, feelings of anxiety, a divided experiences result in state of conflict, feelings of anxiety, a divided self. The personality ceases to grow and to develop in a healthy manner until the conflict is resolved. Rogers is strongly optimistic about human nature. He believes that the most basic drive is to actualize, to maintain, and to enhance the self. He believes that given a chance the individual's own direct experience but have been introjected from parents, teachers, and associates, and have been given distorted symboli-zation with consequent improper intergration in to the self. Consequently, many individuals become divided, unhappy and unable to realize fully their potentialities.

S

Sampling population: The population or entire universe of cases form which a sample is drawn.

Sampling servo: A device for measuring errors in a process and applying corrections at predetermined intervals.

Sampling stability: A state reached when successive sampling from a population give consistent results and are regarded as having reliability.

Sampling theory: The principles involved in drawing representative and adequate samples.

Sampling validity: A determination of how well test items represent the range of behaviour being measured by the test as a whole.

Sampling variability: The degree to which series of samples differs from a truly random sample as estimate from the standard deviation of the series.

Schizophrenia: A general name for a group of psychotic reactions characterized by withdrawal, disturbances in emotional and affective life, and depending upon the type the presence of hallucinations, delusions, negativistic behavior, and progressive deterioration.

In disorganized schizophrenia the symptoms are incoherence in speech and flat, incongrous, or silly emotional reactions with a tendency for social withdrawal and oddities of behaviour. Systematized delusions and hallucinations are absent. In catatonic schizophrenia there is marked withdrawal or decreased reactivity, often to the point to prolonged stupor.

Or the patient may exhibit an agitated or excited phase in which there is a marked increase in purposeless motor activity. In paranoid schizophrenia the prominent symptoms are delusions of grandeur and persecution with hallucinations. In undifferentiated schizophrenia there are pronounced delusions and hallucinations with disorganization of behavior. However, the symptom pattern does not meet the criteria for one of the other types or is a mixture of more than one.

The search for underlying causes of schizophrenia have centered on both functional and organic factors. Functional theories stress psychological maladjustment in parent child relationships with the parents showing either marked psychopathology or immaturity in behaviour, each vying with the other and using the child as an intermediary in the struggle factor theories emphasize numerous studies that shown hereditary predisposition toward developing the disorder.

Particularly striking is the finding that identical twins, even though reared apart, show a much higher incidence of schizophrenia than other children. Moreover, the relatives of schizophrenic individuals in general show a higher likelihood of developing the disorder than individuals from families without a history of the disorder.

In searching for possible biochemical factors in schizophrenia, investigators have searched for products in the blood of schizophrenias that is not found in normal and have attempted to analyze disorders in the neuro-transmitter substances in the brain. Since the antipsychotic drugs have a marked effect on reducing the symptoms of the disorder, many investigators believe that further research in the biochemistry of the brain is promising.

It must be emphasized, however, that the cause or causes of schizophrenia are obscure and may turn out to the result of the interaction of two or more factors. A better understanding of the complex disorder awaits the results of ongoing research.

School: 1. An educational institution. 2. a group of psychologists with common aims and interests who have joined together to promulgate their point of view. Often, but not necessarily, a school of psychology may be located in a certain geographical area. This was particularly true of the older schools. Functionalism, for example, was centered at the University of Chicago, structuralism at Cornell. This is no longer true, since formal school as such have disappeared. Contemporary emphasis in systematic psychology centers around miniature systems or theories and not in the larger, more systems or theories and not in the larger, more programmatic school that flourished in the early part of the century.

School psychologist: A psychologist who specializes in the problems associated with elementary and secondary educational systems. Specifically, he may counsel or advise children, may help to plan curricular units, is alert to serious behavioral disorders, administers tests, and assists in the interpretation of test results to children and parents.

Schwann cell: A cell wrapped around peripheral neurons that forms the neurilemma, providing one layer of the myelin sheath.

Scientific attitude: The attitude characteristic of the sciences-involving chiefly the search for objective facts by empirical the search for objective facts by empirical methods.

Scientific management: The application of scientific methods to improving worker efficiency and conditions of work.

Scientific method: The techniques employed by scientists in the pursuit of knowledge. The scientist may utilize either naturalistic observation or experimentation.

Scientific attitude: The attitude characteristic of the sciences—involving chiefly the search for objective facts by empirical methods.

Scientific management: The application of scientific methods to improving worker efficiency and conditions of work.

Scientific method: The techniques employed by scientists in the pursuit of knowledge. The scientist may utilize either naturalistic observation or experimentation. *Naturalisitc observation* is the objective observing, recording, and interpreting of facts as they are found in nature. In *experimentation,* the scientist manipulates the environment in some way so as to better understand the antecedent conditions that give rise to phenomena. There are, of course, many special procedures utilized in special areas of science.

Scientific psychology: Any system of psychology or body of psychological facts based on the scientific method.

Screening: 1. Selecting test items for exclusion (or inclusion) in the final form of a test. 2. selecting individuals on a preliminary test for a more thorough evaluation.

Screen memory: (*Psychoan*) Fragmentary childhood memories that have been able to overcome the repressive forces of the ego but which, like dreams, are condensed, symbolic, and reveal displacement from the real object of the memory.

Semantic conditioning: The conditioning of a word (conditional stimulus) to the object it symbolizes (unconditional stimulus).

Semantic counseling: Counseling based on the assumption that adjustmental problems are caused by difficulties in the interpretation of meanings.

Semantic differential: A technique for utilizing rating scales in the study of the connotative meanings of works. Words are rated by the subject in terms of such dimensions as strength, action, or pleasantness-unpleasantness.

Semantic therapy: A system of psychotherapy that attempts to readjust individuals by reincorporating the distorted meanings that such individuals have associated with words.

Semantogenic disorder: A mental disorder that has come about through the faulty interpretation of the meaning of emotionally charged words.

Semeiology: 1. The science of signs and sign language. 2. the investigation of symptoms of diseases or the science of symptomology.

Semen: The male sperm cells and the fluid vehicle secreted by the testes and prostate gland respectively.

Sensate focus therapy: In treating sexual dysfunctions, the use of mutual touching and caressing in order to enhance pleasure and reduce anxiety.

Sensation: 1. The elementary process or experience aroused when a stimulus has excited a receptor. 2. the process of sensing. 3. (*Tichener*) with images and feelings, one of the three elements of consciousness. 4. in psychophysics, a discriminable experience.

Sensationalism: 1. The doctrine that all knowledge is derived from sensation. 2. the doctrine that all experience consists of sensations and their derivatives.

Sense: 1. A classification of experiences; a sense modality. 2. the meaning of anything, especially in summary form. 3. a receptor, especially when qualified with a modality, such as the *sense organ for hearing*. 4. a special kind of awareness, such as a *sense of fair play* or a *sense of justice*. 5. intelligence or good judgment.

Sense datum: 1. A sensation. 2. information given by receptor activity.

Sensed difference: A perceived difference in two stimuli that have been presented either successively or simultaneously.

Sensitive: 1. Pertaining to sensitivity. 2. describing an individual whose threshold of emotionality is low and is therefore easily hurt. 3. in psychic research, capable of receiving supernormal information.

Sensory adaptation: 1. A general concept referring to any alteration in a receptor as a result of stimulation. Depending on the condition of the organ and the nature of the stimulus, the effect may be either an increase or a decrease in sensitivity. 2. a reduction in sensitivity of a receptor as a result of prolonged stimulation. 3. in dark adaptation, the increased sensitivity of the rods under conditions of low illumination.

Sensory conditioning: A procedure in which two stimuli are paired over a number of trials until one of the two can be used as a substitute for the other in eliciting a response. For example, a light and a tone are sounded for a large number of trials. No reinforcement is given. Then either the light or the tone is reinforced until the desired response is elicited. If the other stimulus is effective in eliciting the response, *sensory conditioning* has taken place.

Sensory interaction: The mutual interdependence between sensory processes, such as the response of finding a bird in a tree by a combination of listening to it and searching for it with the visual apparatus.

Sentence-completion test: A test in which the subject must supply an appropriate word or phrase to complete a given sentence, or a test in which the subject completes a sentence item in any way that he sees fit. The first type is usually a test of ability, the second is often used as a projective technique.

Sentience: 1. Ability of a nervous system to receive stimuli. 2. the simplest form of cognition, in which there is bare sensing without associated meanings.

Sequence: 1. The following of one phenomenon by another. 2. a temporal series, or the order in which a series of events occurs. 3. a succession of quantities in which each is derived from the preceding by the same operation; a mathematical series.

Serial-anticipation method: In learning, the technique of presenting stimulus-response combinations successively, with each stimulus being the cue for the following response. When the subject can correctly anticipate all responses upon being presented with the stimuli, the list is considered learned.

Serial reinforcement: In a serial-learning problem, a series of reactions that reinforce or increase the probability of each choice. Thus, as the animal runs through the maze, each correct choice becomes a kind of reinforcement or confirming reaction and increases the probability of that choice being made again.

Sex anomaly: 1. A wide deviation from normal in the sexual organs. 2. a functional sexual deviation; a perversion.

Sex character: Any trait, structural or functional, that is typically found in one sex more than in another.

Sex chromosome: The chromosome, or dark staining body bearing the genes, responsible for determining the sex of the individual. In the human being sex is determined by a special pair called the XX chromosomes in the female and the XY in the male. The female chromosomes make a true pair, whereas in the male the Y chromosome is smaller than the X chromosome.

Sex differentiation: The interaction of those biological and environmental factors during development that jointly determine the differences between the sexes. Thus, the male's greater muscular strength is a joint function of inherent biological differences and of training.

Sex education: 1. Instruction in the physiology of reproduction. 2. instruction in the physiology of reproduction and in attitudes promoting good sexual adjustment toward sexuality in general and marriage in particular.

Sex-linked character: A trait transmitted by the sex chromosomes, such as red-green color-blindness.

Sex perversion: Sexual behaviour that differs widely from normal standards and is typically prohibited by law in most states; exhibitionism, fetishism, and rape are examples.

Sexual: 1. Pertaining to reproduction by the union of two different individuals who produce an egg and sperm respectively. 2. in general, pertaining to behaviour, feelings, or emotions associated with stimulation of the genital organs, erogenous zones, or with the process of reproduction.

Sexual aim: The goal of sexual satisfaction or pleasure; the release of sexual tension.

Sexual anesthesia: The inability to enjoy sexual activities; a lack of sexual feeling.

Sexual congress: Sexual intercourse; coition.

Sexual deviation: Any form of sexual behavior differing markedly from the standards set up by a given society. Child molestation, masochism, rape, and fetishism are examples of sexual deviations in our society.

Sexual function: A physiological function performed by members of one sex.

Sexual instinct: 1. (*Psychoam.*) The tendency toward pleasure seeking, particularly through achieving sexual aims and objects. 2. the tendency on the part of the mature organism to seek sexual union with a member of the opposite sex.

Sexual intercourse: 1. The introduction of the penis or male sexual organ into the vagina of the female with accompanying rhythmic pelvic movements to the point of orgasm. 2. the introduction of the penis into the body of another male; technically, anal intercourse.

Sexuality: 1. The capacity to behave sexually or to engage in sexual intercourse. 2. the characteristic of being attractive from the sexual point of view. 3. a tendency toward excessive concern with sex.

Sexual selection: A mating preference favoring certain physical or behavioral traits and eventually resulting in the preponderance of those traits in the population.

Sexual trauma: A highly disturbing or psychically harmful experience related to sex and likely to cause repression and subsequent anxiety.

S factor: A specific or special factor found in factor-analysis studies of ability tests. The specific factor is unique for each test and represents the kind of specialized ability needed to do well on that test.

Shame aversion therapy: In behaviour therapy, an aversive technique primarily applied to sexual deviations in which the behavior to be eliminated is performed in front of a neutral audience. The embarrassment to the patient serves as aversive reinforcement.

Shape constancy: The tendency to perceive objects as having the same shape regardless of wide variations in the conditions of viewing. Thus, plates on a table look round regardless of whether one is sitting or standing, although when one is sitting or standing, although when one is sitting, plates on the far end of the table cast a sharply elliptical image on the retina.

Shaping: (*Skinner*) Teaching a desired response by reinforcing the series of successive steps that lead to the final response.

Sheldon's constitutional theory of personality: Theory that each individual possesses some degree of each of three primary temperamental components: *wiscerotonia*, *somatatonia*, and *cerebrotonia*. *Viscerotonia* is revealed in such traits as relaxation in posture, love of physical comfort, enjoyment in companionship, eating, deep sleep, relaxation under alcohol, and orientation toward childhood and family relations. *Somatotonia* is characterized by assertiveness, love of adventure, need and enjoyment of exercise, love of risk, physical courage, indifference to pain, aggressiveness under alcohol, and orientation toward youth. *Cerebrotonia* is shown in such traits as restraint in posture, overly fast reactions, sensitivity, avoidance of social contacts, hypersensitivity to pain, and resistance to alcohol. Sheldon believes that he has found evidence that the three primary temperaments are related to three basic bodily builds: *ectomorphy*, *mesomorphy*, and *endomorphy*. The ectomorph tends toward a long, stringy, skinny body; the mesomorphy toward stockiness and good muscular development; and the endomorph toward roundness, heaviness, and a preponderance of visceral development.

Each of the temperamental and bodily components is measured on a 7-point scale. An extreme ectomorpy would be rated as a 7-1-1; an extreme viscerotonic, 1-7-1; an extreme endomorpy, 1-1-7. The individual who is average is rated 4-4-4. Sheldon reports correlations of over 80 for relational studies among the following temperamental and bodily traits: Viscerotonia correlates highly with endomorphy; somatotonia with mesomorphy; and cerebrotinia with eciomorphy. However, independent studies of the relation between bodily build and temperament or personality have failed to confirm Sheldon's findings and the matter remains controversial.

Shell shock: Any of several situational neuroses associated with prolonged exposure to battle. The term was used in World War I; the corresponding terms in World War II was *battle fatigue*.

Skinner, Burrhus F.: American psychologist. Skinner was educated at Hamilton College and at Harvard University, where he received a Ph.D. degree in 1931. He has held a Research Fellowship of the National Research Council, a junior fellowship of the Harvard Society of Fellows, and a Guggenheim Fellowship, and during the years 1942-1943 he served as a director of a wartime research project sponsored by General Mills.

Skinner has held academic appointments at the University of Minnesota, at Indiana University, and Harvard, where he delivered the William James Lectures in 1947, and was professor of psychology from 1948 to 1974, when he became professor emeritus. His books include: *The Behavior of Organisms, Walden Two, Science and Human Behaviour, Verbal Behavior, Schedules of Reinforcement* with C. B Ferster, *Cumulative Record, Beyond Freedom and Dignity, Reflections on Behavior and Society,* and *The Shaping of a Behaviorist.*

Skinner's Operant Conditioning: Skinner's system of operant conditioning is a descriptive behaviorism that seeks to establish the laws of behavior through the study of operant learning. An *operant* is an emitted response, in contrast to *respondents,* class of behavior studied by the technique of Pavlovian conditioning.

By contrast, operants may be studied independently of the stimulus conditions that give rise to them--indeed, a in the usual case the stimulus may be unknown. The experimental arrangement for studying operant behavior in the laboratory consists of what has come to be known as a Dkinner box, an enclosure in which the animal is maintained free from distracting stimuli and in which he can receive a reinforcement upon emitting the proper operant. In the case of the rat, the operant is a bar press, and the reinforcement is a pellet of food.

As many times as the rat presses the bar, a magazine will deliver a pellet and conditioning will proceed at a rapid rate. More recently the pigeon has come into extensive use in the Skinner box, and in this case the operant is pecking at a dot, the reinforcement a measured amount of grain.

The fundamental law of operant conditioning is that if the occurrence of an operant is followed by a reinforcing stimulus, the rate of responding will increase. Rate of responding is typically measured during a run to extinction, since the time-consuming process of eating during the reinforcing series obscures the rate of responding. Reinforcers may be both positive and negative. Stimuli such as food, water, or sexual contacts, which serve as positive reinforcers, directly increase the probability of a response. Negative reinforcers strengthen the probability of a response only when they are removed from the situation. Such reinforcers are exemplified by shock, bright lights, loud noises, etc.

Perhaps the most important variable associated with reinforcement is the time schedule on which the reinforcing stimulus is delivered. Continuous reinforcement is the regular presentation of the reinforcement with each operant response. Intermittent reinforcement is irregular reinforcement delivered according to a predetermined time schedule. There are two important types of intermittent reinforcement, *interval* ad *fixed-ratio.* In *interval reinforcement,* the reinforcement is given at certain fixed intervals of time, say every two minutes, regardless of how frequently the animal responds. Under such conditions of periodic reinforcement the shorter intervals yield the highest rates of responding. In *ratio reinforcement*, the animal is given reinforcement after a certain number of responses; for example, the pigeon might get a portion of grain only after pecking ten times. In ratio reinforcement very high rates of responding can be maintained with high ratios, provided these are approached gradually. Reinforcement schedules may also be arranged as *variable intervals* or *variable ratios* under special research conditions. Secondary reinforcement occurs when a stimulus not originally a reinforcer becomes reinforcing through association with a reinforcing stimulus. For example, if a weak light is flashed each time the reinforcement is delivered upon the animal's pressing the bar, the light will come to have reinforcing qualities and can be used to maintain bar pressing for long periods of time in the absence of any primary reinforcer.

Stimulus generalization or induction can be studied by a process of having the reinforcer delivered upon presentation of a positive stimulus and not delivered upon presentation of a neutral or negative stimulus. For example, a tone of 256 Hz may be followed by a delivery of food, while a tone of 100 Hz will not be followed by a delivery of food. The animal will learn to press the bar only in response to the positive tone. The limits of discrimination may be studied by gradually reducing the separation between the stimuli.

The learning of complex skills can be studied by a process called *shaping*. In shaping, a series of acts is gradually brought under control of the reinforcement by reinforcing each separate act in turn. Thus, through shaping, seal can be taught to play "My Country `Tis of Thee'" on a calliope by first reinforcing the animals for approaching the instrument, then for pressing the first correct key, and so forth until the complete performance can be run off for a final single reinforcement.

Skinner's basic techniques of operant conditioning have been extended into the use of human teaching machines that operate on the principle of self-reinforcing learning. The use of reinforcement with speech sounds has made it possible to demonstrate that human symbolic behavior can be learned according to the same principles that apply to more elementary forms of learning. Finally, Skinner and his associates have attempted to extend their methods into the field of behavior therapy (q.v.)

Social habit: A consistent and

relatively automatic form of behavior utilized in social situations.

Social heritage: The institutions, folkways, mores, and cultural patterns transmitted from one generation to the next.

Social immobility: A condition of rigid social systems in which individuals of one class find it difficult or impossible to move to another class.

Social learning theory: Social learning theory grew out of the work of John Dollard and Neal Miller at Yale in the 1940s and more recently of Albert Bandura (q.v.), the leading contemporary exponent of this point of view.

Social learning theory is a modified form of behaviorism that stresses the importance of cognitive processes s causal agents in behavior. In their early work Dollard and Miller emphasized the theoretical importance of imitation in the development of behaviour. Bandura confirmed their hypothesis in a series of well-known experiments on modeling and observational learning conducted on children. Among these studies were experiments showing that children can learn aggression by watching adults model aggressive behavior, an important finding in support of the position that aggression in human beings is not necessarily inherent but may be the result of environmental influences. Modeling has also been shown to be a useful therapeutic technique, as exemplified by subjects who fear objects or situations, are desensitized and taught skills useful in coping with their fears by observing others, then behave toward the same situations without fear.

Bandurahas also stressed beliefs, expectation, choice, and self-reinforcement as important determines of behaviour, in contrast to the radical behaviorists, who assert that reinforcement acts on behavior without regard to conscious or cognitive processes. In part Bandura's emphasis on cognitive processes in the causation of behaviour is a reflection of his extensive use of human subjects as opposed to the traditional use of animals by other behaviourists. His work has received wide critical acclaim and been an important influence in the recent trend toward a cognitive psychology and the development of behavior therapy.

Social psychology: The branch of psychology concerned with psychological processes that occur in groups. It deals with the behavioral interaction of individuals within groups and the interaction between groups. The social psychologist emphasizes those concepts that are derived from the study of individual behaviour, whereas the sociologist tends to emphasize concepts derived from the study of institutions and groups. There is free borrowing of problems and concepts among sociologists, psychologists, and anthropologists.

Social reality: The individual's perception of a situation based on his shared beliefs with others. Does not necessarily conform to physical reality.

Social work: The field of social service that attempts to improve social conditions in a given community.

Socioeconomic status: The individual's relative position in the community. Some of the factors contributing to socioeconomic status are profession, income, place, and cost of residence and relatives.

Socioempathy: Awareness of one's own and another's status.

Sociogenesis: The origination of social behavior.

Sociogenetic: 1. Pertaining to the origin of society. 2. pertaining to behaviour as determined by social experience.

Sociogram: A diagram showing the interactions between members of a group. The two accompanying illustrations show the social interactions of (a) a powerful person and (b) a popular person.

Somatotypology: The classification of individuals on the basis of their bodily build.

Span of consciousness: Historically, the number of objects of which the individual can be simultaneously aware. The term is now obsolete.

Spasm: A localized, involuntary muscular contraction.

Spasmoarthria: The speech characteristic of those suffering from spastic paralysis.

Spasticity: 1. An increased tone in the voluntary muscles, heightened resistance to movement of a joint, and a drawn-up appearance of a limb. 2. spastic paralysis.

Spastic paralysis: A paralysis characterized by increased tension in the muscles due to loss of upper motor neuron control. A limb affected is drawn up and the movements are spasmodic and jerky.

Statistical psychology: The branch of psychology that utilizes statistical models and techniques to derive explanatory constructs. An early example of such a technique was Ebbinghaus' use of the formula $R = k \log t$—or retention is the function of the logarithm of time.

Stress interview: An interview conducted while the interviewee is deliberately put under an emotional strain.

Strees test: A real-life situation in which the individual is put under pressure while his ability to carry out a task is measured. For example, he might be required to build a bridge over a stream during a simulated attack by enemy forces.

Stroboscopic illusion or effect: 1. The apparent motion of two stimuli presented in close succession. Motion pictures are common examples of the stroboscopic effect. 2. the perceptual effect of illuminating a moving object with an intermittent light with the result that it may be made to stand still, reverse itself, or move forward at any desired speed. Thus, if a stroboscopic light is directed on a rotating fan, the blades can be seen as if they were motionless, made to reverse, etc.

Stroke: A sudden cerebral accident caused by the rupture of a blood vessel in the brain. If the damage is extensive, the individual will suffer paralysis on the side opposite that on which the rupture occurred.

Structuralism; structural psychology: A system of psychology associated with the teachings of Wilhelm Wundt (q.v.) and Edward Bradford Tichener (q.v.). Structuralism held that psychology is human experience studied from the point of view of the experiencing person. The method of psychology is introspection, or self-inspection. The aim of psychology, according to the structuralists, was to investigate the *what*, the *how*, and te *why* of experience or consciousness. Under *what* are included the results of introspective analysis of the mental processes. In short, the question of *what* deals with the *content* of experience and the problem of its analysis. *How* is concerned with the manner in which the various mental processes are related to each other—that is, with the problem of synthesis. *Why* is concerned with the cause-and-effect relationships between the mental processes and between experience and underlying physiological processes in the nervous system.

The structuralists resolved the problem of the relation of consciousness to brain or body by invoking the principle of *psychophysical parallelism*, a form of dualism in which mind and body are considered to be separate substances without interaction between them but parallel to each other in such a way that for every event in consciousness there is a corresponding event in body. However, mind does not *cause* states of consciousness. The two are strictly parallel, never interactive. Wundt and Titchener's position on the mind-body problem was made necessary by their separation of mental events from the totality of behavior. It is not possible to use a nonmaterial mind to explain a physical body nor a physical body to explain a nonphysical mind.

The analysis of consciousness into its elements resulted in three irreducibles: sensations, images, and affective states (states of feeling and emotion). Each of these is an element in the sense that it cannot be further broken down by introspective analysis. But each can be described in terms of its attributes.

All elements have the attributes of quality, intensity, and duration. Quality it the most fundamental attribute, which enables the individual to distinguish one experience from another; thus, in the sense of taste, sweet is clearly distinct from sour, and in vision, blue from yellow.

The attribute of intensity is the quantitative aspect of experience; loudness-softness, brightness-dullness, weakness-strength are some of the descriptive terms we utilize to characterize this attribute. The attribute of duration characterizes how long a sensation, image, or affective state persists in time.

For some years structuralism was the dominant school of psychology in the United States and Germany; thereafter it was successfully attacked by rival systems. In the United States, functionalism and behaviorism became the favorite system; in Germany, Gestalt psychology. Structuralism failed because it was too narrow.

It provided excellent subjective reports of sensory, imaginal, and affective states of consciousness, but it could not successfully extend the method to include the behavior of children, or animals, or to provide for mental tests and behavioral studies of learning.

Structure: 1. (*noun*) An enduring organization, pattern, or aggregate of elements. In this usage, *structure* is contrasted with *function*, the latter referring to a *process* that is transitory and does not lend itself to description in terms of elements or organization of parts. However, many psychologists employ *structure* in referring to processes that have stability. Freud, for example, spoke of the structure of the mind in terms of ego, id, and superego, referring thereby to processes rather than entities.

T

T data: Refers to any data based on the use of standardized testing procedures.

T. score: A tipe of score based on the transformation of normalized standard scores to a scale based on a mean of 50 and a standard deviation of 10.

T. test: Refers to me of a number of statistical tests of significance based upon the statistic.

Taboo: Refer any banned or prohibited act, object or behavior.

Tabula Rasa: Means blank tablet.

Tachistoscope: It is an instrument which presents visual materials under conditions of very brief exposures.

Tactile circle: An area on the surface of the skin within which two points presented simultaneously are sensed as one.

Tactual: Pertaining to the sense of touch; tactile.

Tadoma method: A method used for communicating by the deaf and the deaf blind by placing the fingers on the speaker's lips and cheeks.

Tag question: Any interrogative formed by appending a "tag" onto a declarative sentence. For example, in "It's raining out, isn't it?" the 'isn't it?" is a *tag*.

Talbot-Plateau law: Refers to the generalization according to which when the rate of a flickering light is high enough so that a steady light is seen is well have a perceived brightness that is the mean of the periodic impressions.

Talion principle: The principle of retribution, "an eye for an eye and a tooth for a too!th."

Tangentially: Refers to a manner of speaking wherein questions I are answered in inappropriately oblique and irrelevant ways.

Target: Refers to the item which the subject searches for in an array of items. If more than one item is searched for, the several are collectively called the target set.

Tartinal's tone: Difference tone.

The term honors an 18th century Italian violinist who first noted the existence of , difference tones during double-stopping of a violin string he used them as a cue to assist in the tuning of his instrument.

Taurine: It is an amino acid suspected as being a neurotransmitter.

Tautophone: It is a projective device wherein the subject listens to a recording of unintelligible sounds and is asked to elaborate on what they seem to be saying.

Taylor-Russell tables: A set of tables which enables on to asses, 'the value of a particular test in selecting individuals.

Tay-Sach's disease: An inherited disease which is characterized by severe neurological deterioration and accompanying mental and physical retardation.

Teat: Refers to the nipple of a mammary gland.

Telecopisa: A visual disorder wherel, n ol~jects are perceived as being further away then they are and the sense of depth generally is exaggerated.

Telefractor: It is a device which augments sound waves and converts them into vibration patterns which can be felt on the skin. It is used as an aid in teaching speech and language skills to the deaf.

Telencephalon: It is a major subdivision of the forebiain. Its principal structures.

Telencephalon: It is a major subdivision of the forebrain. Its principal structures contain the cerebral cortex, the basal ganglia and the limbic system. Also know as the end brain.

Teleotherapeutics: Refers to the use of hypnotic suggestion in therapy.

Telepathy: Refers to the hypothesized ability for direct mental contact between two or more persons.

Telesis: The assumption of certain values as goals to be attained by conscious striving toward those ends.

Telesthesia: Refers to hyphothesized paranormal abilities to perceive events, objects thoughts, etc. without the use of normal sensory systems, e.g., dairvayance, telepathy.

Tendon: Refers to fibrous connective tissue by which muscles are I attached to bones.

Teratology: It is the study of birth defects, particularly the Nochemical agents that cause them.

Territoriality: Refers to the tendency to defend or protect one's space ageinst invasion or incursion.

Test age: The score obtained on a test that has been standardized in age units.

Test battery: A collection of tests whose results can be combined to produce a single score.

Test scaling: It is the process of setting up a scale for a given test. The usual procedure is to administer the test to a sample group of persons and assign values to each item based on the scores obtained from the sample individuals.

Test sophistication: Refers to the extent to which a person has had experience with (psychological) tests and hence is aware of the general nature and procedures in use.

Test: 1. A set of standardized questions administered to an individual for the purpose of measuring his aptitude or achievement in a given field. 2. more generally, any measurement that yields quantitative data, such as an unstandardized test administered in a school-room. 3. in logic, any operation applied to reasoning in order to assess its validity. 4. a statistical operation designed to assess the significance of a statistic.

Testee: Refers one who takes a test.

Testis: A male gonad or sex organ. One of two reproductive glands located in the scrotum that produce speriatozoa and the male hormone.

Tetanizing shock: Refers to electric shock strong enough to cause tetanus.

Tetanus: Sustained tonic muscular spasms or an acute infectious disease caused by the tetanus bacillus, the primary symptom of which is a state of painful, persistent, tonic spasms of serveral voluntary muscles.

Tetany: It is a condition marked by intermittent tonic mu~cular spasms, generally in the extermities.

Tetartanopia: An extremely rare from of dichromatism wherein reds and grcens are seen normally but blues and yellows are poorly distinguished, with yellow.

Tetrahydrocannabinol (THC): The paychoactive ingredient in marijuana and hashish, which are made from plants of the cannabis family.

Textual: Refers to which are a class of verbal operants controlled by visual verbal stimuli like words or symbols.

Thalamic theory of the emotions: A theory postulated by Cannon and Bard that stresses the role of the hypothalamus as the center of the emotions. It is assumed that emotion-provoking stimuli gives rise to impulses that stimulate the hypothalamus, which, in turn, activates the cortex and the visceral process. The cortical activation arouses the emotional experience; the visceral stimulation readies the individual for an emergency.

Thalamotomy: It is a form of psychosurgery wherein thalamic fibers are severed.

Thanatology: It is the study of the psychological and medical aspects surrounding death and dying.

Thanatomania: Refers to homicidal or suicidal maina or wasting away and ultimate death following awareness that one has transgressed seriously some societal taboo or believing that one has been bewitched.

Thanatophobia: Refers to morbid, pathological fear to death or an irrational fear of dead things, specially human corpses.

The law of effect holds that, other things being equal, those bonds or associations that lead to a satisfying state of affairs are stamped in and those that lead to a dissatisfying or annoying state of affairs are stamped out. The law of exercise—also operative in trial-and-error learning—states that, other things being equal, those associations or bonds that are practiced or exercised are stamped an and those not used fade out.

Thorndike found that practice per se was not effective in stamping in learning. Practice must be accompanies by a reward or by knowledge of results in order to promote learning. Moreover, he discovered in his early research on the law of effect that only the first half of it was correct. Punishment does not stamp out learning; it only inhibits the performance of learning, and when the punishment is removed, the response will reappear.

Thorndike's research in the role of rewards and knowledge of results in learning led to the discovery of the spread of effect, or the carryover of the benefits of reward to adjacent responses in close proximity to the correct one. But he also had to admit—largely as a result of the findings of the Gestalt school of psychology—that the role of reward was not entirely mechanical or blind. Belongingness is also an important factor in facilitating learning, and items that naturally go together are therefore more easily learned than those merely juxtaposed without regard to their relationship to each other. Many of the details of Thorndike's theory of trial-and-error learning have been brought into question by subsequent research, but contemporary authorities in the field of learning rank him as one of the greatest figures in this important area of psychology.

The standardization of an intelligence or other type of

aptitude test used in psychological clinics or schools involves five steps. First, items must be written or selected. Second, a preliminary tryout of the items arranged in test form is held with a large sample of testees. Poor items are weeded out and approximate time limits and scoring standards are determined.

Third, the standardization administration is conducted on a representative sample of testees from all parts of the country. This process may involve years of work by trained specialists and may cost millions of dollars. Fourth, on the basis of the standardization administration, norms or standards are developed.

In the case of individual verbal tests these may be given in mental age units or in IQ units. In the use of group tests they may be in percentile units. Fifth, the validity and reliability of the test are determined. Validity measures the extent to which the test measures what it was designed to measure.

Reliability measures the degree to which the test gives consistent results from time to time. Psychologists employ many different types of tests for the measurement of intelligence and special aptitudes. There are also specialized aptitude and achievement tests for industrial, military, and educational use. Broadly speaking, aptitude and achievement tests may be divided into: (a) *individual tests* and *group tests'* (b) *verbal tests* and *performance tests*. Individual tests are given to a single testee by a trained psychologist. Group tests re given to large numbers of testees simultaneously. Verbal tests require the understanding and use of language in either oral or written form. Performance tests make minimal use of language, utilizing instead concrete nonverbal materials.

Theomania: Delusionary condition wherein the individual considers that he or she is God or has, -more modestly, direct, divine inspiration for thoughts and actions.

Theophobia: Refers to irrational fear of retribution from God for one's sins.

Theorem of escape: The generalization that the self tends not to be influenced by experiences incongruent with its present state of functioning.

Theoretical explanation: A tentative explanation based in part on whatever facts are available, supplemented with hypotheses that fill any gaps in knowledge of the phenomenon under consideration.

Theoretical mode: An estimate of the true mode obtained by fitting a theoretical frequency curve to a set of observations and erecting an abscissa. The mode is at the point of the abscissa.

Theory: A general principle formulated to explain a group of related phenomena.

Theory-begging: A scientific fallacy in which a theoretical assumption is given the name of an established fact, thereby seeming to prove the correctness of the theory.

Therapeutics: Refers to any branch of science or medicine concerned with treatment and cure of disease or other abornal conditions.

Therapy: Refers to all manners and formers of treatment of disease or disorder.

Theriomorphism: The attribution to humans of nonhuman traits which are characteristics and qualities.

Thermanalgesia: A pathological condition wherein the normal painful reaction to hot stimuli is not experienced.

Thermanesthesia: It is the insensitivity to temperature changes an inability to experience normal warmth and cold..

Thinking type: (*Jung*) A category for individuals whose actions and reaction s are dominated by thinking.

Thorndike puzzle box: One of the earliest (if not the earliest) pieces of laboratory apparatus specifically designed to study learning.

Thorndike's Trial-and-Error Learning: Thorndike's system of trial-and-error learning takes as its fundamental principles the laws of effect and exercise developed from the results of his early studies of animal learning typified by his famous experiments on cats in puzzle boxes. Thorndike announced the generalization that the correct response in a puzzle box was only gradually stamped in (imprinted) during a slow process in which the animal proceeded blindly, the correct response selected out of a number of irrelevant responses by the operation of the law of effect.

Thought stopping: In behaviour therapy, a technique in which the therapist stops undesirable thought sequences by shouting "Stop!" The patient is then instructed to apply the technique to himself.

Thought withdrawal: It is experience which somehow one's thoughts have been taken away, from one's head.

Thurstone-type scales: Refers to a number of scales, constructed to measure attitudes. The general procedure for constructing such scales is to take a number of statements reflecting particular attitudes with respect to some topic and have a large number of persons sort them in piles ranging from most strongly agreeing with the statement to most strongly disagreeing with it.

The percentage of judges placing each statement in the various piles calculated and forms the basis for determining the scale values assigned to each statement.

Thymergastic behaviour: A pathological condition of the emotional and affective processes.

Thymus: A ductless gland, located in the lower neck region. Its function is uncertain. It reaches its maximum size about the time of puberty and then atrophies.

Thyroid: An endocrine gland, located in the neck, whose function is the regulation of general metabolism.

Tissue: Refers to any organic structure consisting of cells with similar structures and commcn functions which are organised or bound together in some manner.

Titillate: Means to excite or arouse one sexually or tickle.

T-maze: A maze shaped like a T, make up of an approach alley and two arms, either one of which the subject may choose.

Toilet training: Means training an infant to urinate and defecate in the socially accepted place and manner.

Token economy: The utilization of secondary reinforcement to shape behavior. In the hospital setting the individual may earn tokens that can be utilized for television time, in exchange for passes, special foods, and the like.

Tolerance, drug: Refers to a condition of diminished responsiveness to a particular drug due to repeated tolerance has developed increased, increased doses are needed to produce the effects achieved earlier with small doses.

Tolman's purposive behaviorism: Tolman's Purposive Behaviorism is a systematic treatment of the data of psychology from the point of view of the Gestalt point of view of a molar behaviorism. The systematic framework is a careful blending of the Gestalt point of view with the scientific methodology of the behaviorists. It strongly emphasizes learning, particularly animal learning and more specifically maze learning in rats, a research topic to which its author was devoted.

Tolman's fundamental law of acquisition holds that animal maze learning consists in the building up of sign Gestalts or cognitive processes consisting of learned relationships between environmental cues and the animal's expectations. A pattern of sign Gestalts is called a cognitive map, and it is the animal's cognitive map of the maze that enables him to run it correctly.

The evidence for cognitive processes in animals comes from three types of experiments: place learning, reward expectancy, and latent learning. *Place learning* involves a situation wherein the animal learns a maze whose cues favor going to the same place whether or not the response remains the same. That is, if started from a different direction, the animal may have to learn first to go to a certain place by making a right turn, then to the same place by making a left turn. Such learning, Tolman and his associates claimed, was easier for animals than *response learning*, in which the animal learned to go to different places but always by making the same directional turn. *Reward-expectancy* experiments involve having animals learn to go through a maze for a certain type of reward, whereupon the reward is suddenly switched to a less favored type of food.

The animals' evident disturbance, Tolman holds, indicates the expectancy for a certain type of reward. *Latent learning*, the third type of evidence in favor of cognitive processes, involves having nonhungry animals wander through a maze unrewarded for a number of trials. Upon being made hungry and given a reward, their very rapid catching up to regularly rewarded animals shows that they had been learning incidentally, even though not making the specific responses that led through the maze.

Tomography: An X-ray technique that enables one to obtain a picture of the three dimensional structure of tissue.

Topectomy: A variation of the frontal lobotomy where in small cuts are made through the thalamofrontal tracts.

Topological psychology: A descriptive term often used of Kurt Lewin's filed theory.

Tough-minded: In a formulation by William James, one of two types or categories into which people can be placed. The tough-minded are empirical, materi alistic, skeptical, pessimistic, and fatalistic in their thinking.

Tourette's syndrome: A neurological disorder which characterized in mild from by involuntary tics and movements and, in advanced cases, by large involuntary bodily movements, noises like barks and whistles, and in many instances an uncontrollable urge to utter obscenities.

Toxemla: Refers to an abnormal condition produced by toxi substances carried throughout the body by the blodstream.

Training: 1. The systematic series of activities—instruction, practice, review, examinations, etc.—to which the individual being trained is subjected 2. a program of physical exercise designed to improve physical fitness. 3. the care and instruction of the young. In common speech and informal writing, toilet training may be intended by the concept.

Transactional analysis (TA): It is a form of psychotherapy developed by Eric Brene. It is practiced in a straightforward group setting wherein the I primary goal is to have the client achieve an adaptive, mature and realistic attitude toward life.

Transactional theory of perception: The functionalistic theory of perception that our fundamental perceptions are learned reactions on the basis of our transactions or interactions with the environment. The transactional functionalists hold that we build up probabilities of what we build up probabilities of what to expect perceptually on the basis of our experiences and that we bring these probabilities of what to expect perceptually on the basis of our experiences and that we bring these probabilities to each new situation. The most striking instance of this effect is seen when the individual brings his expectation of rooms as being rectilinear to a distorted room. He will distort the people in it in order to make the room seem perceptually normal.

Transactional therapy: A form of therapy in which the games family members engage in with each other are analyzed and replaced with more adaptive modes of behavior.

Transactonal phychology: An extension of the basic ideas of transactionalism from the study of perception to other areas of human behavior, notably social interaction.

Transcendental Meditation (TM): It is a form of meditation and the techniques for practising it developed and most effectively promulgated by the Maharishi Mahesh Yogi.

Transcendental meditation: The type of meditation involving a mantra as taught by the Maharishi Mahesh Yogi.

Transcortical: Across the cortex: or more properly, from one part of the cortex to another by way of connecting tracts.

Transducer: Refers to any device which converts energy from one from to another.

Transexual: An individual who is physically one sex but psychologically the opposite. A number of such individuals elect to have surgical and hormonal treatments to alter their physical appearance and gender.

Transfer: Learning in one situation carrying over to another situation. In general, there are two broad types of transfer, positive and negative. In positive transfer, learning in one situation facilitates learning in another. Positive transfer is illustrated by learning to drive in one car and then driving in another. There is almost 100 percent positive transfer. Negative transfer occurs when learning in one situation has a detrimental effect on learning in another situation. Negative transfer is illustrated when the individual attempts to draw in a mirror. Because mirrors reverse right and left, he has considerable difficulty since he must build up a new eye-hand coordination that contradicts all his past experience.

Transfer by generalization: The transfer of general principles from one situation to another rather than the transfer of specific behavior patterns.

Transmission: 1. The sequential firing of one neuron in response to the firing of another. 2. the genetic passing of a trait to the offspring. 3. the sending of a message by a transmitter to a receiver. 4. the handing down of customs, mores, and folkways, form generation to generation.

Transpersonal psychology: A cross-cultural approach to psychology blending Eastern and Western conceptions of human nature.

Transposition: 1. Any interchange of position between two or more elements in a system. The change may be temporal, spatial, or psychological. 2. in music, the changing of a tune or composition from one key to another. 3. in learning situations, the subject's reacting to the relationship among the elements of the problem instead of to the elements themselves. Thus, if a hen is taught to peck a grain from the darker of two shades of gray paper, A and B (B being the darker), and is then presented with B and C where C is the darker, the hen will peck at C without difficulty. Reinforcement theory, however, would predict that she would continue to peck at B, since this was the reinforced response. The Gestalt psychologists use transposition experiments to support their theory of transfer of training as based on a transfer of relationships.

Transvestisms: It is a condition marked by a persistent desire to dress in the clothes generally considered by society as appropriate for the other sex.

Trend test: Refers to any of several statistical tests which assess whether two or more trends seen in ~he data can be said to be reliable different from each other.

Triage: It is the process of screening the sick, wounded or injured in times of crisis and classifying them into three groups: those who will likely recover eventually without therapy, those who are expected to die no matter what is done to assist them and those whose recovery is deemed to depend on their receiving adequate cafe.

Tribadism: Means rubbing together of the genitals, particularly when both partners are female.

Trichesthesia: Refers to the tactile sensation experienced in the skin when a hair is touched or moved.

Trichomans vaginalis: A form of vaginitis charactrized by itching, redness and burning, especially around the vulva. It is caused by the Trichmonas protozoa and, although it is not linked directly with sexual intercourse, it is often classified as a venereal disease because it can be communicated through intercourse.

Trichopathophobia: A from of trichophobia seen in women and manifested by abnormal anxiety surrounding any growth of facial hair.

Tridimensional theory of feeling: Woundt's theory according to which all feelings could be represented as being composed of three dimensions, pleasure-displeasure, excitement depression and tension -relaxation.

Triple-X sydrome: A chromosomal anomaly wherein three X chromosomes Are present. Such individuals are phenotypically female, sexually normal and usually fertile, although menstrual problems- and early menopause Are common.

Triskaidekaphobia: Refers to fear of the number that results from the operation of subtracting I from 14.

Troilism: Refers to deep desire to have sexual relations in the presence of others.

Tropin: Combining from used to indicate the stimulating effect of a substance on an organ or other site.

Tryptophan: An amino acid needed for normal growth and development. It functions as a precursor in the production of the inhibitory neurotransmitter serotonin.

Turing's test: It is a "test" of the adequacy of an artificial intelligence device on the question whether or not it can be said to I think.

Turner's syndrome: A cromosomal anomaly in phenotypic females. The basic genetic defect is a missing sex chromosome, so that the total the count is 45, X. The syndrome is marked by short stature and absence of ovaries. With female sex hormones administered at the age of puberty, normal secondary sex characteristics appear, although the sterility cannot be corrected.

Twitch: It is a simple, spasmodic muscular contraction.

Type a personality: A temperament characterized by excessive drive and competiti-veness, an unrealistic sense of time urgency, inappropriate ambition, a reluctance to provide self evaluation, a tendency to emphasize quantity of output over quality and a need for control.

Type b personality: A temprament characterized by a relaxed easy-going approach to life, a focus on quality over quantity, low competitiveness and a tendency for self-reflection.

U

Unconscious inference: A judgment that is not verbalized but is acted upon without awareness.

"Uppers" (or "ups"): Street slang for any drug which is having stimulating, arousing effects. Most of these drugs have been amphetamines or amphetamine-derived.

UCS: Commonly used by psychoanalysts as the shortened form of unconscious stimulus or mind.

Ufibers: Short fibers connecting adjacent gyri in the cerebral cortex.

UG: Probably it has been the-worst acronym ever introduced into science, it stands for universal grammar and would not be included here at all except that such prominent theorists as Chomsky insist upon using it.

UInar reflex: Response when tendon of bent forearm is struck hence not strictly a reflex.

Ulnar muscle: Muscle on inner side of forearm, frequently used as an area for experiments in touch localization.

Ulous: A suffix which means tending toward.

Ultra: Combining for-in which means going beyond, extreme or excessive.

Ultradiad rhythms: Refers to any of the many biologic rhythms that are shorter than one day.

Ultrasonic: (literally, beyond sound) pertaining to sound waves of frequencies beyond the range of human hearing that is, greater than 20, 000 Hz.

Ultraviolet: The electromagnetic radiation the wavelength of which is shorter than that to which the normal human eye responds, *e.g.*, below roughly 400 nm.

Ululation: Animal-like groans and cries of some mental defectives hysterical persons, and, psychotics.

Umklammerungs response: The startle response in an infant.

Umweg behaviour: The detour behaviour or roundabout behaviours.

Umweg: Round about or circuitous.

Umwelt: 1, The environment that is meaningful 2. in existential literature, nature in relation to man.

Unambivalent: (Psychoan.) Not opposite in kind or nature-commonly applied to two motives or affects existing in the same person, as love and respect In contrast, love and hate for a single object, person, or group are considered ambivalent. See also ambivalence.

Unbiased estimate: Any estimate which is made on the basis of adequate and representative sampling.

Unbiased estimator: Any statistic which, in principle, gives a value for any sample which is an unbiased estimate of the true value in the full population. The mean has been an unbiased estimator.

Unbiased: A term used to characterize operations or processes which display no bias, e.g., decision-making that reveals no prejudices.

Uncertainty: 1. Generally, refers to the state of belief when one does not fully believe, when one is unsure. 2. In information theory, refers to the degree to which there are no constraints upon the choices one has available or upon the possible outcomes of a situation.

Uncinate hallucinations: Taste and smell hallucinations, usually unpleasant, caused by pathological condition in the uncinate gyrus of the hippocampal convolution of the temporal lobe.

Uncinate seizures: Convulsions which are caused by organic disease in the uncinate gyrus.

Uncomplicated bereavement: Normal reaction to the death of a loved one in the form of various expressions of sadness, guilt, depression and the like that are deemed appropriate to one's experiences and interactions with the deceased while alive.

Unconditioned response or reflex: A response evoked by a stimulus without the necessity of learning. Thus, salivation to food is a natural, unlearned response that occurs at the beginning of a conditioning series, before learning trials have been initiated. Salivation to the, sound of the bell, by contrast, is a *conditioned* response, dependent upon learning.

Unconditioned stimulus: A stimulus that evokes a response without the necessity of learning or conditioning. In the example provided by Pavlov's dogfood-bell experiment, the food is the unconditioned stimulus, whereas the bell is the conditioned stimulus.

Unconscious cognitive process: Generally, any process which involves thinking, reasoning, judging, problem-solving, etc. which takes place without consciousness, without awareness.

Unconscious knowledge: Knowledge that a person is not aware of possessing, knowledge that Is tacit.

Unconscious memory: (Psychoan.) Repressions; memories that have been forced out of the conscious level of mind into the unconscious.

Unconscious mind: A trouble some and controversial term used, metaphorically, by psychoanalysts to subsume the basic drives, repressed ideas, and unwelcome impulses; it is the part of the psyche in which the id reigns supreme and which is dominated by the pleasure principle Free associations and dream analyses are said, by psychoanalysts, to be the royal road into the unconscious mind.

Unconscious motivation: Motivation of which the individual has been unaware. For example, the individual may forget an unpleasant appointment, convinced that it was a mere accident. The depth psychologist believes that it is revealing of a wish to forget.

Unconscious: A loose term connoting activities which proceed without concomitant awareness, such as digestion, pupilary reflexes, or heart beats. In the older discussions of habit, references were made to the automaticity of well-established habits, no conscious control being considered necessary to maintain them. The adjective has a mentalistic connotation hence it is not used by objectivists.

Uncontrolled: Referring to variables not regulated or held constant by the experimenter.

Underachievement: Performance that does not measure up to the individual's level of aptitude.

Underachiever: A person who does not perform at the level which is indicated by his aptitude.

Underdetermined: Of situations in which there has been insufficient evidence, data or information to determine value or the correct alternative in a set of choices, etc.

Undergeneralization: The term used for the use of a word for & smaller and more specialized category of objects, events or circumstances than it is normally used for. Such under extensions, as they are also called, have been common in young children, for example restricting the label "kitty" to but one cat.

Underproductive: Refers to

unusually poor responses to the inkblots.

Understand: To comprehend, to appreciate the deep meaning of a thing or a process.

Understanding: 1. Refers to the process of apprehending meaning 2. In historical writings, refers to the faculty by means of which the individual apprehends meaning. 3. Sympathy; feeling for another's poins of view.

Underweight: Refers to a condition in which body weight is I or more below the norms for a person's body type and age.

Undifferentiated: Refers to tissues that have not yet developed into characteristic forms and structures according to their her ditary potential.

Undistributed middle, fallacy of. An argument which leads to an invalid conclusion because of the use of a premise that is not distributed. For example, given that "All Communists are atheists" and "Max is an atheist" to conclude that "Max is a Communist", would be to fall prey to the fallacy. To rescue the syllogism one would need to have an additional premise such as, "All atheists are members of the Communist party." The obviously fallacious aspects are shown if the syllogism takes a more blatant form such as : "Max is a: man," "Sam is a man," therefore, "Max is Sam."

Undoing: The process whereby, according to psychoanalysts, the unconscious mind seeks to' wipe out painful thoughts and memories.

Unfinished business: Uncompleted tasks which do not get terminated with a desired degree of finality from the subject's point of view, and which become objects of continuing unpleasant concern or tension.

Unfolding: Refers to a type of multidimensional scaling developed by Clyde Coombs. The technique has been based on having a subject rank order a number of stimuli according to preference. The resulting preference ordering reflects an ideal point and the individual preferences are then "unfolded" mathematically to display the locations of the scaled objects in any number of dimensions relative to the ideal point.

Uni.: Combining form which means one, singular.

Uniaural: Refers to a single ear, monaural (preferred).

Unicellular organisms: Those which have but a single cell. Protozoa.

Unidextrous. Preferring one hand over the other for most actions. Also called handedness.

Uniformity: In social psychology, refers to a condition in which there occurs widespread ("uniform") agreement concerning some belief, practice or fact.

Unigne factor: A factor found in only one test of correlation matrix. Syn. specific factor.

Unilateral. Affecting or pertaining to one side. Opposite of bilateral.

Unimodal: A frequency curve with a single mode or peak.

Unintentional act: According to psychoanalysts, an act which, though consciously unintended, really expresses an unconscious wish.

Unintentional humor: Psycho-analytic theory which holds that amusing slips of tongue are releases for unconscious, repressed tensions. The humor usually having double meaning, resolves or reveals thwarted sex trends. Condensation and displace-ment occur it) unintentional humor, just as they do in dreams.

Uniocular: Refers to a single eye ; monocular (preferred).

Unipolar cell (or neuron): A neuron having a single stalk leading from the soma. This neural process branches with the dendrites at one end and the, axonal terminals at the other.

Unique trait. 1. A personality trait which is found only in a single individual, 2. a trait that shows a zero correlation with all other traite being measured.

Unisexual: Characteristic of a species in which each individual organism has been either male or female but not both.

Unit character: In genetics, a biological characteristic that if transmitted to an offspring, appears as a whole, not partially.

Unit: 1. One of something which is taken as a whole, a datum. 2. A standard amount which is used as the basis of measurement.

Unitary trait: A pattern of behaviour that functions as a whole.

Unitary type: An individual whose afterimages, memory images, and eidetic images are similar in type.

Unity: 1. The state of consisting of one element, without parts or' divisions, 2. harmony or concord in literary or artistic works, 3. a totality or whole.

Univariate: Having but one variable. An experiment using only one variable may be called a univariate study, although the term 8ingle-factor study (or experiment) is more common.

Universal complex: Any complex derived from any instinct.

Universalism: In I sociology, refers to an approach to social theory in which standards of conduct are determined according to sets of principles assumed to reflect universal ethical standards. In this approach the tendency has been to disregard mitigating circumstances or individual contexts.

Universality: The property of being universal, in any of that term's meanings.

Universals, linguistic: Refer to those linguistic aspects that are common to all natural languages. These hypothesized universals have been usually viewed as being of two types, substantive, universals, which are common aspects of description of natural languages such as distinctive features, catalogues of word classes, sets of semantic features, etc., and formal universals, which represent the nature of generative rules found in natural languages, such as transformations.

Universals: A term which is used collectively for any of those aspects of the human condition that the user is asserting are universal.

Universe of discourse: Refers to the full set of things under consideration in a given discus-ion, study or experiment.

Universe, statistical: Refers to the full population from which samples are drawn and about which inferences from the samples are made.

Universe: 1. Most generally, refers to all things everywhere taken as a totality. 2. More specifically, also refers to a collection of things, taken together according to some defining features(s) or characteristic (s). This meaning is close to that of set (1).

Unlearned: Refers to behavior that does not depend upon practice or experience for its appearance. However, all behavior is modified by learning and is dependent upon environmental conditions; hence, the term unlearned is somewhat misleading.

Unlearning: A deliberate attempt to overcome the effect of previous learning-usually attempted in the case of undesirable habits.

Unnatural: Contrary to nature, The term is popular rather than scientific.

Unobtrusive procedure: A general term for any research technique ,r gathering data without the individuals (persons or animals) being observed becoming aware of the procedures.

Unpack: A term borrowed from the computer sciences where it refers to the recovery of original data that have been stored (or "Packed") with other data. It is used as a metaphor for the process of retrieval of specific memories from a large store of other memories and knowledge.

Unpleasant: Characterizing experiences that are disagreeable and which the subject would like to avoid.

Unpleasantness: (Titchener) with pleasantness, one of two poles of feeling or affective tone. Unpleasantness is characterized by dislike and ambient behavior; pleasantness by ambient behavior.

Unpleasure: Refers to the emotional experience that results from the exposure to stimuli that are unpleasant. This experience has been usually treated as basic and primitive and resistant to conscious, introspective analysis.

Unproductive mania: Excitement and hyperactivity without the flight of ideas which usually accompanies mania.

Unreality, sense (or feeling) of: A feeling that things experienced are somehow not "real" or not "right". "When it occurs occasionally in normal living it is usually interpreted as a failure to be able to integrate an experience with one's previous knowledge of things and, indeed, the feeling occurs most often when encountering strange or novel situations. When it takes place frequently or continuously it is regarded as pathological.

Unreflective: Impulsive. With respect to cognitive style.

Unreliability: Ant of reliability in any of the meanings of that term.

Unselected: A term which is used occasionally to characterize a sample that was drawn from a population strictly at random.

Unsocial or unsociable: 1. Characterizing one who avoids the company of others or does not seek others out. 2., Characterizing one who does not fit into the social system.

Unspaced practice: Refers to learning situations in which no rest periods are given between trials.

Unstable: I. Unpredictable in behavior, particularly, in moods, attitudes, or emotional behavior. 2. Suffering from intermittent periods of mental disorder. 3. Unreliable.

Unstressed: In linguistics, a syllable which receives minimal accentuation in a word.

Unstriated muscles: Smooth muscles, often called the involuntary muscles.

Unstructed interview: Refers to interview in which the topics to be covered have been left unspecified at the outset and things are left to the unfolding interaction between the persons involved in the interview.

Unweighted: Refers to scores that have not been multiplied by a constant before being combined with other scores.

Up-and-down method: In psychophysics, refers to a variation on the method of limits in which the ascending stimulus sequence is shifted to descending as soon as the subject changes response category and vice versa. Also termed as the staircase method.

Upper category: In the method of single stimuli in psychophysical experiments, a class of reports that will outnumber other reports as the stimulus magnitude is increased.

Upper threshold: Refers to the upper bound of sensitivity for a particular stimulus dimension.

Upset: Loss of complacency. The drive to action is an upset in the optimum balance ; the end or goal of behavior is the drive to maintain or regain balance.

Ur: A prefix from the German which means original or primitive. Used roughly synonymously with proto.

UR: Abbreviation of unconditioned response.

Uranism: Homosexuality, Karl Heinrichs coined the term in 1862, deboting the male homosexual uraning and the female urinde.

Urethra: The tube which runs from the bladder through which urine is passed.

Urethral complex: H.A. Murray's hypothesized syndrome involving urinal soiling, enuresis and urethral eroticism. Murray regarded it as a minor complex but theorized that it might be related to the Icarus complex.

Urethral eroticism: *(Psychoan) The* centering of sexual feeling in the urethra.

Urethral eroticism: Sexual pleasure by the male in urination. According to psychoanalysts, the male can experience greater pleasure from the act because the urethra is about 8 to 9 inches long in the male ; in the female, it is only about. 11 inches long.

Urge: Non-technical term for any strong desire.

Urning: A male homosexual who takes the role of a woman toward other males.

Urolagnia: The association of sexual excitement with urination or urine.

Urophilia: A paraphilia characterized by the deriving of erotic stimulation from the smell or taste of urine or from the viewing of a person urinating, to the extent that such stimulation has been necessary for maintaining arousal and to achieve orgasm. Also called urolagnia and undinism.

V

Vagus nerve: The Xth *cranial nerve.* A mixed nerve with widely distributed afferent and efferent branches, it innervates the external car, pharynx, larynx, lunds, heart kidneys, spleen, liver, stomach and intestines.

Valence (*Lewin*): Psychological attractiveness of objects. Positive valence signifies attractiveness; negative valence, unattractiveness.

Valence substitute: The valence which is associated with an object that has, for any number of possible reasons, come to serve as a substitute for an original but unreached object.

Valid: Denoting the circumstances in which, by the principles of logic, a statement has been unambiguously implied by the premises.

Validation: 1. Refers to the process of determining whether a measuring instrument measures what it had been designed to measure. 2. More generally, refers to the process of establishing the objective proof of a proposition, process, measuring instrument etc.

Validity: Refers to the characteristic of a proposition, logical argument, etc., that it is founded on truth or is consistent with law or fact. 2. Refers to the property of a measuring device that it measures in fact what it is intended to measure. Validity could be established by correlating the results of the test with an outside criterion or independent measure.

Validity, a priori: A kind of preliminary, intuitive estimate of the => *content validity* of a test. The degree to which the items on the test seem to have an intuitive, a priori relationship to the *behaviours that* are assumed to be being tested.

Validity coefficient of: An index of test's => validity. (3); the coefficient of correlation between the Scores on the test and a set of => *criterion scores* which are taken as reflective of the variable (s) the test is purported to measure. For example, for a test designed to assess scholastic aptitude the correlation would be between the test scores and academic performance as assessed by grade-point average (the criterion scores) and it would provide a measure of the test's validity.

Validity, concurrent: A kind of => *criterion-related validity* in which the relationship between the test scores and the criterion scores is established at the same time. Although similar in spirit to => *predictive validity,* the procedure really uses "post-diction" rather than "Prediction." For example, one way of evaluating the validity of, say, a test for clerical skills would be to see how scores on the test correlate with the known "new math."

Validity, convergent and discriminant: The degree to which any particular testing instrument has validity will reflect the extent to which scores on the test *(a)* correlate highly with factors that they, in principle, should correlate highly with, and (b) correlate poorly with factors that they, in principle, should correlate poorly with. *Convergent validity* is manifested by the former; *discriminant validity* by the latter.

Validity, congruent: A method of establishing the validity of a new test by correlating scores from it with scores from another test of established validity. The most typical case here is in intelligence testing, where newly developed tests are compared with the well-known tests like the Stanford-Binet or the Wechsler.

Validity, consensual: An informal procedure for assessing validity based upon the notion of consensus; that is, it the more persons who concur in a proposition, the more likely is to be valid or the more persons who agree on a perception the more probable that it is real. The term is rarely used in tests and measurements research; it is typically found in social psychology to characterize the principle that systematic support of a particular position grants a greater acceptability to others => *consensual validation.*

Validity, construct: A set of procedures for evaluating the validity of a testing instrument based on the determination of the degree to which the test items capture the hypothetical quality or trait *(i.e., construct)* it was designed to measure. Thus, for example, if a test is supposed to provide a measure cf intelligence one should ask: (a) What traits or qualities (constructs) actually characterize intelligence ? And (b) do the test items actually tap such constructs ? The initial stages of test construction are usually concerned with construct validity.

Note that it provides neither a quantitative nor a static measure of validity unlike measures that depend on a *correlation of validity,* there are no mathematical bases for determining validity and unlike measures that depend on known patterns of behaviour *(e.g., => criterion- related validity)* the estimates of construct validity is always changing with the accumulation of further evidence about the traits and qualities that underlie the construct => *contant validity,* of which it is but one form.

Validity, content: An estimate of the validity of a testing instrument based on a detailed examination of the contents test items. By contents here is meant the actual constituent materials of the test items; the evaluation of them is carried out by reviewing each item to determine whether it is appropriate to the test and by assessing the overall cohesiveness of the several test items. For example, a test of mathematical abilities, in order to have a respectable level of content validity, should not phrase the item in such a way that verbal abilities are critical for the person taking the test to understand what is being asked.

Validity, nomological: A variation of => construct validity that derives from the argument that construct validity actually involves two separate endeavours: one that focuses on validating the constructs or traits (often called trait validity) and one that is concerned with validating the test within a larger a theoretical framework—this latter is known as *nomological validity.*

Validity, predictive: A type of => empirical validity based on determining the extent to which the scores on a, test are Predictive of actual performance. A test designed to measure, say, clerical skills will have high predictive validity if it predicts who will and will not succeed in crerical jobs.

Validity, synthetic: Validity of a complex testing instrument or of a full test battery based on the relationship between a composite score that is takes to represent the various factors that are represented on the test and actual performance. The term derives from the notion that one has synthesized many elements or factors into a single value.

Value: The quality or property of a thing that makes it useful, desired or esteemed, Note the pragmatic aspect implied by this definition; the value of a thing is given by its role in a (social) transaction, the thing itself does not posses value. 2 n. An abstract and general principle concerning the patterns of behaviour within a particular culture or society which through the process of socialisation, the members of that society hold in high regard. These social values, as they are often called, form central principles around which individual and societal goals can become integrated. Classic examples are freedom, justice, education, etc. 5 n. In economics, the net worth of a thing as determined by what it will bring in exchange, either in, other, goods or in some medium of exchange usually money. This meaning combined with 1 above, is very close to the meaning of the term => utility, especially 3. 4n. In mathematics, a quantity or magnitude as represented by a number. 5 n. In the Munsell system for classifying colours, the position along the brightness dimension. 6 vb. To assess the worth of a thing. 7 vb. To hold spine thing in esteem based upon one's evaluation of it.

Value, absolute: A number or => value (4) expressed without regard to its sign. The absolute value of 3 is the same as +3 and is denoted as |3|

.**Value judgment:** A reaction to persons, objects, aesthetic products, etc. in terms of their value or worth, as opposed to their objective characteristics.

1. Property of being true, correct, in conformity with reality. This meaning, common in ordinary parlance, is typically not intended in the technical literature. 2. In logic the property of an argument or conclusion that it is deemed to be => valid because it conforms With proper, logical principles. The fundamental notion here is that the; reasoning process itself must be correct; an argument may have validity in this sense and not correspond with reality but the fault will lie with assumptions and not the reasoning process. 3. In testing, the property of any measuring instrument, device or test that it measures What it purports to measure. Validity here is not a simple notion and it is not a simple "either-or" property as in sense 2 and to ionic extent in sense 1.

Values clarification: A variation on moral education which emphasizes awareness and clarification of moral judgements and ethical considerations.

Values education: An aspect of education focusing on specific instruction in moral and ethical values in society. The term is usually associated with the work of L. Kohlberg on moral *development*, which is based on the assumption that some moral positions are inherently better than others. Hence, the educational curriculum here is oriented toward raising the child's level of morality.

Variability: The characteristic of being subject to change whether continuous or discontinuous. In descriptive statistics, the common measures of variability are the standard deviation, average deviation, and the range.

Variable error: The deviation of a measure from the mean. Variable errors occur on' either side of the mean. Their extent may be predicted by the measures of dispersion, but they cannot be corrected.

Variable interval reinforcement: Reinforcement delivered according to a random sequence of time intervals. Typically the intervals lie between prearranged arbitrary values with a fixed mean.

Variable ratio reinforcement: A type of intermittent reinforcement in which the animal is given reinforcement, such as a pellet of food, after a certain number of responses, the number of responses varying from trial to trial but lying between arbitrary values with a fixed average.

Variance: The square of the standard deviation employed as a measure of the extent to which individual scores in a set of scores differ from each other.

Vascular theory or thermal sensitivity *(Nafe)*: The theory that thermal sensations are correlated with changes in, the constriction and dilation of arterioles and veinules.

Vasopressin: A hormone produced by the posterior pituitary gland that increases blood pressure and decreases the production of urine.

Vector: 1. A directed line or magnitude. 2. In field theory, a symbol of motivation or a representation of a force that causes locomotion toward or away from an incentive. 3. In statistics, the representation of a score by means of a line having direction and length.

Vector field: A field in which there is direction and magnitude of all forces (vectors). Vectors, or directed lines, represent motivational forces in field theory.

Ventricle: 1. Any one of the cavities within the brain that form a continuous channel for the flow of the cerebrospinal fluids. 2. One of the chambers within the heart. 3. More generally, any cavity within an organ of the body.

Verbal generalization: 1. A universal or widely held principle. 2. In verbal conditioning, stimulus generalization that is, responding in the same way to words with the same general meaning.

Verbal intelligence: The ability to deal effectively with words and symbols, the ability to solve problems utilizing verbal symbols.

Verbal summator: A projective technique in which an instrument produces low-intensity vowel sounds in response to which the subject is asked to tell what words he hears.

Verification: 1. The collecting of empirical data for the purpose of testing a hypothesis. 2. One of the states of creative or artistic thinking in which the thinker evaluates the results.

Vertical mobility: Mobility between social or occupational classes. The term covers movement up or down in the social system, but it is most commonly used with the connotation of upward movement.

Vestibular apparatus: The bony cavity in the labyrinth of the inner car, including the two vestibular sacs (the *utricle* and the *saccule)* and the three *semicircular canals.*

Vestibule: 1. Generally, any small cavity at the-front of a canal'. 2. Specifically the middle part of the inner ear in front of the semicircular canals containing the utricle and saccule. Occasionally the term is used to include the whole of the vestibular *apparatus,* which see for details.

Vestige: 1. Generally, a thing that in its present form is a degenerate or imperfect representation *of* a fully developed form which existed in the past. 2. Specifically, in biology, an organ or organ part showing such characteristics.

Viable: 1. Of an organism, likely *to* live. 2. Of a seed or spore, likely to-germinate. 3. Metaphorically, characterizing a theory or a hypothesis likely to stand up under stringent experimental !est.

Vibration: Generally, periodic motion of matter. A full vibration cycle is from a given point through the full cycle and back to, the original point, as in a sine wave, *vibration rate.*

Vicarious: Pertaining to a substitute. May be used in the sense of another attempting to obtain substitutive satisfaction from her daughter's social activities, or in connection with brain mechanisms where one part of the brain may function in place of another that has been injured.

Vicarious trial and error: The substitution of mental performance for overt performance. The average chess player engages in a good deal of vicarious trial and error before making a move.

Vigotsky test: A concept-formation test that requires the subject to sort out blocks of Various shapes, colours, and sizes.

Vincent curve: A group curve constructed by a technique for making comparable the learning curves of different subjects by dividing the individual curves into equal fractions (such as fifths or sixths) and averaging the results, on the assumption that an equal fraction of the total time or trials is equivalent from one individual to another.

Vineland social maturity scale: A rating scale of maturity, based on samples of behaviour characteristic of individuals at specified ages.

Visibility: In a short range of electromagnetic or radiant energy, - the property of being capable of exciting the retinal receptors 2. the property of being easily seen.

Visible, speech: The representation of units of spoken sound by means of patterns of black, white, and gray. Sound waves are transformed into visible light and then photographed for the purpose of making speech visible.

Visual acuity: The ability of the retina to separate or discriminate stimuli. Acuity may be measured by acuity gratings or, more commonly, by means of the Snellen Chart, which employs letters of graded size. If the individual can discriminate letters that can just be discriminated by the normal eye at the standard distance of 20 feet, he is said to have 20/20, or normal, vision. A rating of 20/200 signifies that at 20 feet the individual is able to discriminate only what the normal person can discriminate at 00 feet. Correspondingly, 15/20 signifies that the individual can discriminate at 20 feet what the normal eye cannot discriminate at more than 15 feet.

Visual adaptation: The tendency for the retina to adjust to conditions of continued stimulation or lack of stimulation. For specific types of adaptation, see dark adaptation; brightness adaptation; chromatic adaptation.

Visual displacement: The angles at which the eyes deviate either vertically or horizontally from the primary position when viewing objects.

Visual field: The totality of all objects available to the unmoving eye at-any given time. 2. The subjective, three-dimensional space in which objects are perceived.

Visual induction: The influence of stimulation of one part of the retina on another part. Thus, a small yellow square will make a surrounding gray field take on a bluish tinge.

Visual-righting reflexes: Reflexes associated with the orientation of the bead according to the fixation' of objects in the visual field.

Vitreous humour: The transparent, jellylike material that fills the eyeball between the retina and the lens.

Vocational aptitude test: A test designed to evaluate, through measurement of ability, personality traits, interests, and potential achievement or success in a specific occupation or profession.

Vocational counselling: Counselling as applied to the problems of vocational adjustment. Theoretically, vocational counselling involves only problems connected with employment, but vocational counsellors find that personal problems and home conditions play an important role in job satisfaction.

Vocational maladjustment: A condition resulting from an individual's attempting to work in a job or profession for which he is 'unsuited.

Vocational preference inventory: An interest inventory for grades 12-16 and adults. The examines, indicates like or dislike for 160 occupational titles. There are also built-in personality scales.

Vocational selection: A choice made among applicants for a job or profession in terms of the individual most likely to succeed.

Voice Onset Time (VOT): The time between the beginning of the uttering of a sound and the vibration of the vocal cord's. The easiest way to appreciate VOT is to say "ba" and "pa" with your fingers lightly touching your throat. The vocal cords vibrate at almost the same instant the lips are opened for "ba" but there is a short lag (about 50- 100 msec) in voicing for pa". This lag time is the VOT.

Volume: In psychophysics, the sense of how much space a stimulus appears to take up; the psychological equivalent of the physicist's definition. Volume is experienced most clearly with sounds, where high-pitched tones are perceived as "thin" and hence low in volume and low-pitched tones feel "larger" or "fuller" and hence as more voluminous. The unit for volume is the vol. The persistence of some radio and television manufacturers to mislabel the *loudness* control volume (a confusing practice arising from a mislabelling of the control for compensating for the human ear's deficiencies at low- and high-pitched tones as *loudness*) has produced more than its share of confusion.

Voluntary admission: Admission into a psychiatric institution or hospital undertaken voluntarily by the individual. While there are cases such as this, the term is also used as a euphemism for many borderline instances in which the individual may be told b y the appropriate authorities that either they request., voluntary" admission or a court order will be sought to impose admission. See here *commitment*.

Volunteer bias: A potential bias in any study where the subjects are volunteers rather than persons who have been selected from the population using sampling procedures that protect against non-representativeness. There is considerable evidence that volunteers are a typical; they are generally more highly motivated and tend to perform at a higher level on most tasks than control subjects who are selected at random.

Von restorff effect: The generalization that if, given a series of stimuli to be learned *(e.g.,* a list of words), one of them is made physically distinctive in some way (e.g., printed in large type or in a different colour from the others) it will be easier to learn and recall.

Vowel: A speech sound produced by vibrating the vocal cords without obstructing the passage of air through the vocal tract. Contrast with *consonant.*

Voyeurism: A *paraphilia* characterized by a pattern of sexual behaviour in which one's preferred means of sexual arousal is clandestine observing of others when they are disrobing, nude or actually engaged in sexual activity. Interestingly, a voyeur does not usually derive pleasure from striptease shows, public nudity or pornography; arousal is dependent upon the observed persons not being aware of their being observed.

W

Weber's law: A psychophysical generalization which has been physioligist Ernst Heinrich Weber attributed due to the German physioligist Ernst Heinrich Weber. It states that the just-noticeable differences in stimuli are proportional to be magnitude of the original stimulus. Formally, DI/I=k where I denotes the intensity of the comparision stimulus, DI denotes the increment ·in intensity just detectable and k is a constant.

The law holds true reasonably for the mid-range of most stimulus dimensions but tends to break down when very low-or very high-intensity stimuli have been used; e.g., for very low-intensity tones the Weber fraction is somewhat larger than it is for moderately loud tones. Note that the ratio has been often rendered as DR/R, where R standards for Reiz and as DS/S, where S stands for stimulus.

Wechsler Adult Intelligence Scale (WAIS): An individual general intelligence test which is similar to the stamord-Binet but which yields both Verbal and performance IQ's as well as a total IQ. The test has been also believed to have diagnostic significance for certain psychiatric problem.

Wechsler Intelligence Scale for Children (WISC): An individual intelligence test for children 6-12 years of age similar in mature to the Wechsler Adult intelligence Scale. A preschool test is also available.

Wechler Preschool and Primary Scale of Intelligence (WPPSI): An intelligence which has been designed for use with children below the use of 6.

Wechsler scales: A general label for the various Wechsler teste of intelligence, each of which has been given above. Note that all the Wechsler scales have been individually administered tests.

We group: The group to which the individual who expresses similar ideas, goals, and feelings belongs.

Weight: A multiplicative factor which has been designed to give, more or less relative importance to a score. 2. The relative contribution of a factor toward the final result.

Weighting: The process of determinating the relative influence each item or score in a series should have in determining the total score.

Weight-lifting experiment: A psychophysical experiment in which subjects judge the difference in magnitude between small weights.

Weigl-goldstein-scheerer test: A concept formation test that needs the subject to sort blocks according to colour and shape. Goldstein has employed this and other similar tests in his studies of brain-studies people.

Well-adjusted: A state of hormoneous relationship with one's social and physical environments.

Wernicke's area: A cerebral area which is comprising parts of the first and second temporal gyri and the supramarginal angular gyrus: formerly regarded to be the area for understanding spoken language.

Wernicke's syndrome: The term used for an acute brain disorder with eye-movement dysfunctions, ataxia, orientation problems and general mental confusion being the primary symptoms.

It gets related to severe alcoholism and is, in the classic case, followed by alcholic amnestic disorder, although this sequela can occasionally be prevented large doses of thiamine. Also called nocturnal emissions.

Wetzel grid: A device which is used for plotting height, weight and age with norms for development based on the interrelation ships among these factors.

Wever-Bray Effect: Electrical activities which are generated in the cochlea in response to external stimulus. It is also known as aural micro-phonics.

Whisper test: A crude hearing test in which the subject, with one tar plugged, stands 20 feet away from the examiner who pronounces test words in a distinct whisper. The subject is not allowed to watch the examiner's lips during the test.

White: The visual sensations evoked by a mixture of radient wavelengths approximating those whose physiological action is equivalent to that stimulated by natural daylight, the extreme of the bright end of the series comprising the black- gray-white dimension of visius, experience.

Whole-learning method: Simply, learning material (usually verbal) in its entirety as opposed to learning it one small piece at a time—the so called part-learning method.

Whole-word method: A method of reading instruction in the focus has been on the relationships between articular configurations of letters (the "whole word") and its pronunciation. Often termed as the looks-say method.

Wide-hand procedure: A term applied to the more 'subjective testing and evaluation procedures such as projective techniques, and interviews. The term was borrowed from information theory.

Wilcoxon test: The term is used for an extension the sign test, which evaluates the magnitude of differences as well as their direction in assessing the significance of differences between matched pairs of scores Also termed as the mached-pairs signed-ranks test.

Wild boy of aveyron: One of the more famous case studies in .psychology. Victor a wild child, was found near the town of Aveyron. Estimated to be about 7 years old at the time, he was extensively studied by the French physician/educator Jean-Marc-Gaspard Itard. The growth and development of Victor intellectually, socially and, to a modest extent, verbally, was discussed in loving detail by Itard over a period of many years and had a profound impact on educational, theory and practice. The most likely explanation is that such children were subnormal to begin with and had been taken out and abandoned by the parents.

Windigo: A culture-specific syndrome observed in Algonquin Indians where a hunter thinks that be is in the power of a flesh-eating supernatural monster.

Win-stay loso-shift strategy: The term used for a commonly observed strategy in two-alternative-choice experiments whereby the subject continues to make a response which receives reinforcement ("winstay") but abruptly switches to the other choice if reinforcement does not take place ("lose-shift").

Wisconsin General Test Apparatus (WGTA): A piece of laboratory apparatus which has been designed at the primate research lab at the University of Wisconsin. It houses a single monkey in a cage and is having a fairly flexible set of trays and platforms which hold various stimulus items for presentation to the subject.

Wishful thinking: Thinking which directed by, and along this lines of one's wishes and desires rather than upon the objective constraints of reality.

Witchcraft: Refers to the occult practice or sorcery. Beliefs concerning witchcraft and the role of its practioners which have found in many societies and with a with a wide range of variation ranging from evil or "black" to beneficent or "white" witches.

Witch's milk: An archaic term for the milk-like secretion which is occassionally exuded from an infant' breast. It gets stimulated by locating hormone from the mother.

Withdrawal: 1. A pattern of behaviour which is characterised by the person removing him or herself from normal day-to-day functioning-with all of its attendent frustrations tensions, and disappointments. 2. A conscious removing of oneself from particular situations. 3. In ethology, a pattern of behaviour which is exhibited by the loser of a battle, who gives a display of submission and is allowed to leave the scene unmolested. 4. In, psychopharmacology, refers to the cessation of administration of a drug, especially one for which the individual has developed a dependence.

Withdrawal delirium: Delirium which is caused by the withdrawal of a drug upon which one had built up a severe dependence.

Withdrawal symptoms: Including any of the effects of the cessation of administration of a substance upon which one has built up a dependence.

Wolf-man: Refers to the sobriquet of one of Freud's more famous patients, a man whose dominant symptom was a recurring dream involving a marked fear of wolves. He was a Russ nobleman whom Freud analysed intensely and from whom he gathered much of his "evidence" for childhood sexuality and the Oedipus complex.

Woodworth-Matthews personal data sheet: A neurotic inventory used largely for screening children or adolescents in educational institutions.

Word-building test: A variation on an anagram task in which the subject has been asked to construct as many words as possible from a given letter set.

Word configuration: The term used for the overall shape of a word, its length; location of ascending and descending letters, placement of capital letters, etc.

Word count: Any systematic assessment of the frequency of occurrence of words in written and/or spoken language. Often such counts have been restricted to specific linguistic domains, e.g., first-year primers, parent-child interactions.

Working through: The process of having the patient thoroughly, explore and master the conflict that brought him to therapy.

Work-limit test: A test in which each subject carries out the same task and the subjects are evaluated on the length of time required to complete the tasks.

Work psychology: A term preferred by many European psychologists to industrial/organizational Psychology.

Wurzburg school: A group of researchers at Wurzburg University led by Oswald Kulpe, work around the turn of the century. Although they were *introspectionists* they extended their scope of research beyond that the Wundtian form of structuralism and focused on the so-called "higher mental pro-cesses" problem-solving, cognitive set and the like.

X

Xanthocyanopsia: Yellow vision; red-green color-blindness in which things as seen as yellow or blue.

Xanthopsia: Yellow-sightedness; a heightened sensitivity to yellow.

X coordinate: The use of strange, foreign, or pretentious words.

Xenoglossophobia: A pathological fear of foreign languages.

Xenophobia: A pathological fear of strangers.

X-O test: (*Pressey*) A test of attitudes and interests in which the individual either crosses out or circles certain preferences.

XYZ pattern: A genetic abnormality believed to be related to criminal or aggressive

Y

Yantra: A visual pattern used in meditation.

Y axis: The ordinate.

Yellow: The visual experience aroused by radiant energy of a wavelength of approxi-mately 582 nanometers.

Yellow-sighted: Pertaining to a pathological condition in which there is a heightened sensitivity to yellow.

Yerkes-bridges point scale: an early adaptation of the Binet Scale utilizing points instead of months of mental age.

Yerkes-Dodson law: The generalization that moderate levels of arousal or motivation yield optimal performance.

Z

Zeigarnik effect: The finding that interrupted tasks are remembered better than completed tasks, provided that the subject is ego-involved in the uncompleted tasks.

Zeppia: (*R.B. Cattell*) A factor trait identified as a flexible superego.

zero-order: Pertaining to correlation coefficients computed from data in which neither variable has been held constant. The typical product-moment correlation coefficient is a *zero-order correlation*.

zeta (z): The difference between the squares of the correlation ratio and the correlation coefficient. In terms of a formula:

$$x = (h^2 - r^2)$$

where h = the correlation ratio, or the degree of which the correlation is nonlinear.

r=the correlation coefficient.

Zollner illusion: An illusion of visual space perception in which parallel lines intersected by numerous short diagonal lines slanting in the opposite direction seem to diverge.